HISTORY
of the
OJIBWAY
PEOPLE

William W. Warren

HISTORY
of the OJIBWAY
PEOPLE

WILLIAM W. WARREN

With an introduction by
W. ROGER BUFFALOHEAD

MINNESOTA HISTORICAL SOCIETY PRESS
ST. PAUL • 1984

New material copyright © 1984
    by the Minnesota Historical Society
    First edition 1885
    Reprint edition 1984
    10 9 8 7

First published in 1885 by the Minnesota Historical Society as
    Volume 5 of the *Collections of the Minnesota Historical Society*
Manufactured in the United States of America
International Standard Book Number 0-87351-162-X

Library of Congress Cataloging-in-Publication Data
Warren, William W. (William Whipple), 1825–1853.
    History of the Ojibway people.
    Reprint. Originally published: History of the Ojibways, based upon traditions and oral statements. St. Paul: Minnesota Historical Society, 1885. (Collections of the Minnesota Historical Society; v. 5)
    Includes bibliographical references and index.
    1. Chippewa Indians—History. 2. Indians of North America—History. I. Title.
II. Series: Collections of the Minnesota Historical Society; v. 5.
E99.C6W32   1984   973'.0497   83-27164

CONTENTS

INTRODUCTION

The importance of William W. Warren's *History of the Ojibway People* is well established. First published by the Minnesota Historical Society in 1885, the work is an early and unique contribution to the field of Ojibway or Chippewa history and culture that has been used extensively by succeeding generations of scholars. In his study, Warren summarized and transcribed the Ojibway tribal memory at mid-19th century — a critical time in the tribe's history. He knew his subject well, and he experimented with an approach to oral history methodology that produced impressive results. No one can ever duplicate this feat, and it makes his work all the more valuable as a primary source. In fact, Warren might well have come closer than any other writer to describing Ojibway tribal history from the inside.[1]

Little can be added to the biographical data appearing in "Memoir of William W. Warren," written by J. Fletcher Williams, secretary of the Minnesota Historical Society, for the 1885 edition of this book. Besides providing important facts about Warren's brief life, the memoir illustrates the high regard and popularity that the young man of mixed Ojibway and

[1] Warren preferred to write the tribal name as "Ojibway," arguing that this spelling more closely reflected in English how native speakers pronounced the tribal name in their language (see p. 37, below). At the present time several tribal names are used, including, but not limited to, Chippewa, Ojibwa, Ojibway, and Anishinabe. Ojibway has been used in this introduction, as Warren preferred. For an interesting recent explanation of the aboriginal name, see Edward Benton-Banai, *The Mishomis Book: The Voice of the Ojibway*, 3 (St. Paul, 1979).

Euro-American heritage enjoyed among both Ojibway and white people. It is true that Warren won the friendship, trust, and confidence of tribal members throughout Minnesota and Wisconsin; it is also certain that he was genuinely sympathetic in his fight for tribal interests as an interpreter for the United States government and as an elected member of Minnesota's territorial legislature. But to understand Warren as a full and practicing member of the Ojibway culture would be an error. Rather he suggests in his preface and narrative that he viewed himself as a man whose life integrated features from both Ojibway and non-Indian societies, with emphasis on Euro-American religious, social, and economic traditions. He took pride in the fact that his education and his tribal heritage uniquely equipped him to "elucidate the grand mystery" of the Ojibway past for white readers.[2]

As a child fascinated by his tribal heritage, Warren probably memorized the stories of cultural heroes. Later in young manhood, having returned from the white schools he attended in the East, he took a more direct interest and set out methodically to learn the traditions of the tribe from its leaders and old men. Despite his good intentions, he was not always successful, especially at first. "The [I]ndians generally are reluctant in giving any information respecting their history to the White Man," Warren explained. "During the course of my inquiries I have often been discouraged and would give over the attempt altogether." Such setbacks were temporary, however, and in 1847 Warren received crucial encouragement from Buffalo, the oldest living chief of the tribe. He later recalled the incident that occurred at La Pointe: " 'My Grandson' said the old man. 'You have now become as one of us, you have now

---

[2] For quote, see p. 27, below. On Warren, see also Willoughby Babcock, "William Whipple Warren and His Chippewa Writing," in *Minnesota Archaeologist*, 12:40–42 (April, 1946); *Minnesota Democrat*, July 6, 1853. Williams' biographical data was taken largely from information supplied to him by Warren's sister Mary Warren English; see Correspondence, 1849–84, Minnesota Historical Society (MHS) Archives, MHS. A short biography of Warren is in MHS, *The Ojibwe: A History Resource Unit* (St. Paul, 1973).

arrived to the age of thinking and discretion and see far around
you. . . . You have often asked me what I knew of former
times, but I did not open my heart to you for you [were] then
a child. You are now a man. You know how to write like the
whites. You understand what we tell you. Your ears are open
to our words. And we will tell you what we know of former
times.' . . . The ice of their reserve being thus broken I succeeded thereafter in procuring from them the traditions pertaining to their past History." Through his kinship ties and his
work as an interpreter, he "gained the full confidence of the
Chiefs, and [became] more experienced in questioning and
drawing them out." Before long he began writing himself
memoranda to record the various versions of the same events he
was given.[3]

As a native speaker of Ojibway, Warren felt he "had every
advantage to glean from their story tellers and tradition
keepers, the principle [sic] events of past generations." He
believed, of course, that there was truth in the traditions and
that he was uniquely qualified to understand that truth. By the
time he began writing, he had acquired a sophisticated
understanding of the problems inherent in oral traditions based
upon his own trial-and-error experience. In fact, he had worked
out a method for evaluating his sources and for determining
what is now known as a "composite view." He described the
technique in the *Minnesota Democrat* (St. Paul): "In order to
arrive at the truth of a fact obtained of an Indian, respecting
their past history, a person must go from one old man to
another of different villages or sections of the tribe, and obtain
the version of each; if they all agree in the main fact, even if

[3] Here and two paragraphs below, see William W. Warren to Jonathan E.
Fletcher, May 1, 1850, in "General Correspondence and Related Matters," Henry
R. Schoolcraft Papers, originals in Library of Congress, microfilm copy in MHS;
Minnesota Democrat, February 11, 1851. The latter, the first of a series of weekly
articles that ran until April 1, is reprinted as "A Brief History of the Ojibwas,"
"Sioux and Chippewa Wars," and "Answers to Inquiries Regarding Chippewas,"
in *Minnesota Archaeologist*, 12:45–91, 95–107, 13:5–21 (April, October, 1946,
April, 1947).

they disagree in the details, you can then be certain that the circumstances had happened and the tale has a substantial origin. However vague and unnatural the traditions of the Indians become in the particulars, or details, from a verbal transmission of ages; yet each must have something real and true for its origins, and for this reason their traditions are more worthy of attention than people are generally disposed to accord to them."

Warren solicited from his informants details about "all the events of importance that had happened to their tribe in former times, especially the battles that their ancestors had fought with their many and different enemies." From the mass of data collected, he sorted out that relating to the political and military history of the tribe for the first in a projected series of books. Later volumes, he indicated, would incorporate information on the customs, beliefs, rites, religion, and other aspects of Ojibway society. He then arranged the historical data into an organizational and chronological framework for revealing the principal events of the Ojibway past over five centuries.

The *History of the Ojibways* was greeted on its original publication in 1885 as "a rare book . . . valuable because it is written by one who understood all their history. It is exceedingly interesting as a narrative, and surprises one with the ease and clearness of its style." The assessment is still valid.[4]

Warren's book has much to offer modern readers. On the clan system, principal bands and divisions, patterns of governance and leadership, and other aspects of political organization, the text provides information valuable to any historical or cultural study of the Ojibway. His biographical data on political leaders, fur traders, and members of his Indian family are in many cases the only such information available. Of course the detailed descriptions of intertribal wars carry an Ojibway bias (as Warren recognized) and suffer distortion from perceptions of Indian warfare held by whites in the 19th century. But they contain much useful information about the principal groups in-

---

[4] *American Antiquarian and Oriental Journal,* 8:389 (November, 1886).

volved, especially the Iroquois, Dakota, Sauk and Fox, and French and English traders and explorers. There is also material to be gleaned on the social and economic systems of Ojibway culture. The book offers intriguing reading, full of tantalizing tales. One can only wonder how much more would be known about the Ojibway today if Warren had been able to finish his other volumes, instead of carrying his knowledge of his people into an early grave.

This Borealis Book edition of *History of the Ojibway People* also offers modern readers an opportunity to reassess Warren's work with a critical eye. The need for careful reinterpretation is an immediate one. Problems of understanding and writing about American Indian history and culture rise like specters from the tragedy of the past to haunt the realm of professional scholarship. These problems will remain until the historical knowledge transmitted by the first people of this land secures genuine equality in the intellectual foundations of contemporary knowledge and understanding. While much scholarly revision has taken place in recent years, new perspectives continue to shatter old myths and are themselves called into question. Historians, cultural anthropologists, and contemporary tribal members all have viewpoints and questions that must be taken into consideration; striking a proper balance among these concerned and sometimes contentious parties may, however, be impossible. In this fluid and challenging context, the reexamination of such classics as Warren's history helps us to understand better the people whose life beckons for truth, both to heal the past and to initiate new beginnings in a relationship spanning the whole of American history.[5]

Warren's *History of the Ojibway People* is an apt choice for reconsideration. It describes a people whose cultural heritage and homelands have the widest geographic distribution of any

---

[5] Since the late 1960s an interesting dialogue has developed among historians, cultural anthropologists, and Indian scholars about the nature of Indian history. For a discussion of these viewpoints, see Daniel Tyler, ed., *Red Men and Hat-Wearers: Viewpoints in Indian History* (Boulder, Colo., 1976).

tribal grouping in North America, ranging from the eastern
Great Lakes region in Canada and the United States to the edge
of the Great Plains near Lake Winnipeg in Manitoba and the
Turtle Mountains in North Dakota. This account is relatively
old; it is based upon information obtained directly from tribal
members and fur traders who knew the Ojibway well; its author
was fairly well educated for his time, spoke the tribal language
fluently, and interacted with considerable ease in both Ojibway
and non-Indian societies. Because Warren lived at the time he
did, and because of his abilities and cross-cultural circumstances, his history provides both fascinating insights and
invaluable information about the Ojibway people. For the same
reasons, it raises several questions for today's readers.

For some scholars, Warren's method of research presents a
problem. Professional historians who study American Indians
find few topics more agitating than the validity of oral history;
cultural anthropologists, in contrast, need no convincing of its
value. The primary question is the reliability of the human
memory. To say that memory is totally unreliable suggests that
oral tradition is really—to paraphrase Voltaire—a common and
agreed-upon verbal lie, transmitted from generation to generation. To say there can be complete reliance on oral versions of
the past turns the search for historical truth into an act of faith.
Remembering that Voltaire directed his comment toward written history, we would perhaps be wisest to observe that
somewhere in between these two extreme positions lies the real
value of oral accounts of the tribal past.[6]

From the vantage point of present-day knowledge, scholars
may also question the influence on Warren's work of 19th-
century ideas about, and perceptions of, Ojibway history and
culture. Easily discernible in Warren's narrative is considerable
evidence that he believed in the superiority of American culture
over Ojibway or other Indian ways of life. He stated in his
preface that Indians were fast disappearing "before the onward

---

[6] For a discussion of the validity of oral traditions, see William L. Montell,
Don't Go Up Kettle Creek, 8 (Knoxville, Tenn., 1983).

resistless tread of the Anglo-Saxon," and he predicted that by the mid-1860s it would be too late to save the traditions of the Ojibway forefathers from oblivion. Such statements indicate his acceptance of the then popular theory of Indian extinction, with its underlying assumption that Indian cultures were inferior and unable to endure in the presence of "civilized" society.[7]

Writing for non-Indian readers, Warren embraced the 19th-century concept of history as an account of major political events and wars of the past set forth in a rigid chronology. In doing so, he dismissed the distinction between the tribal view of the past and his own understanding of Indian history as essentially the "somewhat uncertain manner in which the Indians count time" in their oral traditions versus the "more authentic record of the whites." Thus his narrative, with its emphasis on the political developments of the tribe's principal bands and divisions, presents the Indian as the fierce warrior—the "noble savage"—set in a context largely lacking references to social and economic life, religious beliefs and practices, music and art traditions, the roles of women and children, and other important cultural elements that have always been included in the tribal view of history. Perhaps Warren had misgivings about his own abilities as a historian, or perhaps he decided his scheme was the only means to make the material understandable to non-Indian readers. In either case the effect was the same: Warren folded Ojibway history into an American framework, causing some serious distortion in the coverage of the Ojibway past.[8]

Whether Warren would have filled the information gap in succeeding volumes devoted to the cultural life of the Ojibway will never be known. It was not until 76 years after his death that another Minnesotan, ethnologist Frances Densmore, published her cultural studies of the Ojibway conducted with

[7] See p. 23, 25, below.
[8] See p. 26, below; Warren to Fletcher, May 1, 1850, Schoolcraft Papers. For a thorough discussion of non-Indian perceptions of Indians during the 19th century, see Robert F. Berkhofer, *The White Man's Indian*, 3–31 (New York City, 1978).

the vital assistance of Warren's sister, Mary Warren English.[9]

Because none of Warren's notes and memoranda are known to survive, it is not possible to determine whether his narrative is a fair and accurate representation of the information shared with him by Ojibway leaders. In keeping with the practice of his time, he did not annotate his work, and he specifically identified his sources only when he disagreed with written accounts or thought the fame of his informant added credibility to his own narrative. A comparison of Warren's history with later written versions of the same events and with surviving oral traditions among the Ojibway has limited usefulness, at best revealing general conformity in main outlines. Neither preliminary versions nor the final book manuscript is available for study to show if the author made any basic changes in focus, interpretation, or content. Although several differences between the published book and the earlier articles Warren wrote for the *Minnesota Democrat* indicate that he changed his mind about some details, it is clear that the articles served as the nucleus for the larger work.[10]

The responsibility for separating the genuine from the suspect in Warren's history is left to the reader. The sorting process ranges from the easy dismissal of his theory of Indian origins as a mistaken 19th-century notion to the apparently unresolvable controversy over his interpretation of the tribal

[9] Frances Densmore, *Chippewa Customs* (Bureau of American Ethnology, *Bulletins*, no. 45 — Washington, D.C., 1929; reprint ed., St. Paul, 1979).

[10] The original Warren manuscript seems to have been lost or misplaced. Archivists at the MHS are not certain what happened to the original copy but speculate that either it was never returned to the society by the printer or upon return was filed away in the manuscript collections in a place as yet uncovered by researchers. In an attempt to find out if the manuscript was returned to the society, the author examined MHS Correspondence, 1879–87. While much information appears on related matters, such as correspondence between Williams and persons with an interest in the publication, nothing was found to indicate that the manuscript was returned to the society or that copies were made of the original version before it was sent to the printer.

For an example of differences between the *Minnesota Democrat* series and the book manuscript, see February 18, 1851, where Warren proposes yet another definition of the tribal name.

name.[11] It is a task requiring sharp skills and a thorough knowledge of the related literature. As a people who more often than not have been misunderstood or maligned by those unfamiliar with their history and culture, the Ojibway would want Warren's work to be read in conjunction with studies that provide a more balanced and well-rounded interpretation of their past and present. An assessment of the literature is available in Helen Horbeck Tanner's *The Ojibwas: A Critical Bibliography* (Bloomington, Ind., 1976). In addition, publications produced by various branches of the Ojibway in Minnesota, Wisconsin, and Michigan are now accessible in university and public libraries as well as through Indian organizations and tribes in the Great Lakes region.

This Borealis Book edition of Warren's history retains both J. Fletcher Williams' memoir of the author and the explanatory notes provided in the original work by the Reverend Edward D. Neill to clarify the time frame and to provide additional information. Neill's supplementary piece, entitled "History of the Ojibways, and Their Connection with Fur Traders, Based upon Official and Other Records," has been omitted; more recently published works better serve to complement Warren's history. A new, more comprehensive index was prepared for this edition by Sarah P. Rubinstein, editor in the Publications and Research Division of the Minnesota Historical Society.

W. Roger Buffalohead

[11] See p. 35–37, 61–63, below.

MEMOIR

OF

WILLIAM W. WARREN.

BY

J. FLETCHER WILLIAMS,
SECRETARY MINNESOTA HISTORICAL SOCIETY.

(7)

MEMOIR OF WILLIAM W. WARREN.

WILLIAM WHIPPLE WARREN, whose work follows, was a descendant of Richard Warren, one of the "Mayflower" pilgrims, who landed at Plymouth in 1620. From this ancestor a large proportion of the persons bearing the name of Warren, in the United States, have descended. General Joseph Warren, who fell at Bunker Hill, was the descendant of a collateral line of the family. Abraham Warren, a descendant of Richard, born September 25, 1747, fought in the Revolutionary War, as did also his son, Stephen. Lyman Warren, son of Abraham, was born in Hartford, Connecticut, May 25, 1771, and was married in Berkshire, Massachusetts, to Mercy Whipple.

Their son, Lyman Marquis Warren, father of the subject of this memoir, was born at the latter place, Aug. 9, 1794. He came to the Lake Superior region in 1818, with his brother Truman A., younger than himself, to engage in the fur trade. The U. S. government having some time before enacted that no one, not a citizen of the United States, should engage in the fur trade, the British subjects, who were engaged in that trade, employed American clerks to take charge of their posts. The Warren brothers entered the service of Michel Cadotte, an old trader among the Ojibways at La Pointe, and soon became great favorites with the Ojibways. In 1821, each of the brothers married a daughter of Cadotte, and in 1823, the latter sold out all his trading outfit to them, and retired from

(9)

the business. Truman Warren did not live long after this. He died on board a vessel on Lake Superior in 1825, from pneumonia, resulting from the hardship and exposure incident to a trader's life. Rev. Alfred Brunson, in his autobiographical reminiscences, entitled "A Western Pioneer," states that "Lyman M. Warren traded for several years in the Lac du Flambeau, Lac Coutereille and Saint Croix Departments, in opposition to the American Fur Company. He then entered into an arrangement with them and took charge of those three departments as partner and chief factor under a salary, making his depot at La Pointe. This arrangement continued until 1834." La Pointe appears to have been his permanent residence until his death.

The Cadottes, into which family the Warren brothers married, were descendants of a Mons. Cadeau, who, it is stated, came to the Ojibway country in 1671, in the train of the French envoy, Sieur de St. Lusson.[1] His son, John Baptiste Cadotte (as the name was then and subsequently spelled) became a trader among the Ojibways, and was engaged for a time with Alexander Henry, who in his work mentions him very frequently. He was married by a Catholic priest to an Ojibway woman of the A-waus-e clan, and made his residence at Sault Ste Marie. Mrs. Cadotte is described by Henry as being a woman of great energy and tact, and force of character. She aided her husband in his trading operations, sometimes undertaking long expeditions with *coureurs du bois* for him. She bore him two sons, John Baptiste Cadotte, Jr., and Michel Cadotte, who also became traders among the Ojibways, and were men of energy and ability in their calling. Both of them were well educated and had great influence in the Lake Superior region, and northwest, where they were well

---

[1] The full name and title of this officer, as given in a document in The Margry Papers, vol. i. p. 96, is Simon-Francis Daumont, Sieur de St. Lusson.

known. Both J. B. and Michel Cadotte married Ojibway women, the latter the daughter of White Crane, hereditary chief of La Pointe village. Their descendants are quite numerous, and are scattered throughout the northwest. Michel Cadotte died at La Pointe in 1836, æt. 72 years. Though he had once made large profits in the fur trade and was wealthy, he died poor, a result of the usual improvidence which that kind of life engenders, and of his generosity to his Indian relatives.

In 1821, as before remarked, Lyman M. Warren married Mary, daughter of Michel Cadotte. The ceremony was performed by one of the missionaries at Mackinaw. Rev. A. Brunson, in his work before quoted, says of Mrs. Warren : " She was three-fourths Indian. She was an excellent cook, and a neat housekeeper, though she could not speak a word of English." Mrs. Elizabeth T. Ayer, of Belle Prairie, Minn., widow of Rev. Frederic Ayer, the missionary, states that " she was a woman of fine natural abilities, a good mother, though without the advantages of any education. They raised a large family. The children had, added to more than common intelligence, a large amount of *go-ahead-ativeness.*" Mrs. Warren was a believer in the Catholic faith. Mr. Warren, however, was an adherent of the common evangelical belief, and a member of the Presbyterian Church. Rev. Wm. T. Boutwell, the first missionary at Leech Lake, still living in Washington County, Minnesota, near Stillwater, says: " I knew him as a good Christian man, and as one desirous of giving his children the benefits of a Christian education." Mrs. Ayer says : " He was among the first to invite American missionaries into the region of Lake Superior, and he assisted them as he had opportunity, not only by his influence, but sometimes by his purse. He united with the mission church at Mackinaw, where he was married." Rev. Mr. Brunson, who visited him in 1843, says: " Mr. Warren had a large and select library, an unexpected sight in an Indian country, containing some books that I had never before seen."

After dissolving his connection with the American Fur Company, probably about the year 1838, he removed to the Chippewa River, Wisconsin, where he had been appointed as farmer, blacksmith, and sub-agent to the Ojibways, in that reservation. He located his post at a point a few miles above Chippewa Falls, at a place now known as Chippewa City. Here, in connection with Jean Brunett, he built a saw-mill and opened a farm, which was soon furnished with commodious buildings. His wife died there July 21, 1843, and the following winter he took her remains to La Pointe for interment. Mr. Warren died at La Pointe, Oct. 10, 1847, æt. 53. Of the eight children born to them, two died in infancy. Truman A. is now interpreter at White Earth Agency, Minn., and Mary, now Mrs. English, is a teacher at the Red Lake Mission School. Charlotte, Julia, and Sophia are married, and live on White Earth Reservation. Of William, their oldest son, we now propose to give a brief memoir.

William Whipple Warren was born at La Pointe, May 27, 1825. In his very earliest childhood, he learned to talk the Ojibway language, from playing with the Indian children. His father took every means to give him a good English education. Rev. Mr. Boutwell says: "In the winter of 1832, he was a pupil at my Indian School at La Pointe." He subsequently attended, for awhile, the mission school at Mackinaw, when he was only eight years old. In the summer of 1836, his grandfather, Lyman Warren, of New York, visited La Pointe, and on his return home took William with him to Clarkson, New York, where he attended school for two years, and afterwards, from 1838 to 1841, attended the Oneida Institute at Whitesborough, near Utica, a school then in charge of Rev. Beriah Green, a man noted for his anti-slavery views. William remained there until 1841, when he was sixteen years of age, and acquired a good scholastic training. He was then, and always subsequently, greatly devoted to reading, and read everything which he could get, with avidity. "While at school" (says one who knew him well) "he was greatly beloved for his amiable disposition, and genial, happy manners. He was always full of life, cheerfulness, and sociability, and insensibly attracted all who associated with him."

During his absence from home, he had, by disuse, forgotten some of the Ojibway tongue, but soon became again familiar with it, and acquired a remarkable command of it. Speaking it fluently, and being connected with influential families of the tribe, he was always a welcome and petted guest at their lodge-fire circles, and it was here that his taste and fondness for the legends and traditions of the Ojibways were fostered. He speaks in his work of his love for the "lodge stories and legends of my Indian grandfathers, around whose lodge-fires I have passed many a winter evening, listening with parted lips and open ears to their interesting and most forcibly told tales." He was fond, too, of telling to the Indians stories which he had learned in his reading, and would for hours translate to them narratives from the Bible, and Arabian Nights, fairy stories, and other tales calculated to interest them. In return for this, they would narrate the legends of their race, and thus he obtained those traditions which he has, with such skill, woven into his book. He was always a great favorite with the Indians, not only on account of his relationship to them, but from his amiable and obliging disposition to them, and his interest in their welfare, being always anxious to help them in any way that he could.

His familiarity with the Ojibway tongue, and his popularity with that people, probably led him to adopt the profession of interpreter. When Rev. Alfred Brunson visited the Indians at La Pointe in the winter of 1842–3, on an embassy from the government, he selected young Warren, then seventeen years of age, as interpreter, and found him very ready and skillful. Hon. Henry M. Rice writes: " In the treaty of Fond du Lac, made by Gen. Isaac Verplank and myself in 1847, William was our interpreter. (See Statutes at Large.) He was one of the most eloquent and fluent speakers I ever heard. The Indians said he understood their language better than themselves. His command of the English language, also, was remarkable—in fact, *musical*."

In the summer of 1842, in his eighteenth year, Mr. Warren was married to Miss Matilda Aitkin, daughter of Wm. A. Aitkin, the well-known Indian trader, who had been educated at the Mackinaw Mission School. It was during his interpretership under I. P. Hays in 1844–45, his relatives say, that his health began to fail. Frequent exposures, long and severe winter expeditions, connected with the Indian service at that time, brought on those lung troubles, which subsequently ended his life so prematurely, after several years of suffering.

Warren came to what is now Minnesota, with his family, in the fall of 1845, first living at Crow Wing and Gull Lake, where he was employed as farmer and interpreter, by Major J. E. Fletcher, Winnebago agent, then also in charge of the Mississippi Ojibways. He was also employed as interpreter in the attempted removal of the Lake Superior Indians under J. S. Watrous—an act which he did not, however, approve of. After a year or two he established a home at Two Rivers, now in Morrison Co. In the fall of 1850, he was nominated and elected as a member of the Legislature from the district in which he lived—a district embracing more than one-half the present area of the State. In January following (1851), he appeared at St. Paul, and took his seat as a member of the House of Representatives. Up to this time he had been quite unknown to the public men and pioneers of the Territory, but by his engaging manners, and frank, candid disposition, soon won a large circle of friends.

Col. D. A. Robertson, of St. Paul, contributes the following reminiscence of Mr. Warren at this period : " I became acquainted with young Warren in the fall of 1850. I had shortly before established in St. Paul ' The Minnesota Democrat' newspaper. At the date mentioned, some one introduced Mr. Warren to me, and wishing to learn what I could regarding the customs, belief, and history of the Ojibways, I questioned him on these points, and he very lucidly and eloquently gave me the desired information. I was much pleased with him, and talked with him a great deal, at that and other times, on the subject. I was amazed at his information in regard to the Ojibway myths, as well as pleased with his style of narrative, so clear and graphic, which, with his musical voice, made his recitals really engrossing. I asked him, ' how did you get these myths ?' He replied, from the old men of the tribe, and that he would go considerable distances sometimes to see them—that they always liked to talk with him about those matters, and that he would make notes of the principal points. He said this was a favorite pastime and pursuit of his. He had not at this time, it seems, attempted to write out anything connected, and the matter which he had written down was not much more than notes, or memoranda.

" In January, 1851, Mr. Warren took his seat as a member of the Legislature, and I renewed my talks with him about the Ojibway legends. I then said to him, write me out some articles on this subject, to which he consented, and began to do so during his leisure moments, when not engaged in the Legislature. He had up to that

time, probably had little or no practice in writing such
things, but soon acquired a good style. The first of his
papers, or articles, was printed in the Democrat, Feb.
25, 1851, an article of several columns, entitled, ' a brief history of the Ojibways in Minnesota, as obtained from their
old men.' This was followed by other chapters during
the same year. These sketches took well, and seemed to
please all who read them. I finally suggested to him that
if he would gather them up, and with the other material
which he had, work them into a book, it would sell readily, and possibly secure him some profits. The idea
seemed to please him, and I am certain it never occurred
to him before. He at once set about it, and from time to
time when I saw him during the next two years, he
assured me he was making good progress. At this period
he was in poor health and much discouraged at times,
suffering from occasional hemorrhages, as well as from
financial straitness.

"During all my intercourse with Mr. Warren, for two or
three years, I never saw the least blemish in his character.
His habits were scrupulously correct, and his morals
seemed unsullied. He appeared candid and truthful in
everything, and of a most amiable disposition. Though
about that time he was bitterly assailed by some whose
schemes regarding the Indians he had opposed, he never
spoke of them with any bitterness, but kindly, gently,
and forgivingly. In fact, I never heard him speak ill of
any one."

Mr. Warren's widow, now Mrs. Fontaine, of White
Earth, states that when he had once set about writing his
projected book, he pursued his work with an ardor that
rapidly undermined his already feeble health. He read,
studied, and wrote early and late, whenever his official duties
or absence from home did not prevent, and even when suffering from pain and debility. During this period, a corres-

pondent of "The Minnesota Democrat," who visited Mr.
Warren, writes thus under date March 17, 1852:—

"I write you from a most lovely spot, the residence of
my friend, Hon. W. W. Warren. Mr. Warren's house
stands directly opposite the mouths of the two small rivers
which empty into the Mississippi on the western side, a
short distance apart, and hence the name, 'Two Rivers.'
Opposite this point, in the river, is an island of great
beauty of appearance. Near by are countless sugar trees
from which, last spring, Mr. Warren manufactured upwards of one thousand pounds of fine sugar. During my
short sojourn here, I have been the attentive listener to
many legendary traditions connected with the Chippewas,
which Mr. Warren has, at my request, been kind enough
to relate. They have been to me intensely interesting.
He appears to be perfectly familiar with the history of
these noted Indians from time immemorial. . . . . . .
Their language is his own, and I am informed that he
speaks it with even more correctness and precision than
they do themselves. This is doubtless true. . . . As
I write, he is conversing with Esh-ke-bug-e-coshe, or Flat
Mouth, the far-famed old chief of the Pillagers. This old
chief and warrior, now 78 years of age, has performed his
long journey from Leech Lake, to visit 'his grandson,' as
he calls Mr. Warren."

Much interest was felt at this period among Mr. Warren's personal friends, especially among such as had devoted
any attention to the study of the Indian races, regarding
his proposed publication, and he had the good wishes of
all who knew him for its success, as well as their sym-
pathies on account of his health and his pecuniary straits.
In the preparation of his book, also (and he mentions this
fact in his preface), he was much embarrassed for want of
the works of other authors to refer to, for there were no
public libraries in Minnesota at that time, while his lack

of means prevented him from purchasing the desired books himself. It is gratifying to be able to state however, that some of his friends who felt an interest in him and his proposed work, generously aided him at this juncture. Among these should be prominently mentioned Hon. Henry M. Rice, to whose liberal help is probably owing the completion of the work, and into whose hands it subsequently passed, to be by him ultimately donated to this Society.

In the winter of 1852–53, Mr. Warren completed his manuscript, and in the latter part of the winter, proceeded to New York, in hopes of getting the work published there. He had also another object, to secure medical treatment for his rapidly failing health. In both objects he was doomed to disappointment. The physicians whom he consulted, failed to give him any relief, or but little encouragement, while the publishers to whom he applied would only agree to issue his work on the payment by him of a considerable sum. Believing that some of his friends in Minnesota, who had always expressed an interest in the work, might advance such aid, Mr. Warren resolved to return home and lay the case before them. There is little doubt that had he lived to do so, he would have promptly secured the means required. He reached St. Paul on his way home, in the latter part of May, 1853, very much exhausted. He went to the residence of his sister Charlotte, (Mrs. E. B. Price) and was intending to start for Two Rivers on the morning of June 1. Early on the morning of that day, however, he was attacked with a violent hemorrhage, and in a short time expired. His funeral took place the following day, Rev. E. D. Neill officiating, and the remains were laid to rest in the cemetery at St. Paul.

Thus was untimely cut off, at the early age of 28 years, one who, had his life and health been spared, would have made important contributions to the knowledge which we

possess regarding the history, customs, and religion of the
aboriginal inhabitants of Minnesota. He had projected
at least two other works, as noted in his preface, and it is
believed that he had the material, and the familiarity with
the subject, to have completed them in a thorough manner.

The news of Mr. Warren's death was received with
much sorrow by a large circle of friends, and especially
by the Ojibways, to whom he was much endeared, and
whom he had always so unselfishly befriended. They had
always placed the most implicit confidence in him, and
knew that he could be relied on. His generosity in sharing
with them anything that he had, was one cause of his
straitened circumstances.

His death was noticed by the press with just and appropriate eulogies. A memoir in the Democrat, July 6, 1853,
written by the late Wm. H. Wood, Esq., of Sauk Rapids,
says:—

" From his kindly and generous nature, he has ever been
a favorite, especially with chiefs and old men. He spoke
their language with a facility unknown even to themselves,
and permitted no opportunity to pass, of learning from the
old men of the nation, its history, customs and beliefs.
He delighted to listen to their words. Often has the
writer of this tribute found him seated at the foot of an
old oak, with Flat Mouth, the Pillager chief, noting down
upon paper the incidents of the old man's eventful life, as
he related them. Having, by his steadfast friendship to the
Indians, won their confidence, they fully communicated to
him, not only the true history of their wars, as seen by
themselves, and as learned from tradition, but also that
of their peculiar religious beliefs, rites and ceremonies.
Perhaps no man in the United States was so well acquainted with the interior life of the Indian, as was Mr.
Warren. He studied it long and thoroughly. Investing

Indian life with a romance perhaps too little appreciated by less imaginative minds, he devoted himself to the work of preparing and unfolding it, with a poet's enthusiasm.

"Thus animated, he could not be otherwise than enthusiastically attached to the Indians and their interests, and so he was. He was their true friend. While from the treachery of some and the cupidity of others, the Indians were often left with apparently no prospect but sudden destruction, in Mr. Warren they never failed of finding a brother, by whose kinds words of encouragement and sympathy, their hearts were ever gladdened. In his endeavors to contribute to their happiness, he sacrificed all personal interests and convenience, he, with his wife and children, often dividing with them their last morsel of subsistence. With a true philanthropist's heart, he literally went about among them doing good."

Of the four children born to Mr. Warren and his wife, two survive, a son, William Tyler Warren, and a daughter, Mrs. Madeline Uran, both residing on White Earth Reservation, Minn.

He was a firm believer in the truths of the Christian faith, and was a regular and interested student of the sacred Scriptures. He was accustomed, in his intercourse with the Indians, to enjoin upon them the duty and advantage of accepting the religion taught them by the missionaries, and it is believed that his advice had good effect upon them.

I must not close this imperfectly performed task, without acknowledging my obligations to Hon. H. M. Rice, Col. D. A. Robertson, Mrs. Elizabeth Ayer, Rev. W. T. Boutwell, and especially to Truman A. Warren, of White Earth, and Mrs. Mary C. [Warren] English, of Red Lake, for material and aid kindly furnished me in its preparation.

HISTORY OF THE OJIBWAYS,

BASED UPON

TRADITIONS AND ORAL STATEMENTS.

BY

WILLIAM W. WARREN.

(21)

PREFACE.[1]

THE red race of North America is fast disappearing before the onward resistless tread of the Anglo-Saxon. Once the vast tract of country lying between the Atlantic sea-board and the broad Mississippi, where a century since roamed numerous tribes of the wild sons of Nature, but a few—a very few, remnants now exist. Their former domains are now covered with the teeming towns and villages of the " pale face" and millions of happy free-men now enjoy the former home of these unhappy and fated people.

The few tribes and remnants of tribes who still exist on our western frontiers, truly deserve the sympathy and attention of the American people. We owe it to them as a duty, for are we not now the possessors of their former inheritance? Are not the bones of their ancestors sprinkled through the soil on which are now erected our happy homesteads? The red man has no powerful friends (such as the enslaved negro can boast), to rightly represent his miserable, sorrowing condition, his many wrongs, his wants and wishes. In fact, so feebly is the voice of philanthropy raised in his favor, that his existence appears to be hardly known to a large portion of the American people, or his condition and character has been so misrepresented

[1] Written in 1852, before the emancipation of negroes in the Southern States of the Republic.—E. D. N.

(23)

that it has failed to secure the sympathy and help which
he really deserves. We do not fully understand the
nature and character of the Red Race. The Anglo-Amer-
icans have pressed on them so unmercifully—their intercourse with them has been of such a nature, that they have
failed to secure their love and confidence.

The heart of the red man has been shut against his
white brother. We know him only by his exterior. We
have judged of his manners and customs, and of his religious rights and beliefs, only from what we have seen. It
remains yet for us to learn how these peculiar rites and
beliefs originated, and to fathom the motives and true
character of these anomalous people.

Much has been written concerning the red race by missionaries, travellers and some eminent authors; but the
information respecting them which has thus far been collected, is mainly superficial. It has been obtained mostly
by transient sojourners among the various tribes, who not
having a full knowledge of their character and language,
have obtained information through mere temporary observation—through the medium of careless and imperfect
interpreters, or have taken the accounts of unreliable
persons.

Notwithstanding all that has been written respecting
these people since their discovery, yet the field for research,
to a person who understands the subject, is still vast and
almost limitless. And under the present condition of the
red race, there is no time to lose. Whole tribes are daily
disappearing, or are being so changed in character through
a close contact with an evil white population, that their
history will forever be a blank. There are but a few
tribes residing west of the Mississippi and over its headwaters, who are comparatively still living in their primitive state—cherishing the beliefs, rites, customs, and traditions of their forefathers.

Among these may be mentioned the Ojibway, who are at the present day, the most numerous and important tribe of the formerly wide extended Algic family of tribes. They occupy the area of Lake Superior and the sources of the Mississippi, and as a general fact, they still live in the ways of their ancestors. Even among these, a change is so rapidly taking place, caused by a close contact with the white race, that ten years hence it will be too late to save the traditions of their forefathers from total oblivion. And even now, it is with great difficulty that genuine information can be obtained of them. Their aged men are fast falling into their graves, and they carry with them the records of the past history of their people ; they are the initiators of the grand rite of religious belief which they believe the Great Spirit has granted to his red children to secure them long life on earth, and life hereafter ; and in the bosoms of these old men are locked up the original causes and secrets of this, their most ancient belief.

The writer of the following pages was born, and has passed his lifetime, among the Ojibways of Lake Superior and the Upper Mississippi. His ancestors on the maternal side, have been in close connection with this tribe for the past one hundred and fifty years. Speaking their language perfectly, and connected with them through the strong ties of blood, he has ever felt a deep interest in their welfare and fate, and has deemed it a duty to save their traditions from oblivion, and to collect every fact concerning them, which the advantages he possesses have enabled him to procure.

The following pages are the result of a portion of his researches ; the information and facts contained therein have been obtained during the course of several years of inquiry, and great care has been taken that nothing but the truth and actual fact should be presented to the reader.

In this volume, the writer has confined himself altogether to history; giving an account of the principal events which have occurred to the Ojibways within the past five centuries, as obtained from the lips of their old men and chiefs who are the repositories of the traditions of the tribe.

Through the somewhat uncertain manner in which the Indians count time, the dates of events which have occurred to them since their discovery, may differ slightly from those which have been given us by the early Jesuits and travellers, and endorsed by present standard historians as authentic.

Through the difficulty of obtaining the writings of the early travellers, in the wild country where the writer compiled this work, he has not had the advantage of rectifying any discrepancies in time or date which may occur in the oral information of the Indians, and the more authentic records of the whites.

The following work may not claim to be well and elaborately written, as it cannot be expected that a person who has passed most of his life among the wild Indians, even beyond what may be termed the frontiers of civilization, can wield the pen of an Irving or a Schoolcraft. But the work does claim to be one of truth, and the first work written from purely Indian sources, which has probably ever been presented to the public. Should the notice taken of it, by such as feel an interest in the welfare of the red race, warrant a continuation of his labors in this broad field of inquiry, the writer presents this volume as the first of a series.

He proposes in another work to present the customs, beliefs, and rites of the Ojibways as they are, and to give the secret motives and causes thereof, also giving a complete exposition of their grand religious rite, accompanied with the ancient and sacred hieroglyphics pertaining thereto, with their interpretation, specimens of their religious idiom, their common language, their songs. Also their creed of spiritualism or communion with spirits, and jugglery which they have practised for ages, and which resembles in many respects the creed and doctrines of the clairvoyants and spiritualists who are making such a stir in the midst of our most enlightened and civilized communities. Those who take an interest in the Indian, and are trying to study out his origin, will find much in these expositions which may tend to elucidate the grand mystery of their past.

Succeeding this, the writer proposes, if his precarious health holds out, and life is spared to him, to present a collection of their mythological traditions, on many of which their peculiar beliefs are founded. This may be termed the "Indian Bible." The history of their eccentric grand incarnation—the great uncle of the red man—whom they term Man-abo-sho, would fill a volume of itself, which would give a more complete insight into their real character, their mode of thought and expression, than any book which can be written concerning them.

A biography of their principal chiefs, and most noted warriors, would also form an interesting work.

The writer possesses not only the will, but every advantage requisite to procure information for the completion of this series of works. But whether he can devote his time and attention to the subject fully, depends on the help and encouragement he may receive from the public, and from those who may feel an anxiety to snatch from oblivion what may be yet learned of the fast disappearing red race.

HISTORY OF THE OJIBWAYS.

CHAPTER I.

GENERAL ACCOUNT OF THE PRESENT LOCAL POSITION AND
NUMBERS OF THE OJIBWAYS, AND THEIR CONNECTION WITH
OTHER TRIBES.

Divisions among the aboriginal inhabitants of North America—The Algic
family of tribes—Their geographical position at the time of the discovery—
Their gradual disappearance, and remarks on their present fate—Ojibways
form the most numerous tribe of the Algics—The names, with their significations, of the principal tribes of this family—Causes of the difference in
their several idioms—The importance of the Totemic division among the
Algics—Origin of the name Ojibway—Present geographical position of the
Ojibways—Their numbers and principal villages—Subdivisions of the
tribe—Nature and products of their country—Present mode of livelihood.

BEFORE entering into the details of their past history, it
is necessary that the writer should give a brief account of
the present position and numbers of the Ojibways, and the
connection existing between them and other tribes of the
American Indians residing in their vicinity, within the
limits of the United States, Canada, and the British possessions.

Reliable and learned authors who have made the
aboriginal race of America an object of deep study and
research, have arrived at the conclusion, that the numerous
tribes into which they are divided, belong not to the same
primitive family or generic stock, but are to be ranged
under several well-defined heads or types. The well-
marked and total difference found existing between their
several languages, has been the principal and guiding rule

(29)

under which they have been ethnologically divided, one type or family from another.

The principal and most numerous of these several primitive stocks, comprising a large group of still existing tribes, have been euphoniously named by Henry R. Schoolcraft, with the generic term of ALGIC, derived from the word Algonquin, a name given by the early French discoverers to a tribe of this family living on the St. Lawrence River, near Quebec, whose descendants are now residing, partially civilized, at the Lake of the Two Mountains, in Canada.

Judging from their oral traditions, and the specimens of their different languages which have been made public by various writers, travellers, and missionaries, nearly every tribe originally first discovered by the Europeans residing on the shores of the Atlantic, from the Gulf of St. Lawrence, south to the mouth of the James River in Virginia, and the different tribes occupying the vast area lying west and northwest of this eastern boundary to the banks of the Mississippi, from the mouth of the Ohio to Hudson Bay, belong to the Algic family. In this general area the Six Nations of New York, the Wyandots, and formerly the Winnebagoes, who, however, now reside west of the Mississippi, are the principal exceptions.

The red men who first greeted our Pilgrim Fathers on the rock-bound coast of Plymouth, and who are so vitally connected with their early history, were Algics. The people who treated with the good William Penn for the site of the present great city of Philadelphia, and who named him " me guon," meaning in the Ojibway language " a pen" or feather, were of the Algic stock.

The tribes over whom Pow-hat-tan (signifying " a dream") ruled as chief, and who are honored in the name of Po-ca-hon-tas (names so closely connected with that of Capt. John Smith, and the early Virginia colonists), belonged to this wide-spread family, whose former possessions are now covered with the towns and teeming cities of millions of happy freemen. But they—where are they? Almost forgotten even in name: whole tribes have become extinct, and passed away forever—none are left but a few remnants who are lingering out a miserable existence on our far western frontiers, pressed back—moved by the so-called humane policy of our great and enlightened government—where, far away from a Christian and conscientious community, they can be made the easier victims of the unprincipled money-getter, the whiskey dealer, and the licentious dregs of civilized white men who have ever been first on our frontiers, and who are ever busy demoralizing the simple Indian, hovering around them like buzzards and crows around the remains of a deer's carcass, whom the wolves have chased, killed, gorged upon, and left.

This is a strong picture, but it is nevertheless a true one. A vast responsibility rests on the American people, for if their attention is not soon turned forcibly toward the fate of his fast disappearing red brother, and the American statesmen do not soon make a vast change for the better in their present Indian policy, our nation will make itself liable, at some future day, to hear the voice of the Great Creator demanding " Cain, where is Abel, thy brother? What hast thou done? the voice of thy brother's blood crieth unto me from the ground." . . .

The Ojibways form one of the principal branches of the Algic stock, and they are a well-marked type, and at present the most numerous section or tribe of this grand division of the aboriginal inhabitants of North America.

Next to them in numbers and importance, rank the tribes of the O-dah-waug[1] (which name means trading people), best

---

[1] The Outouaes originally lived in the valley of Ottawa River, Canada, and the furs at first received by the French at Quebec and Montreal, came through them.

Duchesneau, Intendant of Canada, in one of his dispatches to France wrote : " The Outawas Indians who are divided into several tribes, and are nearest to

known as (Ottaways), Po-da-waud-um-eeg[1] (Pottawatomies)
(those who keep the fire), Waub-un-uk-eeg (Delawares)
(Eastern earth dwellers), Shaw-un-oag[2] (Shawnees) (South-
erners), O-saug-eeg (Saukies[3]) (those who live at the entry),

us, are those of the greatest use, because through them we obtain beaver ; and
although they do not hunt generally, and have but a small portion of peltry
in this country, they go in search of it to the most distant places, and exchange
it for our merchandise."—N. Y. Col. Docs. ix. 160.—E. D. N.

[1] The Pouteouatami, contracted by the French traders Poux, fled from the
Iroquois, and the trader Nicolet, in the fall of 1634 or winter of 1635, found
them in the vicinity of Green Bay, Wisconsin. After the French settled at
Detroit, a portion of the tribe followed, while another band settled at St.
Joseph, Michigan, and some stragglers near the present city of Milwaukee,
Wis. In 1701, Ounanguissé, the Chief of the tribe, visited Montreal. In 1804,
Thomas G. Anderson traded with the Pottawatomies of Milwaukee. The
tribe was represented when the treaty was made in 1787, at Fort Harmer on
the Muskingum, Ohio, by Governor Arthur St. Clair. By a treaty with them
in October, 1832, the land around Chicago was ceded to the United States.
In 1846 the different bands agreed to remove to a reservation in Kansas. In
1883 a remnant of 100 were living in Calhoun County, Michigan, but the tribe
to the number of 410 persons were in the reservation in Jackson County, Kansas, while 280 wanderers were reported in Wisconsin, and 500 citizen Pottawatomies in the Indian Territory.—E. D. N.

[2] The Shawnees, or Chaouanou of the French. Father Gravier in 1700
descended the Mississippi, and in the account of this voyage writes of the
Chaouanoua living on a tributary of the Ohio which comes from the south-
southwest, now known as the Tennessee. They now live on a reservation
west of the Missouri and south of the Kansas Rivers. In 1883 they were estimated at 720 persons.—E. D. N.

[3] The Sakis or Ousakis were found by the French near Green Bay, and
spoke a difficult Algonquin dialect. The Jesuit Relation of 1666-7 speaks of
them in these words : " As for the Ousaki, they may be called savage above
all others ; there are great numbers of them, but wandering in the forests
without any permanent dwelling places."

The Outagomies, Renards or Foxes, driven by the Iroquois westward,
and settled. southwest of Green Bay, and were the allies of the Sakis. They
gave the name to Fox River in Wisconsin, and for years were hostile to the
French. By a treaty in 1804, the Sacs and Foxes ceded to the United States
lands on both sides of the Mississippi. During the war of 1812, the Chief of
the Sacs and Foxes, Black Hawk, assisted the British. In 1832 this Chief refused to comply with treaty stipulations and leave his village near Rock Island,
Illinois, and after some hostilities delivered himself to the Winnebagoes at La
Crosse, and they brought him to the United States authorities. After this in
Sept. 21, 1832, the confederate tribes of Sacs and Foxes ceded all the eastern
part of the State of Iowa. By a treaty of 1842, they agreed to remove to

O-dish-quag-um-eeg (Algonquins proper), (Last water people), O-mun-o-min-eeg[1] (Minominies) (Wild rice people), O-dug-am-eeg[2] (Foxes), (those who live on the opposite side), O-maum-eeg[3] (Miamies or Maumies), (People who live on the peninsula).

Ke-nis-te-noag (Crees).

Omush-ke-goag (Musk-e-goes), (Swamp people).

These names are given in plural as pronounced by the Ojibways; annexed are their different significations.

The names of many lesser tribes, but who are now almost extinct, could be added to the catalogue. It has been assumed, however, that enough have been named to show the importance of the Algic family or group of tribes. It is supposed, through a similarity of language with the Ojibways, lately discovered, that the numerous and powerful tribe of the Blackfeet, occupying the northwestern prairies at the eastern base of the Rocky Moun-

reservations on the Osage and Great Nemaha Rivers. For thirty years nearly all the Fox tribe have lived in Tama County, Iowa, and in 1883, 368 was the estimated population. In the Indian Territory a census of mixed Sacs and Foxes was made in 1883, and 437 was the number.—E. D. N.

[1] The Menominies called by the French Maloumines, Maroumines, and Folles Avoines were found by the first explorers near Green Bay. In 1831 they ceded to the United States the lands between Green Bay, Lake Winnebago, and Milwaukee River. In 1848 they ceded their remaining lands in Wisconsin, and accepted a reservation above Crow Wing River in Minnesota. Upon examination they were not pleased, and gave it back, the United States giving them, from their old lands in Wisconsin, in 1854, a reservation of 432 square miles. Their number in 1883 was 1392.—E. D. N.

[2] See note 3 on preceding page.

[3] The Miamis, called by the French Oumamis, Oumamik, Miamioueck and Oumiamis, the prefix Ou being equivalent to the definite article in English, were composed of several bands. D'Iberville in 1701 mentions that they were 500 families in number. They belonged to the Illinois confederacy. In 1705 some of them were dwelling at St. Joseph and Detroit, Michigan. In 1751 they were on the Wabash. Selling their lands to the United States, with the exception of a few on Eel River, Indiana, the Miamis went to a reservation on the Osage River. They have dwindled down to 61 persons who live in the Indian Territory.—E. D. N.

tains, above the head of the Missouri, also form a branch of this family.

The Ojibways term them Pe-gan-o, and know the Missouri River by the same name.

The difference between all these kindred tribes consists mostly in their speaking different dialects or idioms of the same generic language; between some of the tribes the difference lies mostly in the pronunciation, and between none of them is the difference of speech so wide, but a direct and certain analogy and affinity can be readily traced to connect them.

These variances occurring in the grammatical principles and pronunciation of their cognate dialects, has doubtless been caused by the different tribes occupying positions isolated from one another throughout the vast area of country over which they have been spread, in many instances separated by long distances, and communication being cut off by intervening hostile tribes.

The writer asserts positively, and it is believed the fact will surprise many who have made these Indians an object of inquiry and research, that the separation of the Algics into all these different and distinct tribes, is but a secondary division, which can be reached and accounted for, in their oral traditions: a division which has been caused by domestic quarrels, wide separations, and non-intercourse for generations together, brought about through various causes.

The first and principal division, and certainly the most ancient, is that of blood and kindred, embodied and rigidly enforced in the system which we shall denominate Totemic. The Algics as a body are divided into several grand families or clans, each of which is known and perpetuated by a symbol of some bird, animal, fish, or reptile which they denominate the Totem or Do-daim (as the Ojibways pronounce it) and which is equivalent, in some respects, to the coat of arms of the European nobility. The Totem descends invariably in the male line, and inter-marriages never take place between persons of the same symbol or family, even, should they belong to different and distinct tribes, as they consider one another related by the closest ties of blood and call one another by the nearest terms of consanguinity.

Under the head of "The Totemic System" this peculiar and important division of the Algics will be more fully explained and illustrated. It is mentioned here only to show the close ties which exist between the Ojibway and the other tribes, who belong with them to the same generic stock.

We have in the preceding remarks briefly explained the general connection which the Ojibways bear with other tribes, and indicated the grand section of which they form a principal part or branch. We will now more particularly treat of them, as a separate tribe, and state their present geographical position, numerical force, and intertribal divisions.

A few remarks will not be inappropriate respecting the definition of their tribal name.

Mr. Henry R. Schoolcraft, the learned author on Indians, who has written much concerning this tribe, says in one of his works: "They call themselves Od-jib-wäg, which is the plural of Od-jib-wa—a term which appears to denote a peculiarity in their voice or manner of utterance." In another place he intimates that the word is derived from "bwa" denoting voice. From this, the writer, through his knowledge of the language, is constrained to differ, though acknowledging that so far as the mere word may be regarded, Mr. Schoolcraft has given what, in a measure, may be considered a natural definition ; it is, however, improbable, for the reason that there is not the slightest perceivable pucker or " drawing up," in their manner of utterance, as the word O-jib would indicate. The word ojib or Ojibwa, means literally "puckered, or drawn up." The answer of their old men when questioned respecting the derivation of their tribal name, is generally evasive ; when hard pressed, and surmises given them to go by, they assent in the conclusion that the name is derived from a peculiarity in the make or fashion of their moccasin, which has a puckered seam lengthways over the foot, and which is termed amongst themselves, and in other tribes, the O-jib-wa moccasin.

There is, however, another definition which the writer is disposed to consider the true one, and which has been corroborated to him by several of their most reliable old men.

The word is composed of O-jib, "pucker up," and ub-way, " to roast," and it means, " To roast till puckered up."

It is well authenticated by their traditions, and by the writings of their early white discoverers, that before they became acquainted with, and made use of the fire arm and other European deadly weapons of war, instead of their primitive bow and arrow and war-club, their wars with other tribes were less deadly, and they were more accustomed to secure captives, whom under the uncontrolled feeling incited by aggravated wrong, and revenge for similar injuries, they tortured by fire in various ways.

The name of Ab-boin-ug (roasters), which the Ojibways have given to the Dahcotas or Sioux, originated in their roasting their captives, and it is as likely that the word Ojibwa (to roast till puckered up), originated in the same manner. They have a tradition which will be given under the head of their wars with the Foxes, which is told by their old men as giving the origin of the practice of torturing by fire, and which will fully illustrate the meaning of their tribal name. The writer is even of the opinion that the name is derived from a circumstance which forms part of the tradition.

The name does not date far back. As a race or distinct people they denominate themselves A-wish-in-aub-ay.

The name of the tribe has been most commonly spelt, Chippeway, and is thus laid down in our different treaties with them, and officially used by our Government.

Mr. Schoolcraft presents it as Od-jib-wa, which is nearer the name as pronounced by themselves. The writer, however, makes use of O-jib-way as being simpler spelled, and embodying the truest pronunciation; where it is ended with *wa*, as in Schoolcraft's spelling, the reader would naturally mispronounce it in the plural, which by adding the *s*, would spell *was*, whereas by ending the word with *y* preserves its true pronunciation both in singular and plural. These are slight reasons for the slight variance, but as the writer has made it a rigid rule to present all his Indian words and names as they themselves pronounce them, he will be obliged often to differ from many long received O-jib-way terms, which have, from time to time, been presented by standard writers and travellers.

The O-jib-ways are scattered over, and occupy a large extent of country comprising all that portion of the State of Michigan lying north of Green Bay and west of the Straits of Michilimackinac, bordering on Lake Superior, the northern half of Wisconsin and the northeastern half of Minnesota Territory. Besides this they occupy the country lying from the Lake of the Woods, over the entire north coast of Lake Superior, to the falls of St. Mary's and extending even east of this point into Upper Canada. They literally girdle the great " Father of Lakes," and the largest body of fresh water in the world may emphatically be called their own, Ke-che-gum-me, or " Great Water."

They occupy, through conquest in war against the Dahcotas, all those numerous lakes from which the Mississippi and the Red River of the North derive their sources.

They number, scattered in different bands and villages
over this wide domain, about fifteen thousand souls; including many of their people interspersed amongst other
tribes, and being isolated from the main body, on the Missouri, in Canada and northward amongst the Crees and
Assineboins, the tribe would probably number full twenty
thousand souls.

Of this number, about nine thousand live within the
limits of the United States, locally divided as follows:—

In Michigan, at their village of Bow-e-ting (Sault Ste
Marie), We-qua-dong (Ance-ke-we-naw), and Ga-ta-ge-te-
gaun-ing (Vieux Desert), they number about one thous-
and.

In the State of Wisconsin, residing at La Pointe, and on
the Wisconsin, Chippeway, and St. Croix Rivers, and their
tributary streams and lakes, they number three thousand.

In the territory of Minnesota, residing at Fond du Lac,
at Mille Lac, Gull Lake, Sandy Lake, Rabbit Lake, Leech,
Ottertail, Red, Cass, Winnepeg, and Rainy Lake and Portage, they count full five thousand souls.

The tribe is subdivided into several sections, each of
which is known by a name derived from some particular
vocation, or peculiar mode of procuring food, or other
characteristic.

Thus, those of the tribe who live on the immediate
shores of Lake Superior are known by the name of Ke-
che-gum-me-win-in-e-wug (Men of the Great Water).
Those residing in the midland country, between Lake
Superior and the Mississippi, are named Be-ton-uk-eeng-
ain-ub-e-jig (Those who sit on the borders).

With these, are incorporated the Mun-o-min-ik-a-sheenh-
ug (Rice makers), who live on the Rice lakes of the St.

Croix River; also the Wah-suah-gun-e-win-in-e-wug (Men of the torches), who live on the Head lakes of the Wisconsin, and the Ottawa lake men, who occupy the headwaters of Chippeway River.

The bands residing immediately on the banks of the Mississippi are named Ke-che-se-be-win-in-e-wug (Great river men); those residing in Leech and Ottertail lakes, are known as Muk-me-dua-win-in-e-wug (Pillagers). A large body living on the north coast of Lake Superior, are named Sug-waun-dug-ah-win-in-e-wug (Men of the thick fir woods). The French have denominated them " Bois forts" (hardwoods).

These are the principal divisions of the Ojibway tribe, and there are some marked and peculiar differences existing between them, which enable one who is well acquainted with them, to tell readily to which division each man in the tribe belongs. The language is the same with all of them.

These several general divisions are again subdivided into smaller bands, having their villages on the bank of some beautiful lake or river, from which, again, as bands, they derive names.

It is unnecessary, however, to enter into minute details, as the only object of this chapter is to give the reader a general knowledge of the people whose history we propose to present in the following chapters.

The O-jib-ways reside almost exclusively in a wooded country ; their lands are covered with deep and interminable forests, abounding in beautiful lakes and murmuring streams, whose banks are edged with trees of the sweet maple, the useful birch, the tall pine, fir balsam, cedar, spruce, tamarac, poplar, oak, ash, elm, basswood, and all the plants indigenous to the climate in which they reside.

Their country is so interspersed with watercourses, that they travel about, up and down streams, from lake to lake, and along the shores of Lake Superior, in their light and ingeniously made birch-bark canoes. From the bark of this useful tree, and rushes, are made the light covering of their simple wigwams.

The bands who live on the extreme western borders of their country, reside on the borders of the vast western prairies, into which they have gradually driven the fierce Dahcotas. The Red Lake and Pembina bands, and also the Pillagers, hunt buffalo and other game on the prairies west of the Red River: thus, as it were, standing one foot on the deep eastern forests, and the other on the broad western prairies.

The O-jib-ways, with the exception of a few Lake Superior and Canada bands, live still in their primitive hunter state.

They have ceded to the United States and Great Britain large and valuable portions of their country, comprising most of the copper regions on Lake Superior and the vast Pineries in Wisconsin. From the scanty proceeds of these sales, with the fur of the marten, bear, otter, mink, lynx, coon, fisher, and muskrat, which are yet to be found in their forests, they manage to continue to live in the ways of their forefathers, though but poorly and scantily.

They procure food principally by fishing, also by gathering wild rice, hunting deer, and, in some bands, partially by agriculture.

CHAPTER II.

TOTEMIC DIVISION OF THE O-JIB-WAYS.

A description of the Totemic System—Tradition of its origin—List of the different Totemic badges—The A-waus-e or "Great Fish" clan—Its subdivisions—Physical characteristics—Tradition of the Awause—Present position and numbers of this clan among the O-jib-ways—Bus-in-as-e, or Crane Totem clan—Their position in the tribe—Physical characteristics—Names of their most noted chiefs—Ah-awh-wauk or Loon Totem clan—Position and claims—Their principal chiefs—Noka, cr Bear Totem—Their numbers and position in the tribe—Physical characteristics—Their war chiefs—The Wolf Totem—Its position and origin—Chiefs—Monsoneeg, or Moose and Marten Totem—Their origin, and names of most noted men—Tradition accounting for their coalition—Addik, or Reindeer Totem—Totemic system deserving of more research.

THERE is nothing so worthy of observation and study, in the peculiar customs and usages of the Algic type of the American aborigines, as their well-defined partition into several grand clans or families.

This stock comprises a large group of tribes, distinct from each other, not only in name and locality, but also in the manner of uttering their common generic language. Yet this division, though an important one and strongly defined, is but a sub-division, which has been caused by domestic quarrels, necessity, or caprice, and perpetuated by long and wide separations and non-intercourse. These causes are related in their traditions, even where the greatest variance is found to exist between tribes. The separation does not date many centuries back. The first grand division is that of blood and kindred, which has been perpetuated amongst the different tribes by what they call the Totemic System, and dates back to the time "when the Earth was new."

Each grand family is known by a badge or symbol, taken from nature; being generally a quadruped, bird, fish, or reptile. The badge or Dodaim (Totem, as it has been most commonly written), descends invariably in the male line; marriage is strictly forbidden between individuals of the same symbol. This is one of the greatest sins that can be committed in the Ojibway code of moral laws, and tradition says that in former times it was punishable with death.[1]

In the present somewhat degenerated times, when persons of the same Totem intermarry (which even now very seldom occurs), they become objects of reproach. It is an offence equivalent among the whites to the sin of a man marrying his own sister.

In this manner is the blood relationship strictly preserved among the several clans in each tribe, and is made to extend amongst the different tribes who claim to derive their origin from the same general root or stock, still perpetuating this ancient custom.

An individual of any one of the several Totems belonging to a distinct tribe, as for instance, the Ojibway, is a close blood relation to all other Indians of the same Totem, both in his own and all other tribes, though he may be

[1] In the *Iroquois Book of Rites*, edited by Horatio Hale, Number 2 of Brinton's *Library of Aboriginal American Literature*, there is the following statement, pp. 51, 52, as to the clan system.

" There are many indications which seem to show that the system is merely an artificial arrangement instituted for social convenience. It is natural, in the sense, that the desire for association is natural to man. The sentiment is one which manifests itself alike in all stages of society. The guilds of the Middle Ages, the Masonic and other secret brotherhoods, religious organizations, trade unions, clubs, and even political parties, are all manifestations of this associative instinct. The Indian clan was simply a brotherhood or aggregate of persons, united by a common tie. What the founders of the Iroquois league did, was to extend this system of social alliances through the entire confederacy. The Wolf clans-man of the Caniengas is deemed a brother of the Wolf clans-man of the Senecas, though originally there may have been no special connection between them."—E. D. N.

divided from them by a long vista of years, interminable miles, and knows not even of their existence.

I am not possessed of sufficient general information respecting all the different groups of tribes in America, to enable me to state positively that the Algics are the only stock who have perpetuated and still recognize this division into families, nor have I even data sufficient to state that the Totemic System is as rigidly kept up among other tribes of the Algonquins, as it is among the Ojibways, Ottaways, and Potta-wat-om-ies.

From personal knowledge and inquiry, I can confidently assert that among the Dakotas the system is not known. There are a few who claim the Water Spirit or Merman as a symbol, but they are the descendants of Ojibways who have in former times of peace intermarried with them. The system among the Winnebagoes, which somewhat resembles this, they have borrowed or derived from the Ojibways during their long intercourse with them while residing about Green Bay and other portions of the present State of Wisconsin.

From these and many other facts which shall be enumerated, the writer is disposed to consider, and therefore presents, the Totemic division as more important and worthy of more consideration than has generally been accorded to it by standard authors who have studied and written respecting the Indians.

The Ojibways acknowledge in their secret beliefs, and teachings to each successive generation, five original Totems. The tradition in which this belief is embodied, is known only to their chief Medas, or priests. It is like all their ancient traditions, vague and unsatisfactory, but such as it is, I will here present it—verbatim—as I received it.

" When the Earth was new, the An-ish-in-aub-ag lived, congregated on the shores of a great salt water. From the bosom of the great deep there suddenly appearèd six beings in human form, who entered their wigwams.

One of these six strangers kept a covering over his eyes, and he dared not look on the An-ish-in-aub-ag, though he showed the greatest anxiety to do so. At last he could no longer restrain his curiosity, and on one occasion he partially lifted his veil, and his eye fell on the form of a human being, who instantly fell dead as if struck by one of the thunderers. Though the intentions of this dread being were friendly to the An-ish-in-aub-ag, yet the glance of his eye was too strong, and inflicted certain death. His fellows, therefore, caused him to return into the bosom of the great water from which they had apparently emerged.

The others, who now numbered five, remained with the An-ish-in-aub-ag, and became a blessing to them; from them originate the five great clans or Totems, which are known among the Ojibways by the general terms of A-waus-e, Bus-in-aus-e, Ah-ah-wauk, Noka, and Monsone, or Waub-ish-ash-e. These are cognomens which are used only in connection with the Totemic system.

Though, according to this tradition, there were but five totems originally, yet, at the present day, the Ojibway tribe consists of no less than fifteen or twenty families, each claiming a different badge, as follows:—

1.	Uj-e-jauk,	Crane.
2.	Man-um-aig,	Catfish.
3.	Mong,	Loon.
4.	Muk-wah,	Bear.
5.	Waub-ish-ash-e,	Marten.
6.	Addick,	Rein Deer.
7.	Mah-een-gun,	Wolf.
8.	Ne-baun-aub-ay,	Merman.
9.	Ke-noushay,	Pike.
10.	Be-sheu,	Lynx.
11.	Me-gizzee,	Eagle.

12. Che-she-gwa,	Rattlesnake.
13. Mous,	Moose.
14. Muk-ud-a-shib,	Black Duck or Cormorant.
15. Ne-kah,	Goose.
16. Numa-bin,	Sucker.
17. Numa,	Sturgeon.
18. Ude-kumaig,	White Fish.
19. Amik,	Beaver.
20. Gy-aushk,	Gull.
21. Ka-kaik,	Hawk.

I have here given a list of every badge that is known as a family totem among the Ojibways throughout their widespread villages and bands.

The crane, catfish, bear, marten, wolf, and loon, are the principal families, not only in a civil point of view, but in numbers, as they comprise eight-tenths of the whole tribe. Many of these Totems are not known to the tribe in general, and the writer has learned them only through close inquiry Among these may be named the goose, beaver, sucker, sturgeon, gull, hawk, cormorant, and white-fish totems. They are only known on the remotest northern boundaries of the Ojibway country, among the Musk-keeg-oes and " Bois Forts."

The old men of the Ojibways whom I have particularly questioned on this subject, affirm that all these different badges are only subdivisions of the five great original totems of the An-ish-in-aub-ag, who have assumed separate minor badges, without losing sight or remembrance of the main stock or family to which they belong. These divisions have been gradually taking place, caused in the same manner as the division into distinct tribes. They are easily classed under the five great heads, the names of which we have given.

Aish-ke-bug-e-coshe, the old and reliable head chief of the Pillager and Northern Ojibways, has rendered me much information on this subject. He is the present living recognized head of the great A-waus-e family. He says that this clan claim the Me-she-num-aig-way (immense fish) which, according to their description, is equivalent or analogical, to the Leviathan mentioned in the Bible. This being is also one of the Spirits recognized in their grand Me-da-we rite. This clan comprises the several branches who claim the Catfish, Merman, Sturgeon, Pike, Whitefish, and Sucker Totems, and in fact, all the totems of the fish species may be classed under this general head. This family are physically noted for being long lived, and for the scantiness and fineness of their hair, especially in old age; if you see an old Indian of this tribe with a bald head, you may be certain that he is an A-waus-e.

Tradition says that many generations ago, all the different clans of the tribe, with the exception of the Ah-ah-wank, formed a league and made war on the Aw-aus-e with the intent to exterminate them. But the Aw-aus-e family proved too strong for their united brethren and prevailed against their efforts, and ever since this event, they have claimed a certain pre-eminence over them in the councils of the tribe. They also claim, that of the six beings who emerged from the great water, and originated the Totems, their progenitor was the first who appeared, and was leader of the others.

Of nine thousand of the Ojibways who reside within the limits of the United States, about the shores of Lake Superior and the headwaters of the Mississippi, full one thousand belong to the Aw-aus-e family.

The Bus-in-as-see, or Crane family, are also numerous, and form an important element of the Ojibway tribe. They reside mostly on the south shores of Lake Superior and toward the east in the Canadas, though they have representatives scattered in every spot where the Ojibways have set foot and lighted their fires. The literal meaning of their totemic name is, " Echo-maker," derived from the word Bus-wa-wag, " Echo," and pertaining to the loud, clear, and far reaching cry of the Crane. This clan are noted as possessing naturally a loud, ringing voice, and are the acknowledged orators of the tribe; in former times, when different tribes met in councils, they acted as inter-- preters of the wishes of their tribe. They claim, with some apparent justice, the chieftainship over the other clans of the Ojibways. The late lamented chief Shin-ga-ba-wos-sin, who resided at Sault Ste. Marie, belonged to this family. In Gov. Lewis Cass's treaty at Prairie du Chien in 1825, he was the acknowledged head chief of his tribe, and signed his name to that treaty as such. Ah-mous (the Little Bee), the son of the late worthy chief of Lac du Flambeau, Waub-ish-gaug-aug-e (or White Crow), may now be considered as head or principal chief of this family.

The old war chief Ba-be-sig-aun-dib-ay (Curly Head), whose name is linked with the history of his tribe, and who died on his way returning home from the Treaty of Prairie du Chien above mentioned, was also a Bus-in-aus-e, and the only representative of his clan amongst that section of his tribe, who so long bravely struggled with the fierce Dakotas for the mastery of the western banks of the Mississippi, which now form the home of the Winne-bagoes. He was the civil and war chief of the Missis-sippi Ojibways. Hole-in-the-day 1st, of later notoriety, and his brother Song-uk-um-ig (Strong ground), inherited his chieftainship by his dying request, as he died childless. Weesh-e-da-mo, son of Aissance (Little Clam), late British Ojibway chief of Red River, is also a member of this family. He is a young man, but has already received two American medals, one from the hands of a colonel of our army, and the other from the hands of the Governor of Minnesota

Territory. He is recognized by our government as chief of the Pembina section of the Ojibway tribe.

These facts are stated to show the importance of this family, and its wide extended influence over the tribe. It can be said of them that wherever they have planted their wigwam on the widespread territory of their people, they have been recognized as chieftains.

They also boast the names of Keesh-ke-mun, chief of the Lac du Flambeau section; Che-suh-yauh and Waub-ij-e-jauk (White Crane), of La Pointe, Shaug-a-waum-ik-ong, all noted chiefs during their first intercourse with the white race.

The small clans who use the eagle as their Totem or badge, are a branch of the Bus-in-aus-e.

The Ah-ah-wauk, or loon totem, also form an important body in the Ojibway tribe; in fact, they also claim to be the chief or royal family, and one of their arguments to prove this position is that nature has placed a color [collar?] around the neck of the loon, which resembles the royal megis, or wampum, about the neck of a chief, which forms the badge of his honor. This dignity, however, is denied by the Cranes and other totems, who aver that the principal chiefs of the Ah-ah-wauk are descended from individuals who were on a certain occasion made chiefs by the French at Quebec, as will be related in the course of the following history. This family do not lack in chiefs who have acted a prominent part in the affairs of the tribe, and whose names are linked with its history.

Ke-che-waish-keenh (Great Buffalo), the respected and venerable chief of the La Pointe band, and principal chief of all the Lake Superior and Wisconsin bands, is the acknowledged head of this clan, and his importance as an individual in the tribe, strengthens the position of the Ah-ah-wauk. The chief of Sandy Lake on the upper Mississippi is also of this family. The Goose and Cormorant

Totems are its subdivisions. The No-ka or Bear family are more numerous than any of the other clans of the Ojibways, forming fully one-sixth of the entire tribe.

In former times this numerous body was subdivided into many lesser clans, making only portions of the bear's body their Totems, as the head, the foot, the ribs, etc. They have all since united under one head, and the only shade of difference still recognized by them is the common and grizzly bear. They are the acknowledged war chiefs and warriors of the tribe, and are keepers of the war-pipe and war-club, and are often denominated the bulwarks of the tribe against its enemies.

It is a general saying, and an observable fact, amongst their fellows, that the Bear clan resemble the animal that forms their Totem in disposition. They are ill-tempered and fond of fighting, and consequently they are noted as ever having kept the tribe in difficulty and war with other tribes, in which, however, they have generally been the principal and foremost actors. They are physically noted, and the writer has observed the fact, that they are possessed of a long, thick, coarse head of the blackest hair, which seldom becomes thin or white in old age. Young Hole-in-the-day (son of the great war-chief of that name), the recognized chief of the Ojibways of the Mississippi, numbering about twelve hundred, is now [A. D. 1852] the most noted man of the No-ka family. Ka-kaik (the Hawk), of Chippeway River, and Be-she-ke (Buffalo), of Leech Lake, have extolled influence as war chiefs.

The Mah-een-gun, or Wolf totem family, are few in number, and reside mostly on the St. Croix River and at Mille Lac. They are looked upon by the tribe in general with much respect. The Ojibways of this totem derive their origin on the paternal side from the Dakotas. Na-guon-abe, the civil chief of Mille Lac, may be considered the principal man of this family. Mun-o-min-ik-a-she

(Rice-maker), who has lately removed from the St. Croix to Mille Lac with his band, is a man of considerable importance amongst his fellows.

The Waub-ish-a-she, or Marten family, form a numerous body in the tribe, and is one of the leading clans. Tradition says that they are sprung from the remnant captives of a fierce and warlike tribe whom the coalesced Algic tribes have exterminated, and whom they denominate the Mun-dua. The chiefs Waub-ish-ash (the Marten), of Chippeway River, Shin-goob (Balsam), and Nug-aun-ub (Sitting-ahead), of Fond du Lac, are now the principal men of the clan. The celebrated Ke-che-waub-ish-ash, of Sandy Lake, Sha-wa-ke-shig, of Leech Lake, and Muk-ud-a-shib (or Black Duck), of Red River, were members of this family. In their days they conduced greatly towards wresting country from the Dakotas, and driving them westward. All three died on battle-fields—the first at Elk River fight, the second at Rum River massacre, and the third fell fighting on the western prairies against immense odds; but one out of forty, who fought with him, escaped a warrior's death.

Under the generic term of Mous-o-neeg, the families of the Marten, Moose, and Reindeer totems are included. Aish-ke-bug-e-coshe, the old Pillager chief, related to me the following tradition, accounting for the coalition or close affinity between the Moose and Marten totems:—

"The family of the Moose totem, denominated Mous-o-neeg, many centuries ago, when the Ojibways lived towards the rising sun, were numerous and powerful. They lived congregated by themselves in one great village, and were noted for their warlike and quarrelsome disposition. They were ill-tempered and proud of their strength and bravery. For some slight cause they commenced to make war on their brethren of the Marten totem. Severely suffering from the incursions, and unable to cope singly with the

Mous-o-neeg, the Martens called together the different clans of the tribe to council, and called on them for help and protection. A general league was made between the different totems, and it was determined that the men of the obnoxious and quarrelsome family of the Moose badge should be exterminated.

"The plan for their sudden and total destruction was agreed upon, and a council lodge was ordered to be built, which was made narrow and just long enough to admit all the warriors of the Mous-o-neeg. The poles of this lodge were planted firmly and deep in the ground, and close together, and lapping over the top they were strongly twisted and fastened together. Over this frame were tied lengthways, and worked in like wicker-work, other green poles, and so close together that a man's hand could scarcely pass through any part of the frame, so close and strong was it constructed. Over this frame, and from the inside, leaving but a long narrow aperture in the top, was fastened a thick covering and lining of dried grass.

"When this lodge had been completed, runners were sent to the village of the Moose Totem family, and all their chiefs and warriors solemnly invited to a national council and feast. This summons was made in such a manner that they could not refuse, even if they so felt disposed; and on the day fixed, the chiefs and all the men of war of the refractory clan arrived in a body at the village of their mortal foes (the Martens), where the council-lodge had been built and made ready.

"They were led into the lodge, where the old men and chiefs of the tribe had collected to receive them. The Mous-o-neeg entered unarmed, and as their great numbers gradually filled the lodge, the former inmates, as if through courtesy, arose and went out to give them room. Kettles full of cooked meat were brought in and placed before them, and they were requested to eat, after the fatigues of

their journey. They entirely filled the long lodge; and
when every one had left it but themselves, and while they
were busy feasting on the good things that had been placed
before them, the doors at each end were suddenly closed
and fastened on them. A chief of the Marten Totem then
addressed them in a loud voice, repeating over all the acts
of blood and wickedness which they had enacted, and
informing them that for these things the national council
had decreed to sweep them from the face of the earth
which they polluted. The lodge was surrounded by the
warriors of the Marten, who acted as executioners; torches
were applied to the thick and dry covering of grass, and,
struggling in the flames unable to escape, the men of the
Moose Totem were dispatched with barbed arrows shot
through the narrow openings between the lodge-poles that
confined them. In this fearful manner were the men of
this wicked clan destroyed. Their women and children
were captured by the Marten family, and adopted into
their clan. In this manner the close consanguinity of
these two Totems commenced, and at this day they are
considered as one family."

The Reindeer family, which is a branch of the Mous-o-
neeg, are few in number, and they reside mostly on the
north coast of Lake Superior. The celebrated Ojibway
war-leader Waub-o-jeeg (White Fisher), whom Mr. Schoolcraft has noticed in his writings at some length, was a
member of this family, descended from a branch who emigrated from the Grand Portage near the mouth of Pigeon
River to La Pointe, Shag-a-waum-ik-ong, where he and his
father, Ma-moug-e-se-do (Big-foot), flourished nearly a century ago as war-leaders and chiefs of their people.

The other badges or totemic symbols which I have enumerated, form inconsiderable families, and are but branches
of the principal clans whom I have noticed in the fore-
going pages.

It will be difficult, till a minute insight is obtained into the totemic history and organization of all the Algic tribes, to decide fully the number of generic or grand Totems which are recognized among them, and the numeric strength of each.

This subject is deserving of close research and study. I consider it a most important link in solving the deep mystery which covers their origin. Even with the imperfect insight which has been given on this subject by different writers, an analogy cannot but be noticed existing in many respects between the totemic division of the Algics, and the division of the Hebrews into tribes. And the remarkable purity with which the system has been kept up for ages, finds no other parallel in the history of mankind.

CHAPTER III.

ORIGIN OF THE OJIBWAYS.

Preliminary remarks—Belief of the Ojibways respecting their origin—Belief in, and causes of a deluge—A code of religion given to them by the Great Spirit—Analysis of their name as a people—Their original beliefs have become mixed with the teaching of the old Jesuit missionaries—Difficulty of obtaining their pure beliefs—Tales which they relate to the whites, not genuine—Non-unity of the human race—Effects of disbelieving the Bible—Differences between the American aborigines—Between the Ojibways and Dakotas—Surmise of their different origin—Belief of the Ojibways in a Great Spirit—Their extreme veneration—Sacrifice—Visions of the Great Spirit—Mode of obtaining guardian or dream Spirits—Fasts and dreams—Sacrificial feasts—Grand rite of the Me-da-we-win—It is not yet understood by the whites—Misrepresented by missionaries and writers—It contains their most ancient hieroglyphics, and the most ancient idiom of their language—Rules of the Me-da-we-win—Tradition of the snake-root—Ojibway medicine sack—Custom among the Blackfeet bearing a resemblance to the ark and the High Priesthood of the Hebrews—Totemic division into families—Their traditions bear a similitude to Bible history—Antagonistical position between the Ojibways and Dakotas—Belief of the Ojibways in a future state—Important facts deduced therefrom.

I AM fully aware that many learned and able writers have given to the world their opinions respecting the origin of the aboriginal inhabitants of the American Continent, and the manner in which they first obtained a footing and populated this important section of the earth, which, for so many thousand years, remained unknown to the major portion of mankind inhabiting the Old World. It is, however, still a matter of doubt and perplexity; it is a book sealed to the eyes of man, for the time has not yet come when the Great Ruler of all things, in His wisdom, shall make answer through his inscrutable ways to the question which has puzzled, and still puzzles the minds of the learned civilized world. How came America to be first inhabited by man? What branch of the great human family are its aboriginal people descended from?

Ever having lived in the wilderness, even beyond what is known as the western frontiers of white immigration, where books are scarce and difficult to be procured, I have never had the coveted opportunity and advantage of reading the opinions of the various eminent authors who have written on this subject, to compare with them the crude impressions which have gradually, and I may say naturally, obtained possession in my own mind, during my whole life, which I have passed in a close connection of residence and blood with different sections of the Ojibway tribe.

The impressions and the principal causes which have led to their formation, I now give to the public to be taken for what they are considered worth. Clashing with the received opinions of more learned writers, whose words are taken as standard authority, they may be totally rejected, in which case the satisfaction will still be left me, that before the great problem had been fully solved, I, a person in language, thoughts, beliefs, and blood, partly an Indian, had made known my crude and humble opinion.

Respecting their own origin the Ojibways are even more totally ignorant than their white brethren, for they have no Bible to tell them that God originally made Adam, from whom the whole human race is sprung. They have their beliefs and oral traditions, but so obscure and unnatural, that nothing approximating to certainty can be drawn from them. They fully believe, and it forms part of their religion, that the world has once been covered by a deluge, and that we are now living on what they term the "new earth." This idea is fully accounted for by their vague traditions; and in their Me-da-we-win or Religion, hieroglyphics are used to denote this second earth.

They fully believe that the Red man mortally angered the Great Spirit which caused the deluge, and at the commencement of the new earth it was only through the medium and intercession of a powerful being, whom they denominate Man-ab-o-sho, that they were allowed to exist, and means were given them whereby to subsist and support life; and a code of religion was more lately bestowed on them, whereby they could commune with the offended Great Spirit, and ward off the approach and ravages of death. This they term Me-da-we-win.

Respecting their belief of their own first existence, I can give nothing more appropriate than a minute analysis of the name which they have given to their race—An-ish-in-aub-ag. This expressive word is derived from An-ish-aw, meaning without cause, or "spontaneous," and in-aub-a-we-se, meaning the "human body." The word An-ish-in-aub-ag, therefore, literally translated, signifies "spontaneous man."

Henry R. Schoolcraft (who has apparently studied this language, and has written respecting this people more than any other writer, and whose works as a whole, deserve the standard authority which is given to them by the literary world), has made the unaccountable mistake of giving as the meaning of this important name, "Common people." We can account for this only in his having studied the language through the medium of imperfect interpreters. In no respect can An-ish-in-aub-ag be twisted so as to include any portion of a word meaning "common."

Had he given the meaning of "original people," which he says is the interpretation of "Lenni Lenape," the name which the ancient Delawares and eastern sections of the Algic tribes call themselves, he would have hit nearer the mark. "Spontaneous man" is, however, the true literal translation, and I am of the impression that were the two apparently different names of Lenni Lenape and An-ish-in-aub-ag fully analyzed, and correctly pronounced by a person understanding fully the language of both sections of the same family, who call themselves respectively by these names, not only the meaning would be found exactly to coincide, but also the words, differing only slightly in pronunciation.

The belief of the Algics is, as their name denotes, that they are a spontaneous people. They do not pretend, as a people, to give any reliable account of their first creation. It is a subject which to them is buried in darkness and mystery, and of which they entertain but vague and uncertain notions ; notions which are fully embodied in the word An-ish-in-aub-ag.

Since the white race have appeared amongst them, and since the persevering and hard-working Jesuit missionaries during the era of the French domination, carried the cross and their teachings into the heart of the remotest wilderness, and breathed a new belief and new tales into the ears of the wild sons of the forest, their ideas on this subject have become confused, and in many instances they have pretended to imbibe the beliefs thus early promulgated amongst them, connecting them with their own more crude and mythological ideas. It is difficult on this account, to procure from them what may have been their pure and original belief, apart from what is perpetuated by the name which we have analyzed. It requires a most intimate acquaintance with them as a people, and individually with their old story tellers, also with their language, beliefs, and customs, to procure their real beliefs and to analyze the tales they seldom refuse to tell, and separate the Indian or original from those portions which they have borrowed or imbibed from the whites. Their innate courtesy and politeness often carry them so far that they seldom, if ever, refuse to tell a story when asked by a white man, respecting their ideas of the creation and the origin of mankind.

These tales, though made up for the occasion by the Indian sage, are taken by his white hearers as their *bona fide* belief, and, as such, many have been made public, and accepted by the civilized world. Some of their sages have been heard to say, that the " Great Spirit" from the earth originally made three different races of men—the white, the black, and red race. To the first he gave a book, denoting wisdom; to the second a hoe, denoting servitude and labor; to the third, or red race, he gave the bow and arrow, denoting the hunter state. To his red children the " Great Spirit" gave the great island on which the whites have found them; but because of having committed some great wickedness and angered their Maker, they are doomed to disappear before the rapid tread and advance of the wiser and more favored pale face. This, abbreviated and condensed into a few words, is the story, with variations, with which, as a general thing, the Indian has amused the curiosity of his inquisitive white brother.

It is, however, plainly to be seen that these are not their original ideas, for they knew not, till they came amongst them, of the existence of a white and black race, nor of their characteristic symbols of the book and the hoe.

Were we to entertain the new belief which is being advocated by able and learned men, who have closely studied the Biblical with the physical history of man, that the theory taught us in the Sacred Book, making mankind the descendants of one man—Adam—is false, and that the human family are derived originally from a multiplicity of progenitors, definitely marked by physical differences, it would be no difficult matter to arrive at once to certain conclusions respecting the manner in which America became populated. But a believing mind is loth to accept the assertions, arguments, and opinions of a set of men who would cast down at one fell swoop the widely-received beliefs inculcated in the minds of enlightened mankind by the sacred book of God. Men will not fall blindly into such a belief, not even with the most convincing arguments.

Throw down the testimony of the Bible, annul in your mind its sacred truths, and we are at once thrown into a perfect chaos of confusion and ignorance. Destroy the belief which has been entertained for ages by the enlightened portion of mankind, and we are thrown at once on a level with the ignorant son of the forest respecting our own origin. In his natural state he would even have the advantage of his more enlightened brother, for he deduces his beliefs from what he sees of nature and nature's work, and possessing no certain proof or knowledge of the manner of his creation, he simply but forcibly styles himself "spontaneous man." On the other hand, the white man, divested of Bible truths and history, yet possessing wisdom and learning, and a knowledge of the conflicting testimony of ages past, descended to him in manuscript and ancient monuments, possessing also a knowledge of the physical formation of all races of men and the geological formation of the earth, would still be at a loss to arrive at certain conclusions; and the deeper he bit into the apple of knowledge, the more confused would be his mind in attempting without the aid of God's word to solve the deep mysteries of Nature—to solve the mystery of the creation of a universe in which our earth is apparently but as a grain of sand, and to solve the problem of his own mysterious existence.

We pause, therefore, before we take advantage of any apparent discrepancy or contradiction in the Bible which may be artfully shown to us by unbelieving writers, and to make use of it to more easily prove any favorite theory which we may imbibe respecting the manner in which America first became peopled.

Assume the ground that the human species does not come of one common head, and the existence of the red race is a problem no longer; but believe the word of the Holy Bible, and it will remain a mystery till God wills otherwise. In the mean time, we can but conjecture and surmise; each person has a right to form his own opinion. Some deduce from the writings of others, and others from personal observation, and by making known the causes which have led to the formation of his opinion, he will add to the general mass of information which has been and is gradually collecting, from which eventually more certain deductions will be arrived at.

Taking the ground that the theory respecting the origin of the human race taught us in the Holy Scriptures is true, I will proceed to express my humble opinion respecting the branch of the human race from which originates that particular type of the aboriginal race of America comprised by the term Algic or Algonquin, of which grand family the Ojibway tribe, of whom I shall more particularly treat, forms a numerous and important section.

During my long residence among the Ojibways, after numberless inquiries of their old men, I have never been able to learn, by tradition or otherwise, that they entertain the belief that all the tribes of the red race inhabiting America have ever been, at any time since the occupancy of this continent, one and the same people, speaking the same language, and practising the same beliefs and customs. The traditions of this tribe extend no further into the past than the once concentration or coalition under one head, of the different and now scattered tribes belonging to the Algic stock.

We have every reason to believe that America has not been peopled from one nation or tribe of the human family,

for there are differences amongst its inhabitants and con-
trarieties as marked and fully developed as are to be found
between European and Asiatic nations—wide differences
in language, beliefs, and customs.

A close study of the dissimilarities existing between
the Ojibways and Dakotas, who have more immediately
come under my observation, has led me fully to believe
that they are not descended from the same people of the
Old World, nor have they ever in America formed one
and the same nation or tribe. It is true that they assimi-
late in color and in their physical formation, which can be
accounted for by their residence in the same climate, and
sustaining life through the same means. Many of their
customs are also alike, but these have been naturally
similarized and entailed on them by living in the same
wild hunter state, and many they have derived from one
another during their short fitful terms of peace and intercourse. Here all similitude between the two tribes ends.
They cannot differ more widely than they do in language;
and the totemic system, which is an important and leading
characteristic among the Ojibways, is not known to the
Dakotas. They differ also widely in their religious beliefs,
and as far back as their oral traditions descend with any
certainty, they tell of even having been mortal enemies,
waging against each other a bloody and exterminating
warfare.

Assuming the ground which has been proved both
probable and practicable by different eminent authors,
that the American continent has been populated from the
eastern and northeastern shores of Asia, it is easy to
believe that not only one, but portions of different Asiatic
tribes found their way thither, which will account for the
radical differences to be found in the languages of the
several stocks of the American aborigines.

Taking these grounds, the writer is disposed to enter-

tain the belief that, while the original ancestors of the
Dakota race might have formed a tribe or portion of a
tribe of the roving sons of Tartary, whom they resemble
in many essential respects, the Algics, on the other hand,
may be descended from a portion of the ten lost tribes of
Israel, whom they also resemble in many important particulars.

Of this latter stock only can I speak with any certainty.
I am fully aware that the surmise which is here advanced
is not new, but is one which has already elicited much discussion; and although later writers have presented it as
an exploded idea, yet I cannot refrain from presenting the
ideas on this subject which have gradually inducted themselves into my mind.

Boudinot and other learned writers, having at their command the books and observations on the Indian tribes
which have been published from time to time since their
first discovery, and possessing an intimate knowledge of
Biblical history, have fallen into the same belief, and
from a mass of book information they have been enabled
to offer many able arguments to prove the Red Race of
America descendants of the lost tribes of Israel. I have
never had the advantage of seeing or reading these books,
and only know of their existence from hearsay, and the
casual remarks or references of the few authors I have
been enabled to consult. The belief which I have now expressed has grown on me imperceptibly from my youth,
ever since I could first read the Bible, and compare with it
the lodge stories and legends of my Indian grandfathers,
around whose lodge fires I have passed many a winter
evening, listening with parted lips and open ears to their
interesting and most forcibly told tales.

After reaching the age of maturity, I pursued my inquiries with more system, and the more information I
have obtained from them—the more I have become ac-

quainted with their anomalous and difficult to be understood characters—the more insight I have gained into
their religious and secret rites and faith, the more strongly
has it been impressed on my mind that they bear a close
affinity or analogy to the chosen people of God, and they
are either descendants of the lost tribes of Israel, or they
have had, in some former era, a close contact and intercourse with the Hebrews, imbibing from them their
beliefs and customs and the traditions of their patriarchs.

To enter into a detailed account of all the numerous and
trivial causes which have induced me to entertain this
idea, would take up much space, and as the subject has
been so much dwelt upon, by those who, from having
made the subject the study of their lives, and who by
their researches have gathered much of the requisite information to arrive at more just conclusions than the
humble writer, I will confine myself to stating a few general facts, some of which may have missed the attention
of my predecessors on this road of inquiry, and which
none but those intimately acquainted with the Indians,
and possessing their fullest confidence, are able to obtain.

It is a general fact that most people who have been discovered living in a savage and unenlightened state, and
even whole nations living in partial civilization, have been
found to be idolaters—having no just conception of a
great first Cause or Creator, invisible to human eyes, and
pervading all space. With the Ojibways it is not so; the
fact of their firm belief and great veneration, in an overruling Creator and Master of Life, has been noticed by all
who have had close intercourse with them since their
earliest discovery. It is true that they believe in a multiplicity of spirits which pervade all nature, yet all these are
subordinate to the one Great Spirit of good.

This belief is as natural (if not more so), as the belief of
the Catholics in their interceding saints, which in some

respects it resembles, for in the same light as intercessors between him and the Great Spirit, does the more simple Red Man regard the spirits which in his imagination pervade all creation. The never-failing rigid fasts of first manhood, when they seek in dreams for a guardian spirit, illustrates this belief most forcibly.

Ke-che-mun-e-do (Great Spirit) is the name used by the Ojibways for the being equivalent to our God. They have another term which can hardly be surpassed by any one word in the English language, for force, condensity, and expression, namely: Ke-zha-mune-do, which means pitying, charitable, overruling, guardian, and merciful Spirit; in fact, it expresses all the great attributes of the God of Israel. It is derived from Ke-zha-wand-e-se-roin, meaning charity, kindness—Ke-zha-wus-so expressing the guardian feeling, and solicitude of a parent toward its offspring, watching it with jealous vigilance from harm; and Shah-wau-je-gay, to take pity, merciful, with Mun-e-do (spirit). There is nothing to equal the veneration with which the Indian regards this unseen being. They seldom even ever mention his name unless in their Me-da-we and other religious rites, and in their sacrificial feasts; and then an address to him, however trivial, is always accompanied with a sacrifice of tobacco or some other article deemed precious by the Indian. They never use his name in vain, and there is no word in their language expressive of a profane oath, or equivalent to the many words used in profane swearing by their more enlightened white brethren.

Instances are told of persons while enduring almost superhuman fasts, obtaining a vision of him in their dreams; in such instances the Great Spirit invariably appears to the dreamer in the shape of a beautifully and strongly-formed man. And it is a confirmed belief amongst them, that he or she who has once been blessed with this vision, is fated to live to a good old age and in enjoyment of ease and plenty.

All other minor or guardian spirits whom they court in their first dream of fasting appear to them in the shape of quadrupeds, birds, or some inanimate object in nature, as the moon, the stars, or the imaginary thunderers; and even this dream-spirit is never mentioned without sacrifice. The dream itself which has appeared to the faster, guides in a great measure his future course in life, and he never relates it without offering a sacrificial feast to the spirit of the dream. The bones of the animal which he offers are carefully gathered, unbroken, tied together, and either hung on a tree, thrown into deep water, or carefully burnt. Their beliefs and rites, connected with their fasts and dreams, are of great importance to themselves, more so than has been generally understood by writers who have treated of the Algics.

These facts are mentioned here to show an analogy with the ancient and primitive customs of the Hebrews—their faith in dreams, their knowledge and veneration of the unseen God, and the customs of fasting and sacrifice. Minor customs, equally similar with the usages of the Hebrews as we read in the Bible, might be enumerated; for instance, the never-failing separation of the female during the first period of menstruation, their war customs, etc. But it is not the intention of the writer to enter with prolixity on this field of inquiry which has been so often trod by able writers.

The grand rite of Me-da-we-win (or, as we have learned to term it, " Grand Medicine) and the beliefs incorporated therein, are not yet fully understood by the whites. This important custom is still shrouded in mystery, even to my own eyes, though I have taken much pains to inquire, and made use of every advantage, possessed by speaking their language perfectly, being related to them, possessing their friendship and intimate confidence, has given me, and yet I frankly acknowledge that I stand as yet, as it were, on the threshold of the Me-da-we lodge. I believe, however, that I have obtained full as much and more general and true information on this matter than any other person who has written on the subject, not excepting a great and standard author, who, to the surprise of many who know the Ojibways well, has boldly asserted in one of his works that he has been regularly initiated into the mysteries of this rite, and is a member of the Me-da-we Society. This is certainly an assertion hard to believe in the Indian country; and when the old initiators or Indian priests are told of it, they shake their heads in incredulity that a white man should ever have been allowed *in truth* to become a member of their Me-da-we lodge.

An entrance into the lodge itself, while the ceremonies are being enacted, has sometimes been granted through courtesy; but this does not initiate a person into the mysteries of the creed, nor does it make him a member of the society.

Amongst the Ojibways, the secrets of this grand rite are as sacredly kept as the secrets of the Masonic Lodge among the whites. Fear of threatened and certain death, either by poison or violence, seals the lips of the Me-da-we initiate, and this is the potent reason why it is still a secret to the white man, and why it is not more generally understood.

Missionaries, travellers, and transient sojourners amongst the Ojibways, who have witnessed the performance of the grand Me-da-we ceremonies, have represented and published that it is composed of foolish and unmeaning ceremonies. The writer begs leave to say that these superficial observers labor under a great mistake. The Indian has equal right, and may with equal truth (but in his utter ignorance is more excusable), to say, on viewing the rites of the

Catholic and other churches, that they consist of unmeaning and nonsensical ceremonies. There is much yet to be learned from the wild and apparently simple son of the forest, and the most which remains to be learned is to be derived from their religious beliefs.

In the Me-da-we rite is incorporated most that is ancient amongst them—songs and traditions that have descended, not orally, but in hieroglyphics, for at least a long line of generations. In this rite is also perpetuated the purest and most ancient idioms of their language, which differs somewhat from that of the common every-day use. And if comparisons are to be made between the language of the Ojibways and the other languages, it must be with their religious idiom.

The writer has learned enough of the religion of the Ojibways to strengthen his belief of the analogy with the Hebrews. They assert that the Me-da-we rite was granted them by the Great Spirit in a time of trouble and death, through the intercession of Man-ab-osho, the universal uncle of the An-ish-in-aub-ag. Certain rules to guide their course in life were given them at the same time, and are represented in hieroglyphics. These great rules of life, which the writer has often heard inculcated by the Me-da-we initiators in their secret teachings to their novices, bear a strong likeness to the ten commandments revealed by the Almighty to the children of Israel, amidst the awful lightning and thunder of Mount Sinai.

They have a tradition telling of a great pestilence, which suddenly cut off many while encamped in one great village. They were saved by one of their number, to whom a spirit in the shape of a serpent discovered a certain root, which to this day they name the Ke-na-big-wushk or snakeroot. The songs and rites of this medicine are incorporated in the Me-da-we. The above circumstance is told to have happened when the " earth was new," and taking into consideration the lapse of ages, and their being greatly addicted to figurative modes of expression, this tradition bears some resemblance to the plague of the children of Israel in the wilderness, which was stopped by means of the brazen serpent of Moses.

The Ojibway pin-jig-o-saun, or as we term it, " medicine bag," contains all which he holds most sacred ; it is preserved with great care, and seldom ever allowed a place in the common wigwam, but is generally left hanging in the open air on a tree, where even an ignorant child dare not touch it. The contents are never displayed without much ceremony. This too, however distant, still bears some analogy to the receptacle of the Holy of Holies of the Hebrews.

I have learned from people who have been resident amongst them, that the tribe known as the Blackfeet, living above the sources of the Missouri, practise a custom which bears a still stronger likeness to the sacred ark and priesthood, as used of old in Israel. The Blackfeet, by comparing portions of their language which has been published by the persevering Father de Smet, and portions that I have learned verbally from others, with the language of the Ojibways, has convinced me that they belong to the same family of tribes, and may be denominated Algics. Any portion, therefore, of their customs which may have fallen under our observation, may be appropriately mentioned here, to strengthen the grounds we have taken respecting their common origin.

A man is appointed by the elders and chiefs of the Blackfeet every four years to take charge of the sacred pipe, pipestem, mat, and other emblems of their religious beliefs. A lodge is allotted for his especial use, to contain these emblems and articles pertaining to his office. Four horses are given him to pack these things from place to place, following the erratic movements of the camp. This functionary is obliged to practise seven fasts, and to live during the term of his priesthood in entire celibacy. Even if he possesses a family, on his appointment as " Great Medicine" he must separate from them during his term, and the public supports them. All religious councils are held in his lodge, and disputes are generally adjusted by him as judge. His presence and voice are sufficient to quell all domestic disturbance, and altogether he holds more actual power and influence than even the civil and war chiefs. His face is always painted black, and he wears his hair tied in a large knot over his forehead, and through this knot is passed a sharp stick with which he scratches his body, should he have occasion, for he is not to use his finger nails for this purpose. None but he can or dare handle the sacred pipe and emblems. At the end of his term the tribe presents him with a new lodge, horses, and so forth, wherewith to commence life anew.

It cannot but strike the attention of an observer, that this custom, this peculiar personage with his lodge and sacred emblems, among the roving sons of the prairies, resembles forcibly the ark and high priesthood of the wandering Israelites of old. I wish again to remark that the fact of this custom being in use among the Blackfeet, has not been obtained under my own personal observation, and therefore I cannot vouch fully for its truth. Having learned it, however, of persons of undoubted veracity, I have deemed it worthy of insertion here. It was corroborated to me during the summer of 1849, by Paul Kane, Esq., a Canadian gentleman,[1] while stopping at my house at Crow Wing on the Mississippi, with Sir Edward Poor and

---

[1] Paul Kane was an artist of Toronto. In the Parliament Library of the Dominion of Canada, at Ottawa, are twelve of his oil paintings representing Indian life toward the Rocky Mountains. In 1859 a book from his pen was published in London, with the title *Wanderings of an Artist among the Indians of North America, from Canada to Van Couver's Island and Oregon.*—E. D. N.

others, en route for Selkirk's Settlement, Oregon and California. He appeared a learned and much travelled man, and having been during the course of former travels, and during a long connection with the Hudson Bay Company, a sojourner more or less among the Blackfeet, he had learned of the existence of the above peculiar custom.

Another peculiar trait among the Algics is that which has already been fully dwelt upon under the head of their Totemic division. There is nothing to which I can compare the purity and rigid conformity with which this division into families has been kept for centuries and probably ages, amongst the Ojibways, as the division of the Hebrews into tribes, originating from the twelve sons of Jacob. Another peculiarity which has most forcibly struck my mind as one worthy of notice, and which in fact first drew my attention to this subject, is the similitude which exists between the oral traditions and lodge stories of the Ojibways with the tales of the Hebrew patriarchs in the Old Testament.

They tell one set of traditions which treat of the adventures of eight, ten, and sometimes twelve brothers. The youngest of these brothers is represented in the many traditions which mention them, as the wisest and most beloved of their father, and lying under the special guardianship of the Great Spirit. In one tradition under the name of Wa-jeeg-e-wa-kon-ay (Fisher skin coat) he delivers his brethren from divers difficulties entailed on them from their own folly and disobedience. In another tradition he is made to supply his brethren with corn. The name of the father is sometimes given as Ge-tub-e. The similarity between these and other traditions, with the Bible stories of Jacob and his twelve sons, cannot fail to attract the attention of any person who is acquainted with both versions.

The tradition of the deluge, and traditions of wars

between the different Totemic clans, all bear an analogy
with tales of the Bible.

To satisfy my own curiosity I have sometimes interpreted to their old men, portions of Bible history, and
their expression is invariably : " The book must be true,
for our ancestors have told us similar stories, generation
after generation, since the earth was new." It is a bold
assertion, but it is nevertheless a true one, that were the
traditions of the Ojibways written in order, and published
in a book, it would as a whole bear a striking resemblance
to the Old Testament, and would contain no greater im-
probabilities than may be accounted for by the loose manner in which these traditions have been perpetuated ;
naturally losing force and truth in descending orally
through each succeeding generation.   Discard, then, altogether the idea of any connection existing or having
existed between the Ojibways and the Hebrews, and it
will be found difficult to account for all the similarities
existing between many of their rites, customs, and beliefs.
Notwithstanding all that has been and may be advanced
to prove the Ojibways descended from the lost tribes of
Israel, or at least, their once having had close communion
with them, yet I am aware that there are many stubborn
facts and arguments against it, the principal of which is
probably their total variance in language.   Never having
studied the Hebrew language, I have not had the advantage of comparing with it the Ojibway, and on this point
I cannot express any opinion.

It is not supposable, however, that the ten lost tribes of
Israel emigrated from the land of their captivity in one
body, and proceeding direct to the eastern shores of Asia,
crossed over to America (by some means which, through
changes and convulsions in nature, have become extinct
and unknown to the present age) there to resume the rites
of their religion, practise the Mosaic laws, and isolated

from the rest of mankind, perpetuated in their primitive purity their language and beliefs.

On the contrary, if the Algics are really descendants of these tribes, it must be only from a portion of them, as remnants of the lost tribes have been discovered in the Nestorians of Asia. To arrive in America, these portions must have passed through strange and hostile tribes of people, and in the course of their long wanderings and sojourns amongst them, they might have adopted portions of their languages and usages, losing thereby the purity of their own. It is natural to surmise that they were driven and followed into America by hostile tribes of Asia, and that they have been thus driven and followed till checked by the waves of the broad Atlantic. This would account for the antagonistical position in which they and the Dakotas were first discovered, and which, as the Algics are now being pressed back by the white race, on the track of their old emigration, has again been renewed more deadly than ever. Truly are they a wandering and accursed race! They now occupy a position wedged in as it were, between the onward resistless tide of European emigration, and the still powerful tribes of the Naud-o-wa-se-wug ("Like unto the Adders"), their inveterate and hereditary enemies. As a distinct people their final extinction appears inevitable, though their blood may still course on as long as mankind exists.

I cannot close these remarks on this subject (though they have already been lengthened further than was at first intended), without offering a few words respecting the belief of the Ojibways in a future state. Something can be deducted from this respecting their condition in former ages, and the direction from which they originally emigrated.

When an Ojibway dies, his body is placed in a grave, generally in a sitting posture, facing the west. With the body are buried all the articles needed in life for a journey.

If a man, his gun, blanket, kettle, fire steel, flint and moccasins; if a woman, her moccasins, axe, portage collar,
blanket and kettle. The soul is supposed to stand immediately after the death of the body, on a deep beaten
path, which leads westward; the first object he comes to
in following this path, is the great Oda-e-min (Heart
berry), or strawberry, which stands on the roadside like a
huge rock, and from which he takes a handful and eats on
his way. He travels on till he reaches a deep, rapid stream
of water, over which lies the much dreaded Ko-go-gaup-o-
gun or rolling and sinking bridge; once safely over this as
the traveller looks back it assumes the shape of a huge
serpent swimming, twisting and untwisting its folds across
the stream. After camping out four nights, and travelling
each day through a prairie country, the soul arrives in the
land of spirits, where he finds his relatives accumulated
since mankind was first created; all is rejoicing, singing
and dancing; they live in a beautiful country interspersed
with clear lakes and streams, forests and prairies, and
abounding in fruit and game to repletion—in a word,
abounding in all that the red man most covets in this life,
and which conduces most to his happiness. It is that kind
of a paradise which he only by his manner of life on this
earth, is fitted to enjoy. Without dwelling further on this
belief, which if carried out in all its details would occupy
under the head of this chapter much unnecessary space, I
will now state the conclusions which may possibly be
educed from it.

The Ojibway believes his home after death to lie westward. In their religious phraseology, the road of souls is
sometimes called Ke-wa-kun-ah, "Homeward road." It
is, however, oftener named Che-ba-kun-ah (road of souls).
In the ceremony of addressing their dead before depositing
them in the grave, I have often heard the old men use the
word Ke-go-way-se-kah (you are going homeward). This

road is represented as passing mostly through a prairie country.

Is it not probable from these beliefs that ages ago the Ojibways resided westward, and occupied a country " flowing in milk and honey "—a country abounding in all that tends to their enjoyment and happiness, and to which they look back as the tired traveller on a burning desert looks back to a beautiful oasis which he has once passed, or as the lonely wanderer looks back to the once happy home of his childhood? May they not forcibly have been driven from this former country by more powerful nations— have been pressed east and still further eastward from Asia in to America, and over its whole extent, arrested by the waves of the Atlantic Ocean? And, like a receding wave, they have turned their faces westward towards their former country, within the past four centuries forced back by European discovery and immigration.

With their mode of transmitting traditions from father to son orally, it is natural to suppose that their present belief in the westward destination of the soul has originated from the above-surmised era in their ancient history. And the tradition of a once happy home and country, being imperfectly transmitted to our times through long lines of generations, has at last merged into the simple and natural belief of a future state, which thoroughly pervades the Indian mind, and guides, in a measure, his actions in life, and enables him to smile at the approach of death.

They have traditions connected with this belief which forcibly illustrate the surmises we have advanced.

In conclusion, I will again remark that though I am fully aware that the subject, and much-disputed point, of the origin of the American Indian is far beyond my depth of understanding and limited knowledge, yet I have deemed it a duty to thus make known the facts embodied in this chapter, and ideas, however crude and conflicting with the received opinions of more learned authors. I offer them for what they may be worth, and if they be ever used towards elucidating this mystery by wise men who may make it an object of study and research, the end of making them public will be satisfactorily fulfilled.

The analogies which have been noticed as existing between the Hebrew and Algic tribes have not struck my attention individually; others whom I have consulted, living as isolated among the Ojibways as I have been, holding daily communion with them, speaking their language, hearing their legends and lodge stories, and, withal, readers of the Bible, have fallen into the same belief, and this simple fact is itself full worthy of notice.

CHAPTER IV.

EMIGRATION OF THE OJIBWAYS FROM THE SHORES OF THE
ATLANTIC OCEAN, TO THEIR OCCUPATION OF THE AREA OF
LAKE SUPERIOR.

Tradition of the sea-shell—Tradition of the otter—Separation of the Ojibways,
Potta-wat-umees. and Ottaways at the straits of Michilimacinac—Origin of
their tribal names—Causes of their emigration from the Atlantic seaboard—
Ojibways settle at Sault Ste. Marie—They separate into two divisions—
Movements of the northern division—Traditional anecdote of the war
between the Marten and the Omush-kas families—Movements of the southern
division—Allegory of the cranes—Copper-plate register of the Crane family—
Era of their first occupation of Point Shaug-a-waum-ik-ong—Tradition of
the extermination of the Mundua tribe.

THE history of the Ojibway tribe, till within the past
five centuries, lies buried in darkness and almost utter
oblivion. In the preceding chapter we have feebly attempted to lift the veil which covers their past, by offering
well-founded facts which can be excusably used in the
formation of conjectures and probabilities. All is, however,
still nothing but surmise and uncertainty, and what of
this nature has been presented, has not been given, nor can
it be considered as authentic history. We will now
descend to times and events which are reached by their
oral historic traditions, and which may be offered as certain,
though not minute history. Through close inquiry and
study of their vague figurative traditions, we have discovered that the Ojibways have attained to their present
geographical position, nearly in the centre of the North
American continent, from the shores of the Atlantic Ocean,
about the Gulf of the St. Lawrence River. The manner in
which I first received a certain intimation of this fact, may

illustrate it more forcibly to the reader, and is presented as follows:—

I was once standing near the entrance of an Ojibway Me-da-we-gaun, more commonly known as the "Grand Medicine Lodge," while the inmates were busy in the performance of the varied ceremonies of this, their chief medical and religious rite. The lodge measured in length about one hundred feet, and fifteen in width, was but partially covered along the sides with green boughs of the balsam tree, and the outside spectator could view without hindrance the different ceremonies enacting within. On a pole raised horizontally above its whole length were hung pieces of cloth, calico, handkerchiefs, blankets, etc.—the offerings or sacrifice of the novice who was about to be initiated into the mysteries of the Me-da-we society. The lodge was full of men and women who sat in a row along both of its sides. None but those who were members of the society and who had regularly been initiated, were allowed to enter. They were dressed and painted in their best and most fancy clothing and colors, and each held in his hand the Me-da-wi-aun or medicine sack, which consisted of bird skins, stuffed otter, beaver and snake skins.

The novice in the process of initiation, sat in the centre on a clean mat facing the Me-da-wautig, a cedar post planted in the centre of the lodge, daubed with vermilion and ornamented with tufts of birds' down. The four old and grave-looking We-kauns, or initiating priests, stood around him with their medicine sacks, drums, and rattles.

As I partially understood, and could therefore appreciate, the meaning and objects of their strange ceremonies, and could partially understand their peculiar religious idiom, I stood, watched, and listened with a far deeper interest than could be felt in the mind of a mere casual observer, who is both unacquainted with the objects of the rites or language of these simple children of nature, and who, in his greater wisdom, deems it but the unmeaning mummery and superstitious rites of an ignorant race, buried in heathenish darkness.

One of the four We-kauns, after addressing a few remarks to the novice in a low voice, took from his medicine sack, the Me-da-me-gis, a small white sea-shell, which is the chief emblem of the Me-da-we rite. Holding this on the palm of his hand, he ran slowly around the inside of the lodge, displaying it to the inmates, and followed by his fellow We-kauns swinging their rattles, and exclaiming in a deep guttural tone, "whe, whe, whe." Circling the lodge in this impressive manner, on coming again to the novice, they stopped running, uttering a deep, sonorous, "Whay-ho-ho-ho." They then quietly walked off, and taking their stand at the western end of the lodge, the leader still displaying the shell on the palm of his hand, delivered a loud and spirited harangue.

The language and phrases used were so obscure to a common listener, that it would be impossible to give a literal translation of the whole speech. The following passage, however, forcibly struck my attention:

"While our forefathers were living on the great salt water toward the rising sun, the great Megis (sea-shell) showed itself above the surface of the great water, and the rays of the sun for a long period were reflected from its glossy back. It gave warmth and light to the An-ish-in-aub-ag (red race). All at once it sank into the deep, and for a time our ancestors were not blessed with its light. It rose to the surface and appeared again on the great river which drains the waters of the Great Lakes, and again for a long time it gave life to our forefathers, and reflected back the rays of the sun. Again it disappeared from sight and it rose not, till it appeared to the eyes of the An-ish-in-aub-ag on the shores of the first great lake. Again it sank from sight, and death daily visited the wigwams of our forefathers, till it showed its back, and reflected the rays of the sun once more at Bow-e-ting (Sault Ste. Marie). Here it remained for a long time, but once more, and for the last time, it disappeared, and the An-ish-in-aub-ag was left in darkness and misery, till it floated and once more showed its bright back at Mo-ning-wun-a-kaun-ing (La Pointe Island), where it has ever since reflected back the rays of the sun, and blessed our ancestors with life, light, and wisdom. Its rays reach the remotest village of the wide spread Ojibways." As the old man delivered this talk, he continued to display the shell, which he represented as the emblem of the great megis of which he was speaking.

A few days after, anxious to learn the true meaning of this allegory, I proceeded one evening to the lodge of the old priest, and presenting him with some tobacco and cloth for a pair of leggings (which is an invariable custom when any *genuine* information is wanted of them, connected with their religious beliefs), I requested him to explain to me the meaning of his Me-da-we harangue.

After filling his pipe and smoking of the tobacco I had presented, he proceeded to give me the desired information as follows:—

" My grandson," said he, " the megis I spoke of, means the Me-da-we religion. Our forefathers, many string of lives ago, lived on the shores of the Great Salt Water in the east. Here it was, that while congregated in a great town, and while they were suffering the ravages of sickness and death, the Great Spirit, at the intercession of Man-ab-o-sho, the great common uncle of the An-ish-in-aub-ag, granted them this rite wherewith life is restored and prolonged. Our forefathers moved from the shores of the great water, and proceeded westward. The Me-da-we lodge was pulled down and it was not again erected, till our forefathers again took a stand on the shores of the great river near where Mo-ne-aung (Montreal) now stands.

" In the course of time this town was again deserted, and our forefathers still proceeding westward, lit not their fires till they reached the shores of Lake Huron, where again the rites of the Me-da-we were practised.

" Again these rites were forgotten, and the Me-da-we lodge was not built till the Ojibways found themselves congregated at Bow-e-ting (outlet of Lake Superior), where it remained for many winters.   Still the Ojibways moved westward, and for the last time the Me-da-we lodge was erected on the Island of La Pointe, and here, long before the pale face appeared among them, it was practised in its purest and most original form.   Many of our fathers lived the full term of life granted to mankind by the Great Spirit, and the forms of many old people were mingled with each rising generation.   This, my grandson, is the meaning of the words you did not understand ; they have been repeated to us by our fathers for many generations."

Thus was it that I first received particular corroborating testimony to the somewhat mooted point of the direction from which the Ojibways have reached their present geographical position.   It is only from such religious and genuine traditions that the fact is to be ascertained.   The common class of the tribe who are spread in numerous villages north and west of Lake Superior, when asked where they originally came from, make answer that they originated from Mo-ning-wuna-kaun-ing (La Pointe), and the phrase is often used in their speeches to the whites, that " Mo-ning-wuna-kaun-ing" is the spot on which the Ojibway tribe first grew, and like a tree it has spread its branches in every direction, in the bands that now occupy the vast extent of the Ojibway earth ; and also that " it is the root from which all the far scattered villages of the tribe have sprung."

A superficial inquirer would be easily misled by these assertions, and it is only through such vague and figurative traditions as the one we have related, that any degree of certainty can be arrived at, respecting their position and movements prior to the time when the tribe first lit their central fire, and built their Me-da-we lodge on the Island of La Pointe.

There is another tradition told by the old men of the Ojibway village of Fond du Lac—Lake Superior, which tells of their former residence on the shores of the great salt water. It is, however, so similar in character to the one I have related, that its introduction here would occupy unnecessary space. The only difference between the two traditions, is that the otter, which is emblematical of one of the four Medicine spirits, who are believed to preside over the Medawe rites, is used in one, in the same figurative manner as the sea-shell is used in the other; first appearing to the ancient An-ish-in-aub-ag from the depths of the great salt water, again on the river St. Lawrence, then on Lake Huron at Sault Ste. Marie, again at La Pointe, but lastly at Fond du Lac, or end of Lake Superior, where it is said to have forced the sand bank at the mouth of the St. Louis River. The place is still pointed out by the Indians where they believe the great otter broke through.

It is comparatively but a few generations back, that this tribe have been known by their present distinctive name of Ojibway. It is certainly not more than three centuries, and in all probability much less. It is only within this term of time, that they have been disconnected as a distinct or separate tribe from the Ottaways and Potta-wat-um-ies. The name by which they were known when incorporated in one body, is at the present day uncertain.

The final separation of these three tribes took place at the Straits of Michilimacinac from natural causes, and the partition has been more and more distinctly defined, and perpetuated through locality, and by each of the three divided sections assuming or receiving distinctive appellations :—

The Ottaways remaining about the spot of their final separation, and being thereby the most easterly section, were first discovered by the white race, who bartered with them their merchandise for furs. They for many years acted as a medium between the white traders and their more remote western brethren, providing them in turn at advanced prices, with their much desired commodities. They thus obtained the name of Ot-tah-way, " trader," which they have retained as their tribal name to the present day. The Potta-wat-um-ees moved up Lake Michigan, and by taking with them, or for a time perpetuating the national fire, which according to tradition was sacredly kept alive in their more primitive days, they have obtained the name of " those who make or keep the fire," which is the literal meaning of their tribal cognomen.

The Ojibways, pressing northward and westward, were soon known as an important and distinctive body or tribe, and meeting with fierce and inveterate enemies, the name of Ojibway, " to roast till puckered up," they soon obtained through practising the old custom of torturing prisoners of war by fire, as has already been mentioned more fully in a previous chapter. The original cause of their emigration from the shores of the Atlantic westward to the area of Lake Superior, is buried in uncertainty. If pressed or driven back by more powerful tribes, which is a most probable conjecture, they are not willing to acknowledge it.

From the earliest period that their historical traditions treat of, they tell of having carried on an exterminating war with the Iroquois, or Six Nations of New York, whom they term Naud-o-waig, or Adders. The name indicates the deadly nature of these, their old and powerful antagonists, whose concentrated strength and numbers, and first acquaintance with the use of the white man's murderous fire arms, caused them to leave their ancient village sites and seek westward for new homes.

Sufficient has been seen and written since their discovery by the white race, of the antagonistical position of these two different families, or group of tribes, to prove the certainty of the above surmise. The name of Naud-o-wa-se-wug, which is sometimes applied to the Dakotas by the Ojibways, is derived from the name by which they have ever known the Iroquois.—Naud-o-waig; it implies "our enemies," but literally, means "like unto the adders." Various definitions have been given to this name by different writers; the above is now presented as the only true one.

It is a well-authenticated fact traditionally, that at the Falls of Sault Ste. Marie, the outlet of Lake Superior, the Ojibways, after separating from the Ottaways and Pottawatumees, made a long and protracted stay. Their village occupied a large extent of ground, and their war-parties numbered many warriors who marched eastward against the Naudoways, and westward against the Dakotas, with whom at this point they first came into collision.

At this point the Ojibway tribe again separated into two divisions, which we will designate as the Northern and Southern. The Northern division formed the least numerous body, and consisted chiefly of the families claiming as Totems the reindeer, lynx, and pike. They proceeded gradually to occupy the north coast of Lake Superior, till they arrived at the mouth of Pigeon River (Kah-mau-a-tig-wa-aug). From this point they have spread over the country they occupy at the present day along the British and United States line, and north, far into the British possessions. A large band early occupied and formed a village at Rainy Lake. Here they first came in contact with the Assineboins (a tribe of seceding Dakotas), and from this point, after entering into a firm and lasting peace with the Assineboins and Knis-te-nos, they first joined their brethren of the Southern division in their wars against the fierce Dakotas. This band have to this day retained the cognomen of Ko-je-je-win-in-e-wug, from the numerous straits, bends, and turnings of the lakes and rivers which they occupy.

A large body of this Northern division residing immediately on the north shores of the Great Lake, at Grand Portage and Thunder Bay, and claiming the Totem of the Ke-nouzhay or Pike, were formerly denominated O-mush-kas-ug. Tradition says that at one time their fellow-Ojibways made war on them. This war was brought about by persons belonging to the Pike family murdering some members of the Marten Totem family. It was but the carrying out of their custom of "blood for blood." It was neither very deadly nor of long duration, and to illustrate its character more fully, I will introduce the following traditional anecdote :—

A party consisting of warriors belonging to the Martin family was at one time collected at Fond du Lac. They proceeded on the war-path against the family of the Omush-kas, living on the north shore of the Great Lake, for this family had lately spilled their blood. They discovered a single wigwam standing on the sandy shores of the lake, and the Martens, having stealthily approached, raised the war-whoop, and as was the custom in battle (to show their greater manhood), they threw off every article of clothing, and thus, perfectly naked, rushed furiously to the attack. The Omush-kas, head of the family occupying the threatened lodge, was busy arranging his fishnet, and not aware that war had been declared, he paid no attention to his yelling visitors, but calmly continued his peaceful occupation.

One of the Martens, rushing into the lodge, and, throwing his arms about him, exclaimed, " Ene-ne-nin-duk-o-nah" (a man I hold), meaning that he took him captive.

The simple Omushkas, looking up, merely remarked, " Let me go ; you are tangling my net." Still the Marten, keeping his hold, more loudly exclaimed, " Ene-ne-nin-duk-o-nah." The Omushkas, now perceiving his nakedness, grasped a sensitive part of his person, in turn jokingly exclaimed, " Nin-sah-eta-in-ne-ne-nin-duk-o-nah " (" 'tis only I who truly hold a man"), and the simple man continued to consider the attack as a mere farce. The war-club, however, of the enraged Marten now descended with fearful force on his head, and he died exclaiming, " Verily they are killing me."

A considerable body of the Northern Ojibways are denominated by their fellow-tribesmen Sug-wau-dug-ah-win-in-e-wug (men of the thick firwoods), derived from the interminable forests of balsam, spruce, pine, and tamarac trees which cover their hunting-grounds. Their early French discoverers named them " Bois Forts," or Hardwoods.

Another section forming the most northern branch of this tribe are denominated Omushke-goes (Swamp-people), derived also from the nature of the country they occupy.

The Northern division, which comprises these different sections, having been separated from the main body of the tribe forming the Southern division, now upwards of eight generations, a difference (though not a radical one), has become perceptible in their common language. This consists mostly in the pronunciation, and so slight is the difference in idiom that one good interpreter, speaking the language of each division, may suffice for both.

The characteristics, also of the northern section of the tribe, differ materially in some important respects from those of their southern and western brethren. Not having been opposed by enemies in the course of their northern emigration, they are consequently not warlike, and the name of Waub-ose (Rabbit), is often applied to them by their more warlike fellows, on account of their mild and harmless disposition.

At the partition of the Ojibway tribe into two divisions, at Sault Ste. Marie, the main body pressed their way gradually up along the southern shores of Lake Superior. They made a temporary stand at Grand Island, near the Pictured Rocks, again at L'Anse Bay, or as they more euphoniously name it, We-qua-dong. This grand division consisted principally of the Crane Totem family, the Bear, the Catfish, the Loon, and the allied Marten and Moose clans. These great families with their several branches, form at least eight-tenths of the whole Ojibway tribe.

The Cranes claim the honor of first having pitched their wigwams, and lighted the fire of the Ojibways, at Shaug-ah-waum-ik-ong, a sand point or peninsula lying two miles immediately opposite the Island of La Pointe. This fact is illustrated by the following highly allegorical and characteristic tradition :—

As a preliminary remark, it is necessary to state that there exists quite a variance between three or four of the principal Totems, as to which is hereditarily entitled to the chief place in the tribe.

At a council (in which the writer acted as interpreter), held some years ago at La Pointe, between the principal chiefs of the Ojibways and the United States Government Agent, the following allegory was delivered by an old chief named Tug-waug-aun-ay, in answer to the mooted question of " who was the hereditary chief of La Pointe?"

Ke-che-wash-keenh (Great Buffalo), the grandson of the

celebrated chief Au-daig-we-os (mentioned in Schoolcraft's works), head of the Loon Totem clan, was at this time, though stricken with years, still in the prime of his great oratorical powers.

On this occasion he opened the council by delivering a most eloquent harangue in praise of his own immediate ancestors, and claiming for the Loon family the first place and chieftainship among the Ojibways. After he had finished and again resumed his seat, Tug-waug-aun-ay, the head chief of the Crane family, a very modest and retiring man, seldom induced to speak in council, calmly arose, and gracefully wrapping his blanket about his body, leaving but the right arm free, he pointed toward the eastern skies, and exclaimed : " The Great Spirit once made a bird, and he sent it from the skies to make its abode on earth. The bird came, and when it reached half way down, among the clouds, it sent forth a loud and far sounding cry, which was heard by all who resided on the earth, and even by the spirits who make their abode within its bosom. When the bird reached within sight of the earth, it circled slowly above the Great Fresh Water Lakes, and again it uttered its echoing cry. Nearer and nearer it circled, looking for a resting place, till it lit on a hill overlooking Boweting (Sault Ste. Marie); here it chose its first resting place, pleased with the numerous white fish that glanced and swam in the clear waters and sparkling foam of the rapids. Satisfied with its chosen seat, again the bird sent forth its loud but solitary cry; and the No-kaig (Bear clan), A-waus-e-wug (Catfish), Ah-auh-wauh-ug (Loon), and Mous-o-neeg (Moose and Marten clan), gathered at his call. A large town was soon congregated, and the bird whom the Great Spirit sent presided over all.

" Once again it took its flight, and the bird flew slowly over the waters of Lake Superior. Pleased with the sand point of Shaug-ah-waum-ik-ong, it circled over it, and

viewed the numerous fish as they swam about in the clear
depths of the Great Lake. It lit on Shaug-ah-waum-ik-ong,
and from thence again it uttered its solitary cry. A voice
came from the calm bosom of the lake, in answer; the bird
pleased with the musical sound of the voice, again sent
forth its cry, and the answering bird made its appearance
in the wampum-breasted Ah-auh-wauh (Loon). The bird
spoke to it in a gentle tone, 'Is it thou that gives answer
to my cry?' The Loon answered, 'It is I.' The bird then
said to him, ' Thy voice is music—it is melody—it sounds
sweet in my ear, from henceforth I appoint thee to answer
my voice in Council.'

" Thus," continued the chief, " the Loon became the first
in council, but he who made him chief was the Bus-in-
aus-e (Echo Maker), or Crane. These are the words of my ancestors, who, from generation to generation, have repeated
them into the ears of their children. I have done."

The old man took his seat in silence, and not a chief in
that stricken and listening crowd arose to gainsay his
words. All understood the allegory perfectly well, and as
the curling smoke of their pipes arose from the lips and
nostrils of the quiet listeners, there ascended with it the
universal whisper, " It is true; it is true."

As an explanation of the figures used in the above traditional allegory, we will add, that the crane, commonly
named in the Ojibway language Uj-e-jauk, is the symbol or
totem of a large section of the tribe. This bird loves to
soar among the clouds, and its cry can be heard when flying
above, beyond the orbit of human vision. From this " far-
sounding cry" the family who claim it as their totem derive their generic name of Bus-in-aus-e-wug (Echo Makers).
This family claim, by this allegory, to have been the first
discoverers and pioneer settlers at Sault Ste. Marie, and
again at Pt. Shaug-ah-waum-ik-ong.

The Loon is the Totem also of a large clan. This bird

is denominated by the Ojibways, Mong, but the family who claim it as their badge, are known by the generic name of Ah-auh-wauh, which is derived by imitating its peculiar cry. This family claim the hereditary first chieftainship in the tribe, but they cannot substantiate their pretensions further back than their first intercourse with the old French discoverers and traders, who, on a certain occasion, appointed some of their principal men as chiefs, and endowed them with flags and medals. Strictly confined to their own primitive tribal polity, the allegory of the Cranes cannot be controverted, nor has it ever been gainsaid.

To support their pretensions, this family hold in their possession a circular plate of virgin copper, on which is rudely marked indentations and hieroglyphics denoting the number of generations of the family who have passed away since they first pitched their lodges at Shaug-a-waum-ik-ong and took possession of the adjacent country, including the Island of La Pointe or Mo-ning-wun-a-kaun-ing.

When I witnessed this curious family register in 1842, it was exhibited by Tug-waug-aun-ay to my father. The old chief kept it carefully buried in the ground, and seldom displayed it. On this occasion he only brought it to view at the entreaty of my mother, whose maternal uncle he was. Father, mother, and the old chief, have all since gone to the land of spirits, and I am the only one still living who witnessed, on that occasion, this sacred relic of former days.

On this plate of copper was marked eight deep indentations, denoting the number of his ancestors who had passed away since they first lighted their fire at Shaug-a-waum-ik-ong. They had all lived to a good old age.

By the rude figure of a man with a hat on its head, placed opposite one of these indentations, was denoted the period when the white race first made his appearance among them. This mark occurred in the third generation, leaving five generations which had passed away since that important era in their history.

Tug-waug-aun-ay was about sixty years of age at the time he showed this plate of copper, which he said had descended to him direct through a long line of ancestors. He died two years since, and his death has added the ninth indentation thereon; making, at this period, nine generations since the Ojibways first resided at La Pointe, and six generations since their first intercourse with the whites.

From the manner in which they estimate their generations, they may be counted as comprising a little over half the full term of years allotted to mankind, which will materially exceed the white man's generation. The Ojibways never count a generation as passed away till the oldest man in the family has died, and the writer assumes from these, and other facts obtained through observation and inquiry, forty years as the term of an Indian generation. It is necessary to state, however, for the benefit of those who may consider this as an over-estimate, that, since the introduction of intoxicating drinks and diseases of the whites, the former well-authenticated longevity of the Indians has been materially lessened.

According to this estimate, it is now three hundred and sixty years since the Ojibways first collected in one grand central town on the Island of La Pointe, and two hundred and forty years since they were first discovered by the white race.

Seventy-seven years after, Jacques Cartier, representing the French nation, obtained his "first formal meeting with the Indians of the interior of Canada," and fifty-six years before Father Claude Allouez (as mentioned in Bancroft's History of America), first discovered the Ojibways congregated in the Bay of Shaug-a-waum-ik-ong, preparing to go on a war excursion against their enemies the Dakotas.

From this period the Ojibways are traditionally well possessed of the most important events which have happened to them as a tribe, and from nine generations back, I am prepared to give, as obtained from their most veracious, reliable, and oldest men, their history, which may be considered as authentic.

In this chapter we have noted the course of their migrations, which, in all likelihood, occupied nearly two centuries prior to their final occupation of the shores of Lake Superior.

These movements were made while they were living in their primitive state, when they possessed nothing but the bow and arrow, sharpened stones, and bones of animals wherewith to kill game and fight their enemies. During this period they were surrounded by inveterate foes, and war was their chief pastime; but so dreamy and confused are their accounts of the battles which their ancestors fought, and the exploits they enacted, that the writer has refrained from dwelling on them with any particularity. One tradition, however, is deemed full worthy of notice, and while offering it as an historical fact, it will at the same time answer as a specimen of the mythological character of their tales which reach as far back as this period.

During their residence in the East, the Ojibways have a distinct tradition of having annihilated a tribe whom they denominate Mun-dua. Their old men, whom I have questioned on this subject, do not all agree in the location nor details. Their disagreements, however, are not very material, and I will proceed to give, verbatim, the version of Kah-nin-dum-a-win-so, the old chief of Sandy Lake:

"There was at one time living on the shores of a great lake, a numerous and powerful tribe of people; they lived congregated in one single town, which was so large that a person standing on a hill which stood in its centre, could not see the limits of it.

" This tribe, whose name was Mun-dua, were fierce and warlike; their hand was against every other tribe, and the captives whom they took in war were burned with fire as offerings to their spirits.

" All the surrounding tribes lived in great fear of them, till their Ojibway brothers called them to council, and sent the wampum and warclub, to collect the warriors of all the tribes with whom they were related. A war party was thus raised, whose line of warriors reached, as they marched in single file, as far as the eye could see. They proceeded against the great town of their common enemy, to put out their fire forever. They surrounded and attacked them from all quarters where their town was not bounded by the lake shore, and though overwhelming in their numbers, yet the Mun-dua had such confidence in their own force and prowess, that on the first day, they sent only their boys to repel the attack. The boys being defeated and driven back, on the second day the young men turned out to beat back their assailants. Still the Ojibways and their allies stood their ground and gradually drove them in, till on the eve of the second day, they found themselves in possession of half the great town. The Mun-duas now became awake to their danger, and on the third day, beginning to consider it a serious business, their old and tried warriors, ' mighty men of valor,' sang their war songs, and putting on their paints and ornaments of battle, they turned out to repel their invaders.

" The fight this day was hand to hand. There is nothing in their traditionary accounts, to equal the fierceness of the struggle described in this battle. The bravest men, probably, in America, had met—one party fighting for vengeance, glory, and renown; and the other for everything dear to man, home, family, for very existence itself!

" The Mun-dua were obliged at last to give way, and hotly pressed by their foes, women and children threw themselves into, and perished in the lake. At this juncture their aged chief, who had witnessed the unavailing defence of his people, and who saw the ground covered with the bodies of his greatest warriors, called with a loud voice on the ' Great Spirit' for help (for besides being chief of the Mún-duas, he was also a great medicine man and juggler).

" Being a wicked people, the Great Spirit did not listen to the prayer of their chief for deliverance. The aged medicine man then called upon the spirits of the water and of the earth, who are the under spirits of the ' Great Spirit of Evil,' and immediately a dark and heavy fog arose from the bosom of the lake, and covered in folds of darkness the site of the vanquished town, and the scene of the bloody battle. The old chieftain by his voice gathered together the remnants of his slaughtered tribe, and under cover of the Evil Spirit's fog, they left their homes forever. The whole day and ensuing night they travelled to escape from their enemies, until a gale of wind, which the medicine men of the Ojibways had asked the Great Spirit to raise, drove away the fog; the surprise of the fleeing Munduas was extreme when they found themselves standing on a hill back of their deserted town, and in plain view of their enemies.

" ' It is the will of the Great Spirit that we should perish,' exclaimed their old chief; but once more they dragged their wearied limbs in hopeless flight. They ran into an adjacent forest where they buried the women and children in the ground, leaving but a small aperture to enable them to breathe. The men then turned back, and once more they met their pursuing foes in a last mortal combat. They fought stoutly for a while, when again overpowered by numbers, they turned and fled, but in a different direction from the spot where they had secreted their families: but a few men escaped, who afterward returned, and disinterred the women and children. This small remnant of a once powerful tribe were the next year attacked by an Ojibway war-party, taken captive, and incorporated in this tribe. Individuals are pointed out to this day who are of Mun-dua descent, and who are members of the respected family whose totem is the Marten."

CHAPTER V.

THE OJIBWAY TOWN AT LA POINTE.

Congregation of the Ojibways in one town at Pt. Shag-awaum-ik-ong and on
La Pointe Island, till their final dispersion into smaller bands and villages—
Comprising three generations—They first light their fires on Pt. Shag-awaum-
ik-ong—Harassed by the Dakotas and Foxes—They finally locate their town
on the Island of La Pointe—Mode of gaining a livelihood—Primitive utensils
and weapons—Means used to kill game—Copper mines of Lake Superior
not worked by them—Primitive usages, rites, and customs—Severely harassed by their enemies—Dakotas even secure scalps on the Island of their
town—Battle of Pt. Shag-awaum-ik-ong and almost total destruction of a
Dakota war party—Foxes take four captives on the island—Pursued by the
Ojibways—Naval engagement near Montreal River—Destruction of Fox war
party—Nature of the warfare between the Ojibways and Foxes—Captives
are tortured with fire—Origin of this horrid custom—Tradition of the uncle
and nephew.

In the previous chapter we have gradually traced the
Ojibways from the Atlantic coast, to their occupation of
the surrounding shores of Lake Superior.

Computing their generations as consisting of forty years
each, it is three hundred and sixty years since the main
body of this tribe first reached Pt. Sha-ga-waum-ik-ong on
the Great Lake, where for many years they concentrated
their numbers in one village.

They were surrounded by fierce and inveterate enemies
whom they denominate the O-dug-aum-eeg (opposite side
people, best known at this day as Foxes), and the " A-boin-
ug" or (roasters), by which significant name they have ever
known the powerful tribe of Dakotas.   These two tribes
claimed the country bordering Lake Superior, towards the

south and west, and of which, the migrating Ojibways now took possession as intruders. The opposition to their further advance westward commenced when the Ojibways first lighted their fires at Sault Ste. Marie, and it is from their first acquaintance with them, while located at this spot, that the Dakotas have given them the appellation of Ra-ra-to-oans (People of the Falls).

At every step of their westward advance along the southern shores of the Great Lake, the Ojibways battled with the Foxes and Dakotas; but they pressed onward, gaining foot by foot, till they finally lit their fires on the sand point of Sha-ga-waum-ik-ong. On this spot they remained not long, for they were harassed daily by their warlike foes, and for greater security they were obliged to move their camp to the adjacent island of Mon-ing-wun-a-kaun-ing (place of the golden-breasted woodpecker, but known as La Pointe). Here, they chose the site of their ancient town, and it covered a space about three miles long and two broad, comprising the western end of the island.

The vestiges or signs to prove this assertion are still visible, and are especially observable in the young growth of trees now covering the spot, compared to trees standing on other portions of the island where oaks and pines apparently centuries old, rear their branches aloft, or lie prostrate on the ground.

In the younger days of old traders and half-breeds still living, they tell of deep beaten paths being plainly visible in different parts of the island and even the forms of their ancient gardens, now overgrown with trees, could still be traced out. When my maternal grandfather, Michel Cadotte, first located a trading post on this island, now upwards of sixty years ago, these different signs and vestiges were still discernible, and I have myself noticed the difference in the growth of trees and other marks, as I have a thousand times wandered through this, the island of my nativity.

While hemmed in on this island by their enemies, the Ojibways lived mainly by fishing. They also practised the arts of agriculture to an extent not since known amongst them. Their gardens are said to have been extensive, and they raised large quantities of Mun-dam-in (Indian corn), and pumpkins.

The more hardy and adventurous hunted on the lake shore opposite their village, which was overrun with moose, bear, elk, and deer. The buffalo, also, are said in those days to have ranged within half a day's march from the lake shore, on the barrens stretching towards the headwaters of the St. Croix River. Every stream which emptied into the lake, abounded in beaver, otter, and muskrat, and the fish which swam in its clear water could not be surpassed in quality or quantity in any other spot on earth. They manufactured their nets of the inner bark of the bass and cedar trees, and from the fibres of the nettle. They made thin knives from the rib bones of the moose and buffalo. And a stone tied to the end of a stick, with which they broke branches and sticks, answered them the purpose of an axe. From the thigh-bone of a muskrat they ground their awls, and fire was obtained by the friction of two dry sticks. Bows of hard wood, or bone, sharp stone-headed arrows, and spear points made also of bone, formed their implements of war and hunting. With ingeniously made traps and dead-falls, they caught the wily beaver, whose flesh was their most dainty food, and whose skins made them warm blankets. To catch the moose and larger animals, they built long and gradually narrowing inclosures of branches, wherein they would first drive and then kill them, one after another, with their barbed arrows. They also caught them in nooses made of tough hide and hung from a strong bent tree, over the road that these animals commonly travelled to feed, or find water. Bear they caught in dead-falls, which were so unfailing that they have retained their use to this day, in preference to the steel traps of the pale faces.

Their old men tell of using a kind of arrow in hunting for the larger animals in those primitive days, which I have never seen described in books. The arrow is made with a circular hole bored or burnt in the end, in which was loosely inserted a finely barbed bone. Being shot into an animal, the arrow would fall off leaving the barb in the body, and as the animal moved this would gradually work into its vitals and soon deprive it of life.

In those days their shirts and leggins were made of finely dressed deer and elk skins sewed together with the sinews of these animals. They made their wigwam covering of birch bark and rushes; their canoes of birch bark and thin strips of cedar wood, sewed together with the small roots of the pine tree, and gummed with the pitch of the pine, balsam, or tamarac. They made kettles from clay and pulverized stone, and judging from specimens found occasionally throughout the country, they give evidence of much proficiency and ingenuity in this line of manufacture. Copper, though abounding on the lake shore, they never used for common purposes;[1] considering

---

[1] The tribes of the lakes were workers in copper at an early period. Champlain in an account published in 1613, at Paris, writes: "Shortly after conferring with them about many matters concerning their wars, the Algonquin Savage, one of their chiefs, drew from a sack a piece of copper a foot long, which he gave me. This was very handsome and quite pure. He gave me to understand that there were large quantities where he had taken this, which was on the bank of a river, now a great lake. He said they gathered it in lumps, and having melted it, spread it in sheets, smoothing it with stones."

Pierre Boucher, the grandfather of Sieur Verendrye, the explorer of the Lake Winnipeg region, in a book published in 1664, at Paris, writes that "in Lake Superior there is a great island fifty leagues in circumference, in which there is a very beautiful mine of copper. There are other places in those quarters where there are similar mines; so I learned from four or five Frenchmen, who lately returned. They were gone three years, without finding an opportunity

it sacred, they used it only for medicinal rites, and for ornament on the occasion of a grand Me-da-we.

They are not therefore, the people whose ancient tools
and marks are now being discovered daily by the miners
on Lake Superior; or, if they are those people, it must
have been during a former period of their ancient history;
but their preserving no traditional account of their ancestors ever having worked these copper mines, would most
conclusively prove that they are not the race whose signs
of a former partial civilized state, are being daily dug up
about the shores of the Great Lake.

During this era in their history, some of their old men
affirm that there was maintained in their central town, on
the Island of La Pointe, a continual fire as a symbol of
their nationality. They maintained also, a regular system
of civil polity, which, however, was much mixed with
their religious and medicinal practices. The Crane and
Aw-ause Totem families were first in council, and the brave
and unflinching warriors of the Bear family, defended them
from the inroads of their numerous and powerful enemies.

to return; they told me they had seen an ingot of copper, all refined, which
was on the coast, and weighed more than eight hundred pounds, according to
their estimate. They said that the savages, in passing it made a fire on it,
after which they cut off pieces with their axes."

Isle Royale abounds in pits containing ashes, coals, stone hammers, and chips
of copper, and in some places the scales of the fishes, which had been eaten by
the ancient miners. The vein rock appears to have been heated by fire, and
the water dashed thereon, by which the rock was fractured, and the exposed
copper softened.

Talon, Intendant of Justice in Canada, visited France, taking a voyageur with
him, and while in Paris on the 26th of February, 1669, wrote to Colbert, Minis-
ter of the Colonial Department, "that this voyageur had penetrated among the
western natives farther than any other man, and had seen the copper mine on
Lake Huron," and on the 2d of November, 1671, Talon writes from Quebec :
" The copper which I sent from Lake Superior and the river Nantaouagan
[Ontonagon], proves that there is a mine on the border of some stream. More
than twenty Frenchmen have seen one lump at the lake which they estimate
weighs more than eight hundred pounds." Alexander Henry also alludes to
copper working on Lake Superior.—E. D. N.

The rites of the Me-da-we-win (their mode of worshipping the Great Spirit, and securing life in this and a future world, and of conciliating the lesser spirits, who in their belief, people earth, sky, and waters) was practised in those days in its purest and most original form. Every person who had been initiated into the secrets of this mysterious society from the first to the eighth degree, were imperatively obliged to be present on every occasion when its grand ceremonies were solemnized. This created yearly a national gathering, and the bonds which united one member to another were stronger than exist at the present day, when each village has assumed, at unstated periods, to perform the ceremonies of initiation. Tradition says that a large wigwam was permanently erected in the midst of their great town, which they designated as the Me-da-we-gun, wherein the rites of their religion were performed. Though probably rude in its structure, and not lasting in its materials, yet was it the temple of a numerous tribe, and so sacredly was it considered, that even to this day, in their religious phraseology, the island on which it stood is known by the name of Me-da-we-gaun.

In those days their native and primitive manners and usages were rigidly conformed with. Man nor woman never passed the age of puberty without severe and protracted fasts, in which they sought communion with some particular guardian spirit whom they considered in the light of a medium spirit between them and the " One Great Master of Life," toward whom they felt too deep a veneration, than to dare to commune with directly. Sacrificial feasts were made with the first fruit of the field and the chase. When a person fell sick, a small lodge was made, apart from the village, purposely for his sole use, and a medicine man summoned to attend and cure, and only he, held intercourse with the sick. If a person died of some virulent disease, his clothing, the barks that covered his lodge, and even the poles that framed it, were destroyed by fire. Thus of old did they guard against pestilence; and disease of all kinds appears to have been less common among them than at the present day; and it is further stated that many more persons than now, lived out the full term of life allotted to mankind by the "Great Spirit." Many even lived with the "weight of over a hundred winters on their backs."

The council of the Me-da-we initiators, partook of the spirit of the ten commandments which were given to the children of Israel, amidst the thunders of Mount Sinai. There was consequently less theft and lying, more devotion to the Great Spirit, more obedience to their parents, and more chastity in man and women, than exist at the present day, since their baneful intercourse with the white race. Even in the twenty years' experience of the writer, he has vividly noticed these changes, spoken of by the old men, as rapidly taking place. In former times there was certainly more good-will, charity, and hospitality practised toward one another; and the widow and orphan never were allowed to live in want and poverty. The old traditionists of the Ojibways, tell of many customs which have become nearly or altogether extinct. They dwell with pleasure on this era of their past history, and consider it as the happy days of "Auld lang syne."

I have already stated that they located their town on the island of La Pointe, for greater security against the harassing inroads of their enemies, but though the island is located at its nighest point, about two miles from the main shore of the Great Lake, yet were the Ojibways not entirely secure from the attacks of their inveterate and indefatigable foes, who found means, not only of waylaying their stray hunters on the main shore, but even to secure scalps on the island of their refuge itself. On one occasion a war party of Dakotas found their way to a point of the main shore directly opposite the western end of the island, and during the night, two of their number crossed over, a distance of two miles and a half, each swimming by the side of a log, and attacked a family who were fishing by torchlight along the eastern shore of the island.

With four scalps, and the canoe of those they had killed, they returned to their friends, who immediately retreated, satisfied with their success. Early in the morning, the mangled bodies of the slain were discovered, and the Ojibways, collecting their warriors, made a long but unavailing pursuit.

Shortly after this occurrence, a party of one hundred and fifty Dakota warriors again found their way to the lake shore, and taking a position on the extreme point of Shag-a-waum-ik-ong, immediately opposite the Ojibway village, they laid in ambush for some stray enemy to come within their reach. Shag-a-waum-ik-ong is a narrow neck or point of land about four miles long, and lying nearly parallel to the island of La Pointe, toward the western end of which it converges, till the distance from point to point is not more than two miles. In former times the distance is said to have been much less, the action of the waves having since gradually washed away the sand of which it is composed.

It lays across the entry to a deep bay, and it has derived its name from the tradition that Man-ab-osho created it to bar the egress of a great beaver which he once hunted on the Great Lake, and which had taken refuge in this deep bay. The name signifies " The soft beaver dam," as the great beaver had easily broken through it, making the deep gap which now forms the entry of the bay. This point or peninsula does not average in width more than twenty rods, and in many places it is not more than six rods across. It is covered with a growth of scrubby oak and pine, and the extreme end where the Dakotas lay in ambush, is said in those days to have been covered with numerous sand hillocks, which the winds and waves have since nearly blown and washed away.

Early one morning, two Ojibway lads crossed over to the point to hunt ducks: on landing they were attacked by the ambushed war-party of the Dakotas with loud yells. For some time the two youths, protected by the numerous sand-hills, defended themselves, and evaded the attempts of their enemies, who wished to take them captives. In the mean time, the Ojibway town being aroused by the distant yelling, and seeing the point covered with the forms of numerous men, the startling cry of Aboin-ug! Aboin-ug! was shouted from wigwam to wigwam, and the men of war, grasping their bows and arrows, spears and war-clubs, jumped into their canoes and paddled with great speed to the scene of action. They crossed over in two divisions, one party proceeding straight to the point where the Dakotas were still to be seen hunting the two lads, while the other party living at the lower end of the great village, crossed over to that portion of the peninsula lying nearest to their wigwams. These landed about two miles below the extreme point, and taking their position where Shag-a-waum-ik-ong is but a few rods wide, and covered with scrubby oaks, they entirely cut off the retreat or egress of the Dakotas. Meanwhile the two unfortunate boys had been dispatched and scalped; but their friends who had crossed straight over from the village, landed on the point and proceeded to revenge their death, by bravely attacking the now retreating Dakotas. These being pressed by an enemy increasing in numbers every moment, turned their backs and fled down the point, merely keeping up a running fight, till they were met by the main body of the Ojibways who had collected in their rear, and cut them off effectually from escape. Discovering, too late, the fearful position which their rashness and want of foresight had brought them to, the Dakota warriors took shelter in a thick grove of scrubby oak, and fought to the last gasp. Overwhelmed by numbers, all were killed but two, who were seen to throw themselves into the lake and swim off towards the opposite shore of the deep bay. They were never heard of afterwards, but the probability is that by swimming two miles to the nearest point of the main shore, they saved their lives, and returned to their people with the sad tale of the almost total destruction of their war-party. Over the whole point of Shag-a-waum-ik-ong, are still strewn small particles of bones, which are said to be the remains of the warriors who fell in this bloody fight.

An anecdote is told of an old man, who was the father of one of the lads waylaid by the ambushed party on the point. He was not at home when the alarm was first sounded, and when he arrived, the warriors had all gone, and taken all the canoes belonging to the village. Burning to know the fate of his beloved child, he lashed his weapons of war to his back, amd notwithstanding the entreaties of the women, he threw himself into the lake, and swam over to the scene of action. He arrived too late to join in the fight, but he was ever afterward noted for this almost superhuman feat, and his name is preserved amongst his people even to this day.

On another occasion a party of four hundred Fox warriors floated down the Ontonagun River in their small inland bark canoes, and coasting along the lake shore, they landed in the night time on the island of La Pointe, and at early dawn in the morning, they succeeded in waylaying and capturing four young women who had gone from the village to cut wood. The spot is pointed out to this day, where they were taken. The Foxes satisfied with their success, hastily retreated to their canoes, and under cover of a dense fog, they silently paddled homeward. Confident, however, in their numbers, and full of exultation at having bearded their enemies even on the island of their refuge, feeling also secure of escape in the fog, when still within hearing distance of the Ojibway village, they yelled back the whoop of derision and defiance, and commenced singing a stirring scalp song.

The town of the Ojibways became instantly a scene of commotion, and the eager warriors quickly arming themselves, hastily embarked in their large lake canoes, and silently but swiftly pursued their enemies under cover of the dense fog.

The lake was perfectly calm, and they could hear the loud talking and laughter of the Foxes from a long distance. Guided by the noise thus kept up by their careless and confident enemies, the Ojibways silently straining on their paddles, gradually neared them. By the wise advice of their leaders, they deferred the attack, till the Foxes had arrived opposite the rock-bound coast one mile below Montreal River, and twenty-two miles from La Pointe, where the steep and slippery banks would prevent them from making their escape by land. Here the Ojibways fell on them with great fury, and easily upsetting their small canoes, they dispatched the surprised and now fear stricken Foxes as they struggled in the water. They killed and drowned this large war-party, nearly to a man.

This is the only naval engagement in which the Ojibways tell of ever having been engaged ; and their great success on this occasion, they attribute not only to superior numbers, but to the great advantage which they possessed in the size of their canoes, compared with those of the Foxes. Theirs were made large and strong, sitting firmly on the water, made to withstand the storms of Lake Superior, and capable of holding from five to twenty men each, while on the other hand, the canoes of their enemies, though made of the same material (birch bark), were constructed frail and crank, made to be taken across long portages on a man's head, and capable of containing but two or three persons. These, therefore, were easily upset, and their owners struggling in the deep water, were easily knocked on the head with war-clubs.

These two successful battles materially strengthened the foothold which the Ojibways had obtained in this portion of the Lake Superior country. The Dakotas and Foxes received thereby a check on their war propensities, and they learned to respect the prowess and bravery of the Ojibways. Their war-parties to the lake shore became less frequent than formerly, and they were more cautious in their attacks. On the island of La Pointe, they never again secured scalp nor prisoner, for never again did they dare to land on it.

The war carried on at this period between the Ojibways and Foxes, was fierce and bloody in the extreme, and it was marked with every cruelty attendant on savage warfare. The Foxes tortured their captives in various ways, but principally by burning them by fire. Of old, the Ojibways did not practise these cruelties, and they only learned them at this period from the Foxes. The hellish custom of torturing prisoners with fire, originated amongst them as follows :—

" A noted warrior of the Ojibways was once taken prisoner by his own nephew, who was a young warrior of the Foxes, son of his own sister, who had been captured when young, adopted and married in this tribe. This young man, to show to the Foxes his utter contempt of any ties of blood existing between him and his Ojibway uncle, planted two stakes strongly in the ground, and taking his uncle by the arm, he remarked to him that he ' wished to warm him before a good fire.' He then deliberately tied his arms and legs to the two stakes, as wide apart as they could be stretched, and the unnatural nephew built a huge fire in front of his uncle. When he had burnt his naked body to a blister on this side, he turned him with his back toward the fire, and when this had also been cruelly burned, he untied him, and turning him loose, he bade him to ' return home and tell the Ojibways how the Foxes treated their uncles.' "

The uncle recovered from his fire wounds, and in a subsequent war excursion, he succeeded in capturing his cruel nephew. He took him to the village of the Ojibways, where he tied him to a stake, and taking a fresh elk skin, on which a layer of fat had purposely been left, he placed it over a fire till it became ablaze; then throwing it over the naked shoulders of his nephew, he remarked. " Nephew, when you took me to visit the village of your people, you warmed me before a good fire. I now in return give you a warm mantle for your back."

The elk skin, covered with thick fat, burned furiously, and " puckering," it tightened around the naked body of his nephew—a dreadful " mantle" which soon consumed him.[1] This act was again retaliated by the Foxes, and death by fire applied in various ways, soon became the fate of all unfortunate captives.

[1] It is not unnatural to suppose that the tale of this occurrence being spread amongst the surrounding tribes, gave the name of Ojibway—" to roast till puckered up," to this tribe. Tribes have derived their names from circumstances of lesser note than this.—AUTHOR.

CHAPTER VI.

DISPERSION OF THE OJIBWAYS FROM THE ISLAND OF LA POINTE.

Causes of the sudden evacuation of their ancient town, as given by old traditionists—Different account obtained from old half-breeds and traders—Evil practices become in vogue—Poisoning—Feasts of human flesh—Ojibways fall under the power of their Satanic priesthood—Anecdote of the old man watching by the grave of his victimized child—The Ojibways become panic-stricken, and suddenly desert the island.

For the space of three generations, or one hundred and twenty years, the Ojibways remained congregated on the island of La Pointe, in one extensive town.

At the end of this period, we come to a dark chapter of their history, on which the old men dislike to linger. They are loth to tell the causes which led to the complete and sudden evacuation of their great village, and scattered them in bands and smaller villages on the adjacent shores of the Great Lake, and sent many families back on the track of their former migration to resettle the almost deserted villages of We-qua-dong and Bo-we-ting (Ance-ke-we-naw and Sault Ste. Marie).

The old men from whom I have collected the annals of this tribe, the better to get over this fearful portion of their history, assert that the dispersion from the island, was the immediate consequence to their first knowledge of the white race. Through the medium of their more eastern co-tribes, who first obtained the commodities of the " white spirits," they obtained a few guns and with this fearful weapon they all at once became formidable to their old enemies, the Dakotas and Foxes, whom they gradually drove from the vicinity of the lake shore, and caused to retreat inland toward the Mississippi. As the war parties of these tribes came less frequently to attack them, the Ojibways gained courage, and leaving La Pointe, they pitched their lodges in the adjacent Bay of Shaga-waum-ik-ong, and hunted, with comparative impunity, the larger animals which abounded in the vicinity.

According to other accounts, the dispersion of the Ojibways from the island of their refuge, was sudden and entire. The Evil Spirit had found a strong foothold amongst them, during the latter years of their residence on this island. Evil practices became in vogue.—Horrid feasts on human flesh became a custom. It is said by my informants, that the medicine men of this period had come to a knowledge of the most subtle poisons, and they revenged the least affront with certain death. When the dead body of a victim had been interred, the murderer proceeded at night to the grave, disinterred it, and taking it to his lodge he made a feast of it, to the relatives, which was eaten during the darkness of midnight, and if any of the invited guests became aware of the nature of the feast, and refused to eat, he was sure to fall under the ill-will of the feaster, and become the next victim. It is said that if a young woman refused the addresses of one of these medicine men, she fell a victim to his poison, and her body being disinterred, her relatives were feasted on it by the horrid murderer.

Such a taste did they at last acquire for human flesh, that parents dared not refuse their children if demanded by the fearful medicine man for sacrifice. And numerous anecdotes are related of circumstances happening during this horrid period, which all tend to illustrate the above assertions, but which the writer has not deemed proper to introduce, on account of the bloody and unnatural scenes which they depict. The Ojibways, at this period, fell entirely under the power of their Satanic medicine men, and priesthood, who even for some time caused themselves to be believed invulnerable to death. This, however, was finally tested one night, by a parent whose beloved and only child had just fallen a victim to the insatiable longing for human flesh, of one of these poisoners. After interring his child, he returned at night with his bow and arrow and watched near the grave. At midnight he saw what appeared to be the form of a black bear, approach and commence digging into the grave. It was also believed that these medicine men possessed the power of transforming themselves into the shapes of animals.

But the determined father, overcoming his fear, launched his barbed arrow into the body of the bear, and without waiting to see the consequence of his shot, he fled to his wigwam. The next morning, the body of one of the most malignant and fearful poisoners was found clothed in a bearskin, weltering in his blood, on the grave of the old man's child, whom he had made a victim.

Whether or not these evil practices were at this particular period caused by dire necessity, either through a failure of their crops, or by being entirely hemmed in by their enemies, as to be prevented from hunting on the main shore, the writer is not enabled to state, though he should be but too happy to give this as a palliating excuse for the horrid custom he is obliged to relate, as once having been in such vogue in the tribe of whom he is writing.

It is further stated that these evil practices were carried on to such an extent, that the Che-bi-ug, or "souls of the victims," were at last heard nightly traversing the village, weeping and wailing. On this the inhabitants became panic stricken, and the consequence was that a general and complete desertion of the island of their refuge took place, which left their town and fields entirely desolate, and from that time, they have become overgrown with trees and bushes, till scarcely a vestige of their former site is to be seen.

How far the nightly weeping of the dead, which caused this sudden fear and panic, was drawn from the imagination of the wicked inhabitants, or originated in the nightly secret wailings of fond parents for victimized children, we are not able to affirm, certain it is however, that from that time, the Ojibways considered the island as haunted, and never resided on it till after the first old French traders had located and built their trading establishment thereon.

When my maternal grandfather, Michel Cadotte, first built his trading post and resided on the island of La Pointe, seventy years ago, not an Indian dare stop over night on it alone, for fear of the Che-bi-ug, which were even then supposed to haunt it. At that time, however, it is necessary to state that this fear had been lately increased by a bloody tragedy which had occurred among the first French traders who located on the island, as will be hereafter narrated. Mons. Cadotte located on the site of the ancient Ojibway town, and at this time the ground on which had stood their numerous wigwams, and waved their fields of corn, was covered with a comparatively young growth of trees, and the stumps of the ancient pines which they had cut down, were in one spot still plainly discernible.

I have already stated that the old men of the tribe are not over communicative respecting the bad practices of their ancestors, which we have noted in this chapter, yet though backward to mention them, they do not altogether deny the truth of these tales, which I have learned from the lips of old half-breeds and traders, who received the information many years ago, from old men and women whose parents had been actors in the bloody scenes and feasts of this period. I vividly recollect in my childhood while residing on the very spot where these scenes had occurred, that my mother often stilled my importunities for a story, with tales of this period which would fairly make my hair stand on end, and which she had learned from an old woman who was then still living, and who was considered to be at least one hundred and twenty years of age, from the fact of her relating events which had occurred a century past, when she was a young woman.

CHAPTER VII.

ERA OF THE DISCOVERY.

Preliminary remarks—Visit of Claude Allouez to the Bay of Shag-a-waum-ik-ong, as known to the Ojibways—Definition of "Wa-me-tig-oshe," the Ojibway name for Frenchman—Antique silver crucifix found near La Pointe—Ancient prophecy foretelling the coming of the white race—The singular dream of Ma-se-wa-pe-ga—He goes in search of the white spirits—Finds them and returns to his people with presents—He makes a second journey and returns with the fire-arms and fire-water—Anecdote of the first trial and effect of fire-water—Anecdote of the effect of the fire-arm among the Dakotas—Two white traders found starving on the island of La Pointe—First white visitors to the Ojibways in the Bay of Shag-a-waum-ik-ong—Two hundred years ago—Establishment of traders and priests at the Ojibway village—Remarks, etc.

THE era of their first knowledge of, and intercourse with the white race, is one of most vital importance in the history of the aborigines of this continent.

So far as their own tribe is concerned, the Ojibways have preserved accurate and detailed accounts of this event; and the information which their old men orally give on this subject, is worthy of much consideration, although they may slightly differ from the accounts which standard historians and writers have presented to the world, and which they have gleaned from the writings of the enterprising and fearless old Jesuit missionaries, and from the published narratives of the first adventurers who pierced into the heart of the American wilderness. This source of information may be considered as more reliable and authentic than the oral traditions of the Indians, but as we have undertaken to write their history as they themselves tell it, we will do so without respect to what has already been written by eminent and standard authors. The writer is disposed to consider as true and perfectly reliable, the information which he has obtained and thoroughly investigated, on this subject, and which he will proceed in this chapter to relate in the words of his old Indian informants.

A few preliminary remarks are deemed necessary, before fully entering into the narrative of the Ojibway's first knowledge and intercourse with his white brother.

Those who have carefully examined the writings of the old Jesuit missionaries and early adventurers, who claim to have been the first discoverers of new regions, and new people, in the then dark wilderness of the west, or central America, have found many gross mistakes and exaggerations, and their works as a whole, are only tolerated and their accounts made matters of history, because no other source of information has ever been opened to the public

It is a fact found generally true, that the first adventurer who is able to give a flaming account of his travels, is handed down to posterity as the first discoverer of the country and people which he describes as having visited, when mayhap, that same region, and those same people had been, long previous, discovered by some obscure and more modest man, who, because he could not blazon forth his achievements in a book of travels, forever loses the credit of what he really has performed.

Many instances of this nature are being daily brought to light, and might be enumerated. Among others, Mr. Catlin claims in his book (and is believed by all who do not know to the contrary), to have been the first white man who visited the Dakota pipestone quarry, when in fact, that same quarry had been known to, and visited by white traders for nearly a century before Catlin saw it and wrote his book.

In the same manner also, Charles Lanman, of later notoriety, claims to have been the first white man who visited

the Falls of the St. Louis River, when in fact Aitkin,
Morrison, Sayer, and a host of others as white as he, had
visited, and resided for fifty years within sound of those
same falls.[1] It is thus that a man who travels for the purpose of writing a book to sell, and who, being a man of
letters, is able to trumpet forth his own fame, often plucks
the laurels due to more modest and unlettered adventurers.

Mr. Bancroft in his standard " History of the United
States," mentions that in the year 1665, the enterprising
and persevering Jesuit missionary, Claude Allouez, with
one companion, pushed his way into Lake Superior and
discovered the Ojibways congregated in a large village in
the Bay of Shag-a-waum-ik-ong, and preparing to go on a
war party against the Dakotas; that he resided two years
among them, and taught a choir of their youths to chant
the *Pater* and *Ave.*

This is the first visit made by white men to this point
on Lake Superior, of which we have any reliable *written*
testimony. The account as given in Bancroft's " History"
is not altogether corroborated by the Ojibways. It is only
through minute and repeated inquiry, that I have learned
the fact from their own lips, of this early visit of a " black
gowned priest," but not of his having resided with them
for any length of time. And they assert positively that it
was many years after the first visit of the white men to
their village in the Bay of Shag-a-waum-ik-ong, that the
" priest" made his appearance among them. And I am
disposed to doubt that as long a stay as two years was
made by Father Allouez among their people, or that any of
them learned to chant canticles, for the reason that the Ojibways, who are so minute in the relation of the particulars
of any important event in their history, comprised within
the past eight generations, do not make any mention of

---

[1] The allusion is to Lanman's *Summer in the Wilderness*, published in New
York, 1847.—E. D. N.

these facts. It is probable that the two years stay of this Jesuit in the Bay of Shag-a-waum-ik-ong, amounted to an occasional visit from Sault Ste. Marie, or Quebec, which place had already at this period, become the starting and rallying point of Western French adventurers.[1]

In those days there appears to have been a spirit of competition and rivalry among the different sects of the Catholic priesthood, as to who would pierce farthest into the western wilderness of America to plant the cross.

Imagination in some instances, outstripped their actual progress, and missionary stations are located on Hennepin's old map, in spots where a white man had never set foot. That the Catholic priests appeared amongst their earliest white visitors, the Ojibways readily acknowledge. And the name by which they have ever known the French people is a sufficient testimony to this fact, Wa-me-tig-oshe. For many years this name could not be translated by the imperfect interpreters employed by the agents of the French and English, and its literal definition was not given till during the last war, at a council of different tribes, convened by the British at Drummond's Isle. The several Ojibway interpreters present were asked to give its definition. All failed, till John Baptiste Cadotte, acknowledged to be the most perfect interpreter of the Algics

---

[1] Mr. Bancroft erroneously wrote in the 14th edition of the History of the United States, that Allouez " on the first day of October arrived at the great village of the Chippewas in the Bay of Chagouamigon," but Mr. Warren is also wrong in his supposition.

Allouez upon invitation of traders, came with them to Chagouamigon Bay in October, 1665. At that time there was no permanent Ojibway village beyond Sault Ste. Marie. He built a bark chapel on the shores of the Bay between a village of Petun Hurons, and a village comprised of three bands of Ottawas. On the 30th of August, 1667, he returned to Montreal, and in two days departed again for Lake Superior, where he remained until 1669, when a mission was established among the Ojibways at Sault Ste. Marie. In 1669 Marquette succeeded Allouez, in the words of the Relation of 1669–70, " at Chagouamigong where the Outaouacs and Hurons dwell." He remained with them until they were driven out of Lake Superior in 1671 by the Sioux.—E. D. N.

in his time, arose and gave it as follows: " Wa-mit-ig-oshe is derived from wa-wa, to wave, and metig, wood or stick, and means literally, people or ' men of the waving stick,' derived from the fact that when the French first appeared among the Algonquins who have given them this name, they came accompanied with priests who waved the Cross over their heads whenever they landed at an Indian village."

The circumstance also is worthy of mention, that a few years ago, an old Indian woman dug up an antique silver crucifix on her garden at Bad River near La Pointe, after it had been deeply ploughed. This discovery was made under my own observation, and I recollect at the time it created quite a little excitement amongst the good Catholics of La Pointe, who insisted that the Great Spirit had given this as a token for the old woman to join the church. The crucifix was found about two feet from the surface of the ground, composed of pure silver, about three inches long and size in proportion. It has since been buried at Gull Lake, in the grave of a favorite grandchild of the old Indian woman, to whom she had given it as a plaything.

The Ojibways affirm that long before they became aware of the white man's presence on this continent, their coming was prophesied by one of their old men, whose great sanctity and oft-repeated fasts, enabled him to commune with spirits and see far into the future. He prophesied that the white spirits would come in numbers like sand on the lake shore, and would sweep the red race from the hunting grounds which the Great Spirit had given them as an inheritance. It was prophesied that the consequence of the white man's appearance would be, to the An-ish-in-aub-ag, an " ending of the world." They acknowledge that at first their ancestors believed not the words of the old prophet foretelling these events; but now as the present generation daily see the foretold events coming to pass in all their details, the more reflective class firmly believe that they are truly a "doomed race." It was through harping on this prophecy, by which Te-cum-seh and his brother, the celebrated Show-a-no prophet, succeeded so well in forming a coalition among the Algic and other tribes, the main and secret object of which, was the final extermination of the white race from America.

The account which the Ojibways give of their first knowledge of the whites, is as follows:—

While still living in their large and central town on the Island of La Pointe, a principal and leading Me-da-we priest, whose name was Ma-se-wa-pe-ga (whole ribs), dreamed a dream wherein he beheld spirits in the form of men, but possessing white skins and having their heads covered. They approached him with hands extended and with smiles on their faces. This singular dream he related to the principal men of the Ojibways on the occasion of a grand sacrificial feast to his guardian dream-spirit. He informed them that the white spirits who had thus appeared to him, resided toward the rising sun, and that he would go and search for them. His people tried to dissuade him from undertaking what they termed a foolish journey, but firm in his belief, and strong in his determination, he was occupied a whole year in making preparations for his intended journey. He built a strong canoe of birch bark and cedar wood; he hunted and cured plenty of meat for his provisions; and early in the spring when the ice had left the Great Lakes, and he had completed his preparations, Ma-se-wa-pe-ga, with only his wife for a companion, started on his travels in quest of the white spirits whom he had seen in his dream.

He paddled eastward down the Great Lakes in the route

of the former migration of his tribe, till he entered into a large river which flowed in the direction of the rising sun. Undiscovered he passed through the hostile tribes of the Naud-o-ways. At last when the river on which he floated, had become wide and like a lake, he discovered on the banks, a hut, made of logs, and he noticed the stumps of large trees which had been cut by sharper instruments than the rude stone axes used by the Indians.

The signs were apparently two winters old, but satisfied that it was the work of the spirits, for whom he was in search, Ma-se-wa-pe-ga proceeded on his journey, and he soon came to another hut and clearing, which though deserted, had been built and occupied during the previous winter. Much encouraged, he paddled on down stream till he discovered another hut from the top of which arose a smoke. It was occupied by the "white spirits," who, on his landing, cordially welcomed him with a shake of the hand.

When about to depart to return home, presents of a steel axe, knife, beads, and a small strip of scarlet cloth were given him, which, carefully depositing in his medicine bag, as sacred articles, he brought safely home to his people at La Pointe. Ma-se-wa-pe-ga again collected the principal men of his tribe in council, and displaying his curious presents, he gave a full narrative of his successful journey and the fulfilment of his dream. The following spring a large number of his people followed him on his second visit to the supposed " white spirits." They carried with them many skins of the beaver, and they returned home late in the fall with the dread fire-arm, which was to give them power over their much feared enemies. It is on this occasion also, that they first procured the fire-water which was to prove the most dreadful scourge and curse of their race.

It is related that on the arrival of this party at La Pointe, with the fire-water, none dare drink it, thinking it a poison which would immediately cause death. They, however, to test its virtues, made an experimental trial on a very aged woman who—as they reasoned—had but a short time to live at all events, and whose death would be a matter of no account. The old woman drank it, appeared perfectly happy and in ecstasies, got over the effects of it, and begged for more. On which the men took courage, and drank up the remainder themselves. From that time, fire-water became the mammon of the Ojibways, and a journey of hundreds of miles to procure a taste of it, was considered but as boy's play.

They tell, also, the effect of the first gun, which they procured from the whites and introduced among the more remote and ignorant Dakotas, with whom at this time they happened to be on terms of peace. A peace party of the Ojibways visited a village of these people on the St. Croix river, and took with them as a curiosity, the dreadful weapon they had procured. While enjoying their peaceful games, the young men of the Ojibways informed the Dakotas of the fearful and deadly effects of the gun; but they, thinking that the Ojibways wished to intimidate them with an imaginary fear, reviled and laughed at the instrument, and in their disbelief they even offered to bet against its deadly effects. The dispute becoming high, the bet was taken, and a Dakota brave in utter derision, insisted on offering the back part of his body as a prominent mark. He was shot dead on the spot. With difficulty the peace-party succeeded in returning safely home, for the wrath of the Dakotas was aroused at the death of their warrior, and the old feud was again renewed, though from this time they evinced a mortal fear of the gun, which their remoteness from the white strangers precluded them from obtaining, till many years after the Ojibways had been fully supplied.

About this time, the old men of the tribe date the sudden evacuation of their town on the island of La Pointe, and the planting of their lodges in the adjoining Bay of Shag-a-waum-ik-ong, which occurrence I have fully mentioned in the preceding chapter. The first white men whom they tell of having visited them, came after this dispersion, and while they were congregated on the shores of the Bay.

One clear morning in the early part of winter, soon after the islands which are clustered in this portion of Lake Superior and known as the Apostles, had been locked in ice, a party of young men of the Ojibways started out from their village in the Bay of Shag-a-waum-ik-ong, to go, as was customary, and spear fish through holes in the ice, between the island of La Pointe and the main shore, this being considered as the best ground for this mode of fishing. While engaged in their sport, they discovered a smoke arising from a point of the adjacent island, toward its eastern extremity.

The island of La Pointe was then totally unfrequented, from superstitious fears which had but a short time previous led to its total evacuation by the tribe, and it was considered an act of the greatest hardihood for any one to set foot on its shores. The young men returned home at evening and reported the smoke which they had seen arising from the island, and various were the conjectures of the old people respecting the persons who would dare to build a fire on the spirit-haunted isle. They must be strangers, and the young men were directed, should they again see the smoke, to go and find out who made it.

Early the next morning, again proceeding to their fishing ground, the young men once more noticed the smoke arising from the eastern end of the unfrequented island, and led on by curiosity, they ran thither and found a small log cabin in which they discovered two white men in the last stages of starvation. The young Ojibways filled with compassion, carefully conveyed them to their village, where, being nourished with great kindness, their lives were preserved.

These two white men had started from Quebec during the summer with a supply of goods, to go and find the Ojibways who every year had brought rich packs of beaver to the sea-coast, notwithstanding that their road was barred by numerous parties of the watchful and jealous Iroquois. Coasting slowly up the southern shores of the Great Lake late in the fall, they had been driven by the ice on to the unfrequented island, and not discovering the vicinity of the Indian village, they had been for some time enduring the pangs of hunger. At the time they were found by the young Indians, they had been reduced to the extremity of roasting and eating their woollen cloth and blankets as the last means of sustaining life.

Having come provided with goods they remained in the village during the winter, exchanging their commodities for beaver skins. The ensuing spring a large number of the Ojibways accompanied them on their return home.

From close inquiry, and judging from events which are said to have occurred about this period of time, I am disposed to believe that this first visit by the whites took place about two hundred years ago. It is, at any rate, certain that it happened a few years prior to the visit of the " Black gowns" mentioned in Bancroft's History, and it is one hundred and eighty-four years since this well-authenticated occurrence.

If thorough inquiry were to be made, it would be found that the idea which is now generally believed, that the pious missionaries of those olden times, were the first pioneers into the Indian country about the great chain of Lakes, and Upper Mississippi, and were only followed closely by the traders, is a mistaken one. The adventurous, but obscure and unlettered trader, was the first pioneer. He cared only for beaver skins, and his ambition not leading him to secure the name of a first discoverer by publishing his travels, this honor naturally fell to those who were as much actuated by a thirst for fame, as by religious zeal.

The glowing accounts given by these traders on their return with their peltries to Quebec, their tales of large villages of peaceable and docile tribes, caused the eager Jesuit and Franciscan to accompany him back to the scene of his glowing accounts, and to plant the cross amongst the ignorant and simple children of the forest.

In making these remarks, we do not wish to deteriorate from the great praise which is nevertheless due to these pious and persevering fathers, who so early attempted to save the souls of the benighted Indians.

In the separation of the Ojibway tribe into two divisions, upwards of three centuries ago at the outlet of Lake Superior, which has been fully treated of in a previous chapter, a considerable band remained on their ancient village site at Bow-e-ting or Falls of St. Marie; and here, some years prior to the first visit of the white men and "Black Gowns" to the greater village in the Bay of Shag-a-waum-ik-ong, traders and priests had established themselves, and this circumstance naturally conduced to draw thither from their more western and dangerously situated villages, many families of this tribe, till they again numbered many wigwams, on this, the site of their ancient town. It was the first discovery of this tribe, at this point, which has given them the name, by the French, of Saulteaux, from the circumstance of their residing at the "Falls."

This band have ever since this period, remained detached by the intervening southern shores of Lake Superior, from the main body of the tribe who have radiated northward,

westward and southward, from their central town of La
Pointe.

Aided by the French, Ottawas, Potawatumies, and Wyandots, they succeeded in checking the harassing incursions of the war-like Iroquois, and as they became equally
possessed of the fire-arm, instead of being pressed westward, as they had been for centuries before, they retraced
the eastern track of their ancestors' former emigration, and
rejoined the remnants of their race who had been for
many years cut off from them by the intervening Iroquois,
and who had first greeted the French strangers who
landed in the river St. Lawrence, and who termed them
Algonquins.

From this period, the communication between the
eastern section or rear of the Algic tribes, occupying the
lower waters of the River St. Lawrence, and the great
western van who occupied the area of Lake Superior,
became comparatively free and open, for villages of the
Algic tribes lined the shores of the great chain of Lakes
and also the banks of the great river which forms the outlet into the "salt water."

In one of their traditions it is stated that "when the
white man first came in sight of the 'Great Turtle' island
of Mackinaw, they beheld walking on the pebbly shores,
a crane and a bear who received them kindly, invited them
to their wigwams, and placed food before them." This
allegory denotes that Ojibways of the Crane and Bear
Totem families first received the white strangers, and
extended to them the hand of friendship and rites of hospitality, and in remembrance of this occurrence they are
said to have been the favorite clans with the old French
discoverers.

CHAPTER VIII.

THE IMMEDIATE CONSEQUENCE OF THEIR FIRST INTERCOURSE WITH THE WHITE RACE.

The Ojibways discard their primitive utensils and weapons—They learn the value of the furred animals—Yearly visits to Quebec for purposes of trade—They radiate in bands from the bay of Shag-a-waum-ik-ong—The fur trade the main cause of their future movements and conquests—Mode of carrying on their wars—Tradition of BI-AUS-WAH—He dies for his son—A war party raised to revenge his death—Six Fox villages destroyed—Foxes retire to Wisconsin—Wa-we-gis-ug-o locates a village at Fond du Lac—Nature of their intercourse with the whites at this period—Great convocation of tribes at Sault Ste. Marie 1671—Object of the French in this movement—Words addressed to the Ojibway chief by the French envoy—Ojibways learn to love the French—Causes thereof—Remarks on the nature of their treatment and intercourse, as compared with that of the British and United States Governments.

WE have now come to that period in their history, when the important consequences of their discovery and intercourse with the white race began to work their effects upon the former even, monotonous, and simple course of life, which the Ojibways had pursued for so many generations.   Their clay kettles, pots, and dishes were exchanged for copper and brass utensils; their comparatively harmless bow and arrow, knives and spears of bones, were thrown aside, and in their place they procured the fire-arm, steel knife, and tomahawk of the whites.   They early became aware of the value of furs to the white strangers, and that the skins of animals, which they before used only for garments, now procured them the coveted commodities of the pale-faced traders, and the consequence was, that an indiscriminate slaughter, from this period commenced, of the beaver and other fur animals, which had grown numerous because molested only on occasions when their warm fur had been needed to cover the nakedness of the wild Indian, or their meat required to satisfy his hunger.

In the early part of the seventeenth century the Ojibways had already commenced the custom of yearly visiting Quebec, and afterwards Montreal, taking with them packs of beaver skins, and returning with the fire-arms, blankets, trinkets, and firewater of the whites. This custom they kept up for many years, gradually curtailing the length of their journeys as the whites advanced toward them step by step, locating their trading posts, first at Detroit, then at Mackinaw, then at Sault Ste. Marie, till at last the smoke of their cabins arose from the island of La Pointe itself, when these periodical journeys came comparatively to an end.

It was many years before the first French traders located a permanent trading post among the Ojibways of Shag-a-waum-ik-ong, and in the mean time, as this tribe became supplied with fire-arms, and killed off the beaver in the vicinity of their ancient seat, they radiated in bands inland, westward and southward towards the beautiful lakes and streams which form the tributaries of the Wisconsin, Chippeway, and St. Croix rivers, and along the south coast of the Great Lake to its utmost extremity, and from thence even inland unto the headwaters of the Mississippi. All this was the country of the Dakotas and Foxes, and bravely did they battle to beat back the encroaching Ojibways from their best hunting grounds, but in vain; for the invaders, besides having increased in numbers, had become possessed of fearful weapons, against which they feared to battle with their primitive bow and arrow.

For a number of years the Ojibways continued to consider the bay of Shag-a-waum-ik-ong as their common home, and their hunting parties returned thither at different seasons of the year. Here also, and only here, were their grand medicine rites performed, and their war-parties collected to march against, and drive further back, their numerous foes. The fur trade has been the mainspring and cause which has led the Ojibways westward and more westward, till they have become possessed through conquest, and a persevering, never-relaxing pressure on their enemies, of the vast tracts of country over which they are scattered at the present day. Their present proud position in this respect they have not gained without an equivalent price in blood and life, and the Ojibway exclaims with truth when asked by the grasping " Long Knife" to sell his country, that " it is strewed with the bones of his fathers, and enriched with their blood."

Their wars at this period were generally carried on by small and desultory parties, and it was only on occasions when smarting under some severe blow or loss, inflicted by their enemies, that the warriors of the tribe would collect under some noted leader, and marching into the Dakota or Fox country, make a bold and effective strike, which would long be remembered, and keep their enemies in fear and check.

A circumstance happened, about this time, which, in the regular course of our narrative, we will here relate. A few lodges of Ojibway hunters under the guidance of Bi-aus-wah, a leading man of the tribe, claiming the Loon Totem, was one spring encamped at Kah-puk-wi-e-kah, a bay on the lake shore situated forty miles west of La Pointe.

Early one morning the camp was attacked by a large war-party of Foxes, and the men, women and children all murdered, with the exception of a lad and an old man, who, running into a swamp, and becoming fastened in the bog and mire, were captured and taken in triumph by the Foxes to their village, there to suffer death with all the barbarous tortures which a savage could invent.

Bi-aus-wah, at the time of the attack, was away on a hunt, and he did not return till towards evening. His feelings on finding his wigwams in ashes, and the lifeless, scalpless remains of his beloved family and relatives strewed about on the blood-stained ground, can only be imagined. He had lost all that bound him to life, and perfectly reckless he followed the return trail of the Foxes determined to die, if necessary, in revenging the grievous wrong which they had inflicted on him. He arrived at the village of his enemies, a day after their successful war-party had returned, and he heard men, women, and children screaming and yelling with delight, as they danced around the scalps which their warriors had taken.

Secreting himself on the outskirts of the village, the Ojibway chieftain waited for an opportunity to imbrue his hands in the blood of an enemy who might come within reach of his tomahawk. He had not remained long in his ambush, when the Foxes collected a short distance from the village, for the purpose of torturing and burning their two captives. The old man was first produced, and his body being wrapped in folds of the combustible birch bark, the Foxes set fire to it and caused him to run the gauntlet amid their hellish whoops and screams; covered with a perfect blaze of fire, and receiving withal a shower of blows, the old man soon expired.

The young and tender lad was then brought forward, and his doom was to run backwards and forwards on a long pile of burning fagots, till consumed to death. None but a parent can fully imagine the feelings which wrung the heart of the ambushed Ojibway chieftain, as he now recognized his only surviving child in the young captive who was about to undergo these torments. His single arm could not rescue him, but the brave father determined to die for or with his only son, and as the cruel Foxes were on the point of setting fire to the heap of dry fagots on which the lad had been placed, they were surprised to see the

Ojibway chief step proudly and boldly into their midst and address them as follows:—

"My little son, whom you are about to burn with fire, has seen but a few winters; his tender feet have never trodden the war path—he has never injured you! But the hairs of my head are white with many winters, and over the graves of my relatives I have hung many scalps which I have taken from the heads of the Foxes; my death is worth something to you, let me therefore take the place of my child that he may return to his people."

Taken totally by surprise, the Foxes silently listened to the chief's proposal, and ever having coveted his death, and now fearing the consequence of his despairing efforts, they accepted his offer, and releasing the son, they bade him to depart, and burnt the brave father in his stead. The young man returned safely to his people at La Pointe, and the tale of his murdered kindred, and father's death, spread like wild fire among the wide scattered bands of the Ojibways.

A war party was gathered and warriors came, even from distant Ste. Marie and Grand Portage, to join in revenging the death of their chief.

They marched toward the headwaters of the St. Croix and Chippeway rivers, and returned not home till they had attacked and destroyed six villages of the Foxes, some of which were composed of earthen wigwams, which now form the mounds which are spread so profusely over this section of country. They reaped a rich harvest of scalps, and made such an effective strike, that from this time the Foxes evacuated the rice lakes and midland country about the St. Croix and Chippeway rivers, and retired south to the Wisconsin.

Soon after the above occurrence, the Ojibways pressed up the lake shore, and Wa-me-gis-ug-o, a daring and fearless hunter, obtained a firm footing and pitched his wigwam permanently at Fond du Lac, or Wi-a-quah-ke-che-gume-eng. He belonged to the Marten Totem family, and the present respected chiefs of that now important village, Shin-goob and Nug-aun-ub, are his direct descendants. Many families of his people followed the example of this pioneer, and erecting their wigwams on the islands of the St. Louis River, near its outlet into the lake, for greater security, they manfully held out against the numerous attacks of the fierce Dakotas, whose villages were but two days' march toward the south on the St. Croix River, and the west, at Sandy Lake. During this time, comprised between the years 1612 (at which I date their first knowledge of the white race), and 1671, when the French made their first national treaty or convocation at Sault Ste. Marie with the northwestern tribes, no permanent trading post had as yet been erected on the shores of Lake Superior; the nearest post was the one located at Sault Ste. Marie, which as early as the middle of the seventeenth century, had already become an important depot and outlet to the Lake Superior fur trade. Their intercourse with the whites consisted in yearly visits to their nearest western posts. The trade was partially also carried on through the medium of the intervening kindred tribe of Ottaways, or by adventurous traders who came amongst them with canoes loaded with goods, made a transient stay, sometimes even passing a winter amongst them, following their hunting camps, but returning in the spring of the year to Quebec with the proceeds of their traffic. No incident which the old men related as connected with the whites, is worthy of mention, till a messenger of the "Great French King" visited their village at Shag-a-waum-ik-ong, and invited them to a grand council of different tribes to be held at Sault Ste. Marie. Some of the words of this messenger are still recollected and minutely related by the Ojibways.

Early the following spring, a large delegation proceeded to Ste. Marie to attend the council, and hear the words of the "Great King of the French." Ke-che-ne-zuh-yauh, head chief of the great Crane family, headed this party, and represented the nation of the Ojibways. It is his descendants in the fourth generation, from whom I have obtained the few detached items which are here given respecting this important event.

Michel Cadotte (son of the Mons. M. Cadotte whom we have already had occasion to mention), who is now the oldest man of mixed Ojibway and French blood in the northwest, states that his great-grandfather, a Mons. Cadeau, on this occasion first came into the Ojibway country in the train of the French envoy Sieur du Lusson. The name has since been spelled Cadotte, and the wide spread family of this name claims their connection with the Ojibway tribe from this period. From this old half-breed, still living at La Pointe, I have obtained much reliable information, corroborating with that obtained from the Indians themselves.

The envoy of the French king asked, in the name of his nation, for permission to trade in the country, and for free passage to and from their villages all times thereafter. He asked that the fires of the French and Ojibway nations might be made one, and everlasting.[1]

He promised the protection of the great French nation against all their enemies, and addressing himself to the Chippeway chieftain from La Pointe, he said :—

" Every morning you will look towards the rising of the sun and you shall see the fire of your French father reflecting towards you, to warm you and your people. If you are in trouble, you, the Crane, must arise in the skies and cry with your 'far sounding' voice, and I will hear you.

The fire of your French father shall last forever, and warm his children." At the end of this address a gold medal shaped like a heart was placed on the breast of Ke-che-ne-zuh-yauh, and by this mark of honor he was recognized as the chief of the Lake Superior Ojibways.[1] These words have been handed down from generation to generation, to his present descendants, and it will be readily seen by them that the French had already learned to use the figurative and forcible style of expression of the Ojibways, and understood their division into Totemic clans, with the peculiarities on which each clan prided themselves.

The Ojibways received the "heart" of their French brethren, and accepted their proposals of peace, amity, and mutual support and protection. From this period their country became more free and open to French enterprise, and they learned to term the French king "father."

The Ojibways learned to love the French people, for the Frenchmen, possessing a character of great plasticity, easily assimilated themselves to the customs and mode of life of their red brethren. They respected their religious rites and ceremonies, and they "never laughed" at their superstitious beliefs and ignorance. They fully appreciated, and honored accordingly, the many noble traits and qualities possessed by these bold and wild hunters of the forest. It is an acknowledged fact, that no nation of whites have ever succeeded so well in gaining the love and confidence of the red men, as the Franks. It is probable that their character in many respects was more similar, and adapted to the character of the Indian, than any other European nation. The "voyageur du Nord," as were then termed the common class

[1] Note by Mr. Warren.—On the death of this chieftain, this gold medal was buried with him, through a superstitious notion that he should appear in the land of spirits with the same honors which had attended him on earth. His grave was located on the shores of Shag-a-waum-ik-ong Bay. In 1850 it was carefully searched for by some of his descendants to recover the medal, but the grave was found to have been swept away by high water.

of the French who visited them for the purposes of trade, were nearly as illiterate, ignorant, and superstitious as themselves, and many of them were far beneath the red man in strength of character and morality.

Their aim was not so much that of gain as of pleasure, and the enjoyment of present life, and mainly in this respect will be found the difference between the nature of their intercourse with the natives of America, and that which has since been carried on by the English and Americans, who, as a general truth, have made Mammon their God, and have looked on the Indian but as a tool or means of obtaining riches, and other equally mercenary ends.

In their lack of care for the morrow, which in a measure characterized the French " voyageur," and in their continual effervescence of animal spirits, open-heartedness, and joviality, they agreed fully with the like characteristics possessed by the Ojibways. Some of my readers may be surprised at my thus placing the Indian on a par with the laughter-loving Frenchman, for the reason that he has ever been represented as a morose, silent, and uncommunicative being. It is only necessary to state that this is a gross mistake, and but a character (far different from his real one), assumed by the Indian in the presence of strangers, and especially white strangers in whom he has no confidence. Another bond which soon more firmly attached them one to another with strong ties of friendship, was created by the Frenchmen taking the women of the Ojibways as wives, and rearing large families who remained in the country, and to this day, the mixture and bonds of blood between these two people has been perpetuated, and remains unbroken.

The days of the French domination was the Augustan era of the fur trade, and beavers were so plenty and the profits arising from the trade were so large, that the French traders readily afforded to give large presents of their coveted commodities, their beloved tobacco and fire-water to the Indians who visited them at their posts, or on occasions when they visited them at their own villages. In those days along the lake shore villages of the Ojibways, from Mackinaw to Fond du Lac of Lake Superior, there was no music so sweet to the ears of the inhabitants, as the enlivening boat song of the merry French " voyageurs," as they came from the direction of Quebec and Montreal each spring of the year—rapidly looming up from the bosom of the calm lake, laden with the articles so dearly valued among the wild hunters. They recognized in these yearly visits the " rays of the fire of their great French father," which he bade them to " look for each morning (spring) towards the rising of the sun."

No strangers were more welcome to the Ojibways, and warm were the shaking of hands and embraces on these occasions between the dusky son of the forest, and the polite and warm-hearted Frank. The dark-eyed damsels, though they stood bashfully in the rear of those who thronged the beach to welcome the new-comers, yet with their faces partly hidden they darted glances of welcome, and waited in the wigwams impatiently for their white sweethearts to come in the darkness and silence of night, to present the trinkets which they had brought all the way from Quebec, to adorn their persons and please their fancy.

After the Ojibways became possessed with fire-arms and ammunition, the arrival of a French " Bourgeois" with the flag of France flying at the stern of his canoe, was saluted with a volley of musketry, and in turn, when any chief approached the " posts" or " forts" accompanied with the same ensign, discharges of cannons were fired in his honor by the French. Thus, interchanges of good-will and polite attention were continually kept up between them.

The French early gained the utmost confidence of the Ojibways, and thereby they became more thoroughly acquainted with their true and real character, even during the comparative short season in which they mingled with them as a nation, than the British and Americans are at this present day, after over a century of intercourse. The French understood their division into clans, and treated each clan according to the order of its ascendency in the tribe. They conformed also to their system of governmental polity, of which the totemic division formed the principal ingredient. They were circumspect and careful in bestowing medals, flags, and other marks of honor, and appointing chiefs, and these acts were never done unless being first certain of the approbation of the tribe, and it being in accordance with their civil polity. In this important respect the British, and American government especially, have lacked most wofully. The agents and commissioners, and even traders of these two nations, have appointed chiefs indiscriminately or only in conformity with selfish motives and ends, and there is nothing which has conduced so much to disorganize, confuse, and break up the former simple but well-defined civil polity of these people ; and were the matter to be fully investigated, it would be found that this almost utter disorganization has been one of the chief stumbling-blocks which has ever been in the way of doing good to the Indian race. This short-sighted system has created nothing but jealousies and heart-burnings among the Ojibways. It has broken the former commanding influence of their hereditary chiefs, and the consequence is, that the tribe is without a head or government, and it has become infinitely difficult to treat with them as a people. No good has resulted from this bad and thoughtless policy even to the governments who have allowed it to be pursued by its agents. On the contrary, they are punished daily by the evil consequences arising from it, for in this is to be found the true and first cause of the complaints which are continually at this day being poured into the ears of the " Great Father" at Washington, and it is through this that misunderstandings and non-conformity have arisen to treaties which have been made by the United States, not only with the Ojibways, but other tribes, and which are of the same nature that eventually led to the Creek, Seminole and Black Hawk wars.

CHAPTER IX.

ACCOUNT OF THE FIRST FRENCH TRADING POSTS BUILT ON LAKE SUPERIOR.

A post is built at Grand' Portage by a company of French traders—Their inducements for its location—The French first open a communication with the tribes of the Ke-nis-te-no and Assine-boins—First communication of the northern division of the Ojibways with these allied tribes—They join the alliance—Tradition of the manner in which the Assine-boins became detached .from their .kindred Dakotas—They become close allies of the Ke-nis-te-no and Ojibways—A trading post is located at La Pointe—French work the copper mines on Lake Superior—Bloody tragedy enacted at this post in 1722—Which results in its evacuation.

A FEW years after the great convocation of northwestern tribes, and treaty with the French nation at Sault Ste. Marie, a company of French traders proceeded up the west coast of Lake Superior, and built a trading post or " fort" (as these establishments were termed in those days), on a beautiful bay situated on the lake shore a few miles above Kah-man-a-tig-wa-yah (or Pigeon River), and known as the " Grand Portage" or Ke-che-o-ne-gum-eng, from the fact that a portage of ten miles is here made to Pigeon River, to avoid the rapids which preclude navigation even for canoes, for many miles above the entry of this " bad winding stream."

This is probably the first permanent post erected by the white man in the region of country comprised within the present limits of Minnesota Territory. It was built, as near as I can judge from the information of the Indians and old traders, upwards of one hundred and fifty years ago.

The great quantity of beaver, existing at this period on all the streams emptying into Lake Superior, and especially throughout the country watered by Kah-man-a-tig-wa-yah and its tributaries, together with the great docility, harmless character and friendly disposition of the section of the Ojibways occupying this district, who comprise the northern division of the tribe, were without doubt, the leading causes which induced the French here to build their first "fort" in preference to any other spot on Lake Superior.

From this point, also, a vast region of unexplored country became open to their indefatigable enterprise, in a northern direction. It is by this route that they first became acquainted with the remote northern tribes, of the Ke-nis-te-no and Assineboins, with whom they soon opened a communication.

Long before this, the Ojibways of the northern division had already reached in their northward progress, the country of the Ke-nis-te-no and Assineboins, the former of whom belonged to the same stock as themselves, and though the latter were of Dakota extraction, yet finding the two tribes in close alliance and carrying on a war against the Dakotas, they entered their wigwams in peace, and joined in alliance with them.

I recollect of having read in some book that the Assineboins had been forced into an alliance by the Ke-nis-te-no who first received fire-arms from the British by the route of Hudson's Bay. This led me to make close inquiries on this subject, and I find that Indian tradition says differently. Esh-ke-bug-e-coshe, the present aged and respected chief of the Pillager Ojibways, lived many years in his youth among these tribes; and he gives the following account of the manner in which this singular alliance between an Algic with a Dakota tribe, first happened.

"Many winters before they became aware of the presence of the white man on this great island, the Yankton division of the great Dakota tribe, resided on the borders of the great western prairies near the Red River of the North. They numbered many hundred lodges, and their warriors prevailed against the Ke-nis-te-no toward the north and west, and caused them to keep under the shade of the forests and swamps which covered their hunting grounds. At one time it happened, as it often does, that two young men quarrelled about a woman, and one in the heat of passion and jealousy, took the life of the other. Both belonged to numerous and important families, and in accordance with the law of ' blood for blood,' notwithstanding his relatives wished to buy him off, the murderer was killed.

" Generally a case of this kind ends after the death of the first murderer, but in this instance, the drawer of his fellow's blood was a great warrior, and his loss being severely felt by his relatives, the person who had taken his life was in turn murdered. The matter had gone beyond the usual length, and notwithstanding the interference of the old men and chiefs, the person who drew the last blood suffered death for his act, at the hands of a relative to the person whom he had killed. The great Yankton camp became a scene of excitement, and murders occurred daily, till the weaker party consisting of a thousand lodges, left the main camp and retired by themselves, to pursue their hunt for meat to feed their women and children.

" The feud did not end here, but continued with greater fury ; the larger camp even sending war parties to attack the straggling hunters of their former brethren. Scalps were also taken, and this is equal in Indian custom to a declaration of open and exterminating war. The smaller camp, therefore, to prevent their total eventual destruction at the hands of the more numerous Yanktons, moved towards the country of Ke-nis-te-no, with whom they had always waged a never-ending warfare ; and preferring to trust themselves to their generosity rather than to the vindictive hatred of their own kindred, they collected the women and children whom in former years they had captured from them, and adopted in their families. These they placed on horses, and loaded with presents, they were sent to the great Ke-nis-te-no town on Dead River (Ne-bo-se-be), with the peace pipe of the seceding Dakotas, requesting to be received 'in their lodges' and protected from the 'fire that raged in their rear, on the western prairies.'

" The manly and compassionate Ke-nis-te-no sent forty of their warriors to receive them into their country, and escort them into their village. A grand council was held, where the Assineboins told their grievances, asked for protection, and promised to fight by the side of the Ke-nis-te-no against the Yanktons forever.

" Their words were listened to with deep attention and pity, and they were accepted as allies and brothers. The peace pipe was smoked, ' their council fire was made one,' and they ' ate out of the same dish' and reposed thereafter under the ' shade of the same forests and swamps' till their united prowess eventually drove the Dakotas from the northern plains, and the Ke-nis-te-no and Assineboins could then go out occasionally to ' bask in the sun on the prairies, and taste the meat of the buffalo.' Shortly after this first alliance, the Ojibway made his appearance among them, and he too became a party to the mutual compact which has been kept unbroken to this day."

We will now return to the regular course of our narrative, from which we have digressed in relating the above tradition.

Soon after the location of the trading post at Grand Portage, the same company of traders built a " fort" on the island of La Pointe, at the mouth of a small creek or pond midway between the present location of the " American Fur Company's" establishment, and the mission house of the " American Board of Foreign Missions." Strong palisades of cedar are said to have been planted around this post, and a cannon mounted for its defence. The

Ojibways who had resided on this island, and who occupied the surrounding shores of the lake, now traded at this
establishment, and they learned to pitch their lodges once
more on the spot which they had on a previous occasion so
suddenly evacuated.

Many, it is true, had been drawn back to Sault Ste.
Marie, Mackinaw, and even further east, to visit the spots
which the feet of their ancestors had once trodden, and on
which they had left their bones to moulder and decay,
Yet those that remained still formed a formidable body
numbering many hundreds of warriors and hunters, and
their trade for many years made the post located on the
island of their ancient town, a most important and lucrative one.

At this time it is said that the French worked the copper mines on Lake Superior extensively, and doubtless
many, if not all of the signs which are at the present day
being discovered by the American miners, are the remains
of the former works of these old French pioneers.   When
the British subsequently conquered this section of country
in 1763, the Indians state that the French miners carefully
covered the mines which they had been working, so that
their conquerors might not have the advantage of their
discoveries.

The first old French "Fort" at La Pointe was not
maintained many years before a bloody murder was enacted within its walls, which resulted in its final disman-
tling and evacuation.   The clerk or trader in charge was
named Joseph. He passed his last winter there with his
wife, two children, and with but one Canadian " Coureur
du Bois." This man, it appears from his after confession,
had conceived an unlawful passion for his master's wife,
and he took occasion one morning when the unsuspecting
Joseph had gone to shoot ducks in an adjacent pond, to
press his suit to the wife, who, however, threatened to in-

form her husband of his treachery. On this the wretch attempted to force her to his wishes, but she, seizing an Indian spear which happened to stand in a corner of the room where this scene was being enacted, defended herself in such a manner and jeoparded his life to such a degree, that he was forced in self-defence to take her life.

Having performed this bloody deed, he loaded a gun, and placing himself behind the gate of the " Fort," he awaited anxiously the return of his unsuspecting master, whom, as he entered the gateway, he shot in the back, causing his immediate death. He next murdered the eldest child, a girl about six years of age, and was proceeding to finish his bloody work by taking the life of the youngest, when his black heart misgave him. The child had been his pet, and was just beginning to run about and lisp its childish prattle, and at first he could not find it within him to take its innocent life. His qualms of conscience, however, did not last long, for becoming tired of its ceaseless cries for its parents, after he had preserved its life three days, he murdered the little one in cold blood, and made its grave with his other victims in a heap of shavings and other rubbish, which had accumulated in a corner of the Fort.

This bloody tragedy was perpetrated in the spring of the year, when the Indians were all away at their sugar camps on the main shore, and at a time when the ice on the lake had become so weak and rotten as to make it unsafe to cross or travel on it. Notwithstanding the state of the ice, the guilty man, who could not bear to remain in solitude surrounded with the evidences of his bloody deed, attempted to make his escape, but having twice broken through the ice, and with difficulty saved his life, and (as he confessed) being drawn back by an invisible power, he returned to the scene of his crime, to patiently await its consequence.

When the ice had disappeared and melted away under the rays of the spring sun, the Indians once more frequented the Fort, and on their inquiring for the trader, the murderer told them the plausible story, that his master had started with his family on a dog train, while the ice was still on the lake, to pay them a visit at their sugar camps. And as he had never arrived amongst them, all naturally supposed that he had broken through the bad ice, and drowned with his family.   The Ojibways faithfully hunted the shores of the island and adjacent main land, for the remains of their lost trader, but as may be supposed, they searched in vain.

In the course of the spring a light canoe arrived from Montreal by way of Grand Portage, containing one of the factors of the fur company, to whom belonged the post.

At first the plausible tale of the murderer was credited, but marks of blood having been discovered on the walls of the room where the trader's wife had been murdered, and his evident confusion on being asked the cause of them, led immediately to suspicion, and he was from that time arrested and confined.

Shortly after this, the factor, while walking around the precincts of the fort, endeavoring to discover further traces of the murder, happened to push his sword cane into the pile of rubbish where the murderer had buried the bodies of his unfortunate victims, and the stench on the end of his cane led to a complete discovery. The bodies were immediately disinterred in presence of the guilty wretch, who now confessed his crime.

The fort was evacuated, and the cannon and iron works were thrown into the adjacent pond, which having a deep and miry bottom, they have never been discovered by the Indians, who often afterwards searched for them. The site of this old post is still plainly discernible from small mounds of stone and rubbish which once formed the chimneys of the

dwellings, which are still to be found on the spot where it
once stood. The murderer was taken to Montreal, and
the Indians at this day say that he was torn to pieces by
horses being attached to each of his arms and legs, and
caused to pull in different directions.

Another account has it, and coming from the lips of old
traders and half-breeds, I am disposed to believe it as the
truth, that the guilty wretch managed to escape from his
keepers on the route to Montreal, and seeking refuge
among the Hurons, he adopted their dress and customs,
and learned to speak their language. On one occasion
being present at a war-dance, when the Indian warriors
were striking the "red stake" and telling their different
exploits performed in war against their enemies, the murderer stepped into their midst, and likewise striking the
stake, he related his deed of treachery and blood, expecting to be honored by the red men as a brave man, for the
exploit. He was however mistaken, for before he had
finished his tale of the bloody deed, an Indian warrior
arose, and stepping up to him with the single exclamation
of " Dog," he buried a tomahawk deep into his brain. The
narrative of this event has been carefully preserved and
handed down by the old traders, and it is presented here
as I have learned it from them.

The tale as the Indians tell it, is somewhat mixed with
the superstitious and unnatural, though in the main incidents they fully agree with the trader's account. They
give as a cause for the murder, that the "Coureur du Bois"
had pilfered goods during the winter to such an amount
that his master threatened to report his conduct to the
Factors on their first visit, and have him taken to Quebec
as a culprit. To prevent this disgrace and punishment,
the man first killed his master, as has been related, and
then attempted rape on his wife, who forced him to kill her
by her active self-defence with the Indian spear. Only in

this respect do the Indians differ in the account from that which I have given, and which is said to have been the confession of the murderer himself.[1]

I learn from Michel Cadotte, and the venerable John Baptist Corbin, who came into the Ojibway country when he was twenty years of age and has remained fifty-six years, that this event occurred just one hundred and thirty years ago, in the year 1722.

[1] This story as told by the trader, William Morrison, in August, 1822, appeared in the Detroit Gazette, and is reprinted in Vol. VIII. of *Wisconsin Historical Collections*. The published account says the tragedy of killing the trader, his wife and child, occurred during the winter of 1760–61, and that on his way to Montreal for trial he was released on the St. Lawrence River, and fought with the Indians against the British. His boasting of his murders took place at a dance near Sault Ste. Marie. The Indians, disgusted with his tale of cruelty, invited him to a feast, and as soon as he commenced to eat, he was informed by the chief that as soon as he stopped, he would be killed. He ate for a long time, but at last had to stop, when he was soon lifeless. His body was boiled, but the young men would not eat, for they said "he was worse than a bad dog."—E. D. N.

CHAPTER X.

WARS OF THE OJIBWAYS WITH THE IROQUOIS AND O-DUG-AM-EES, OR FOXES.

Warfare between the Ojibways and Iroquois—Ojibways, Pottawatumies, Ottaways, and Wyandots join in alliance against the Iroquois, to open the route to Quebec—Iroquois driven from Canada—Tradition of the last battle fought between the Ojibways and Iroquois—The French favor the Algic tribes against their enemies—War between the Ojibways and O-dug-am-ees or Foxes—Tradition of the old hunter—He with his family are attacked by the Foxes—Indian fight—Revenge of the old hunter—Foxes are driven from the Wisconsin—They retire to the Mississippi and ask to be incorporated with the O-sau-kies.

BESIDES carrying on an inveterate and exterminating warfare with the powerful Dakotas and cruel Foxes, the Ojibways were obliged to keep up their ancient feud with the Naudoways, or Iroquois, towards the east. For a time the powerful confederation of Six Nations prevailed against the Algic tribes who had taken possession of the great northern chain of lakes, mostly through their having been first supplied with fire-arms by the Dutch and British of New York.

They became possessed of the country bordering the Ottaway River, and effectually barred their enemies from communication with the French who resided on the St. Lawrence. Their anxiety to open the road to the white traders, in order to procure fire-arms and their much coveted commodities, induced the Ojibways, Ottaways, Pottawatumies, Osaukies, and Wyandots to enter into a firm alliance. They sent their united forces against the Iroquois, and fighting severe and bloody battles, they eventually forced them to retire from Canada.

From this time, now upwards of five generations ago, the route from Lake Superior to the French settlement on the St. Lawrence became comparatively free and open, though the trading parties were often waylaid by the ambushed warriors of the Iroquois on the Ottaway River.

The warlike, confederated tribes whom the French early designated with the name of Iroquois, gave not up their long contest with the allied Algics, without a severe and protracted struggle. They often collected their forces, and marching westward, their hardy warriors became familiar with the shores of Lake Huron, the banks of the Ste. Marie, and often even procured scalps on the shores of Lake Superior. At one time the Ottaways were forced to retire from the Straits of Mackinaw, and the islands of Lake Huron, through fear of these redoubtable eastern warriors. The last important battle between the Ojibways and the Iroquois, took place about one hundred years ago at a point on Lake Superior, a short distance above its outlet, which has to this day retained the name of Point Iroquois. The Sault Ste. Marie Ojibways are probably better acquainted with the details of this occurrence than those from whom I have obtained the account which is here given, as they are locally interested in the tradition.

Ke-che-wash-keenh or Great Buffalo, chief of La Pointe, briefly gives the following version of the affair :—

" The Ojibways, one time collected a war party on the shores of the Great Lake, which proceeded eastward against their old enemies the Naud-o-ways. On their road to the country of these people, they one evening encamped on a point of the lake shore a short distance above Bow-e-ting (Ste. Marie). They had lighted their fires for the night and commenced cooking their suppers, when the sounds of distant yelling and laughter came indistinctly to their ever-listening ears. The noise appeared to come from the other side of the point, immediately opposite the

spot where they had encamped.   Scouts were sent to reconnoitre the noisy party, whom they supposed to be traders proceeding up the lake to trade with their people.

" These scouts soon returned on a run, and informed their
party that they had seen a large war party of Naud-o-ways,
who were encamped, drinking firewater, and carousing
with perfect carelessness, and apparently with every sense
of security.   The Ojibways quickly extinguished their
blazing fires, and making their usual preparations for a
desperate fight, they noiselessly approached and surrounded
the encampment of their boisterous and drunken enemies.
They silently awaited the moment when nearly all had
drunk themselves insensible, and the remainder had fallen
asleep, for the war whistle to sound the onset.   They attacked them with great fury, and it is said that but few of
the Naud-o-ways escaped the Ojibways' tomahawk and
scalping knife on this bloody occasion."

The " Six Nations" never after this made incursions into
the country of the Lake Superior Ojibways, and from this
occurrence may be dated the ending of the long and fierce
warfare which these two people had been waging against
one another.[1]

The French always favored the Ojibway and other Algic
tribes in their war with the New York tribes, and for
this, they often suffered at the hands of the Iroquois, who
waylaid their canoes laden with merchandise on the route
up the Great Chain of Lakes.

For providing the Ojibways also with fire-arms, and
through this causing them to become too powerful for their
western enemies, the French incurred the dislike and
hatred of the Dakota and O-dug-am-ee tribes, who on one
occasion made their deep enmity evident, by making war

---

[1] Perrot gives a history of this conflict.   See *Memoirs* edited by Tailhan,
pp. 97, 98.—E. D. N.

on them and attacking their fort at Wow-e-yat-ton-ong or
Detroit, which was only saved by the combined efforts of
the O-dah-wahs and Ojibways under the leadership of the
renowned Pontiac, who had already at this period, 1746,
commenced to carve out the renown which he eventually
attained.

It is shortly after this period that the O-dug-am-ees
again incurred the vengeance of the Ojibways, who a
second time attacked and swept away their villages. It
has been stated that on their being driven from the headwaters of the St. Croix and Chippeway rivers, they had
retired to the Wisconsin and into the country bordering
on Lake Michigan. The tradition of their second invasion
by the Ojibways, is given as follows by the old Indian story
tellers :—

An old Ojibway hunter with his wife, two sons, and
their families, were one winter hunting about the head
lakes of the Wisconsin River. As they searched for game
they moved from camp to camp by slow and easy stages,
and being of a fearless disposition, they formed the southern vanguard of numerous other families similarly employed and following slowly in their wake.

They had arrived in the vicinity of the usual hunting
grounds of the O-dug-am-ees, and now at every camp they
formed a barrier of logs and bushes to shield them from a
sudden attack of their enemies. One morning early, one
of the sons of the old hunter, as usual, put on his moccasins,
tied his blanket around his body, and, shouldering his gun,
started on his day's hunt. It was snowing heavily, and the
rest of the family remained at home. The hunter had
been gone but a short time when he returned, and, without
saying a word, sat down in his usual place, and commenced
whittling his bullets so that they could be easily and
quickly thrown into his gun. When he had finished this
work, he took his gun, drew out the load, and carefully

cleansed it. He then sharpened his knife, and placed his war-club and spear ready at hand for immediate use.

The old hunter watched the singular preparations of his silent son, and suspecting that he had discovered signs of an enemy, arose, and saying that he would go and cut a few sticks of the red willow to smoke, he left the lodge to go and see with his own and more experienced eyes, what were the signs of danger. He had proceeded but a few steps in the adjacent forest, when he discovered a strange track in which there were but a few flakes of the fast falling snow. His Indian sagacity told him that it was the foot-print of an O-dug-am-ee, and returning to the wigwam, he proposed to his family an immediate flight to some neighboring camp of their friends. The silent son now spoke, and told his father that flight had become imprac. ticable, for they were entirely surrounded by a very large war-party of their enemies. "All we can do," said he, "is to prepare for death ; for I have seen the trail of the O-dug-am-ee warriors, and it is deep-beaten and wide ; many feet have trodden it."

Determined to defend their women and children to the last gasp, the Ojibway hunters cut down a few more trees and strengthened the barrier around their wigwam. Night gradually came and covered everything in deep darkness and gloom, yet still was the expected attack deferred. The imitated hootings of the owl, and howling of wolves which resounded from different parts of the forest, but too plainly told the hunters that the O-dug-am-ee wolves had surrounded their camp, and only waited the first dawn of day (the Indian's favorite hour), to make the attack.

The old hunter being anxious to save a portion of his kindred, took two girls—his grandchildren—each by the hand and silently led them some distance into the surrounding woods, amid . the darkness, and informing them the direction they were to go—to be judged by the wind, and fast falling flakes of snow, he bade them save their lives by flight and inform their people of his fate.

The old man then turned to his lodge, and he listened anxiously for the yell that would denote the discovery and death of " the little birds which he had let out to fly away." That expected yell came not, and the old man became satisfied that his two grandchildren were safe.

At the first dawn of morning, the O-dug-am-ees commenced the attack with loud and thrilling war whoops. The Ojibways defended themselves bravely, and as long as their ammunition lasted, they kept their numerous assailants at bay, and sent many of their more hardy warriors to the land of Spirits; but as soon as their powder gave out they ceased firing, the O-dug-am-ees rushed into their camp, and leaping over their barrier of logs and brush, the work of death and scalping commenced. The Ojibways died not without a desperate struggle, for even the grandmother of the family cut down an enemy with her axe before she received the death stroke. All perished but the old hunter, who, during the last brave struggle of his two sons, miraculously escaped through the dense ranks of his eager foes, entirely naked and covered with blood from numerous wounds.

He had not proceeded far before he met a small party of his friends, who had been informed of the desperate situation of his camp, by the two girls whom he had caused to escape during the previous night. At the head of this party, though almost dead with fatigue and loss of blood, the old man returned, and found his wigwam in ashes. The O-dug-am-ee wolves had already done their work and departed, and the bodies of his murdered kindred scalped, dismembered, cut and hashed into a hundred pieces, lay strewn about on the blood-stained snow.

At this horrid spectacle the Ojibway party, though feeble in numbers, recklessly followed the return trail of the perpetrators, depending for help, should they enter into a premature engagement with them, upon the different camps of their tribe, to whom runners had been sent during the night. They had not proceeded far on the deep-beaten trail of their enemies, when they beheld one of their number who had been left in the rear, walking leisurely along; perfectly deaf and unconscious to the approach of the avenging Ojibways, he fell an easy victim under their tomahawks.

They still ran on, till hearing a distant halloo, which was repeated nearer and nearer, they hid themselves in the deep snow near the trail.

The O-dug-am-ees having stopped to smoke, and missing one of their number, first hallooed to him, and on his not answering, they sent two of their young men to go back and bring him up. These two men were dispatched by the ambushed Ojibways, and as they too, did not return, the impatient O-dug-am-ees sent three more of their party to go and see what kept them, and they likewise met the same fate as their fellows. Becoming yet more impatient for the return of their companions, a large number of the O-dug-am-ees arose and ran back in search of them. On these, the ambushed Ojibways were obliged to fire, and immediately retreating, a running fight commenced. The whole force of their enemies now hearing the firing of guns, joined their fellows, and the Ojibways would soon have been annihilated, had not a large party of their friends, guided by the noise of the fight, arrived to their rescue. This timely reinforcement wisely ambushed themselves behind the trees near the trail, and as the O-dug-am-ees were eagerly following the retreating party, the hidden Ojibways fell on them with great fury, and in the first surprise succeeded in killing a large number, and they eventually forced the remainder to retreat and fly back to their villages with the black paint of mourning on their faces.

Though having partially revenged the death of his kindred in this fight, yet the old Ojibway hunter was not satisfied. For two years he secluded himself from his people, and accompanied only by his two grandchildren, he made his hunts where beaver was to be found in the greatest plenty. During this time he laid by the fruits of his solitary hunts, and having collected sufficient for his purposes, he loaded a large canoe with large packs of beaver skins, and made a journey to Detroit, which was then a grand depot for the fur trade, and contained a garrison of French soldiers.

Blacking his face with coal, placing ashes on his head, and gashing his body with his knife, causing himself to be covered with blood as a sign of deep mourning and affliction, he presented himself before his " French father," told him the tale of his wrongs, and presenting his packs of rich beaver, he asked for help to revenge himself against his foes.

The O-dug-am-ees had always evinced a bad feeling toward the French, and on several occasions they had plundered and murdered their traders. They were a restless and troublesome tribe, continually embroiled in mischief, and a short time previous they had attempted with the assistance of the Dakotas and O-saug-ees to take the French fort at Detroit. The appeal of the old Ojibway hunter, therefore, was listened to by willing ears. Ammunition and guns were freely given him, and a number of Frenchmen were promised to aid him in his intended invasion of the O-dug-am-ee country. The old hunter, being supplied with the necessary means, easily raised a large war party of his people, and being joined by his French allies, he proceeded to the hunting grounds of his enemies, and after severe fighting destroyed two of the principal O-dug-am-ee villages, and drove the remnants of this obnoxious tribe from the shores of Lake Michigan, and the Wisconsin River.

Enfeebled in numbers, the O-dug-am-ees retired westward to the Mississippi River, and fearing a total extinguishment of their national fire, it is at this time that they first joined the lodges of the Osaugees, and requested to be incorporated into that tribe. Their petition was denied, though the Osaugees allowed them to remain in their villages till they had in some degree regained, by a long term of quiet and peace, their former strength and numbers.

CHAPTER XI.

TAKING OF MILLE LACS BY THE OJIBWAYS.

A description of Mille Lacs, and its advantages as a home for the Indian—It is occupied by the Dakotas in 1680—Traditions of the Ojibways detailing the manner in which they, in turn, finally obtained possession.

MILLE Lacs, the M'dé Wakan, or Spirit Lake of the Dakotas,[1] and the Missi-sag-i-egan or "the lake that spreads all over" of the Ojibways, is one of the largest and most beautiful sheets of water in Minnesota Territory.[2] It lies imbedded in deep forests, midway between the Mississippi and the head of Lake Superior. Its picturesque shores are skirted with immense groves of valuable sugar maple, and the soil on which they grow is not to be surpassed in richness by any section of country in the northwest.

The lake is nearly circular in form, though indented with deep bays, and the view over its waters broken here and there by bold points or promontories. It is about twenty miles across from shore to shore, and a person standing on its pebbly beach on a clear, calm day, can but just discern the blue outlines of the opposite side, especially as the country surrounding it is comparatively low and level. Its waters are clear and pure as the waters of Lake Superior, and fish of the finest species are found to abound

[1] Mille Lacs so called because it is the largest of the numerous lakes, Mille Lacs (Thousand Lakes) of this region. Upon Franquelin's Map of 1688, it is called Buade, the family name of Count Frontenac then governor of Canada, and Rum River its outlet is called Rivière des François (French River) or Sioux River. Upon Hennepin's Map Rivière des François is R. de St. Francis. —E. D. N.

[2] Written in A. D. 1852. Minnesota in 1858 was admitted as one of the United States of America.—E. D. N.

thereih. Connected with it is a string of marshy, or mud-
bottomed, lakes in which the water is but a few feet deep,
and wherein the wild rice of the north grows luxuriantly,
and in the greatest abundance.

Possessing these and other advantages, there is not a
spot in the northwest which an Indian would sooner choose
as a home and dwelling place, than Mille Lacs. It is not
then to be wondered at, that for nearly two centuries, it
has formed a bone of strife and contention between the
Ojibways and Dakotas.

The name of the still large and important band of Dakotas known as the Mdé wakantons, has been derived
from this lake; they now dwell on the Mississippi and the
lower portions of the Minnesota River.[1] Their ancestors
were dwellers on Spirit Lake, and their bones have enriched
the soil about its shores.

I gather from " A sketch of the early trade and traders
of Minnesota," by the Rev. Edward D. Neill, of St. Paul,
published in the Annals of the Minnesota Historical Society for 1852, that in the year 1680, the Franciscan priest
Hennepin, with two companions named Michael Ako[2] and
Picard du Gay, were taken captive by the Dakotas of Mille

---

[1] The M'déwakantons (Spirit Lake People), in 1852 were divided into seven
bands, who dwelt on the western banks of the Mississippi and in the lower
Minnesota valley. The Ki-yuk-sa band lived below Lake Pepin. Another
band dwelt at Re-mni-ca (Hill, water and wood) now Red Wing, a few miles
above Lake Pepin. Kaposia band, four miles below St. Paul, Grey Iron's
band at Black Dog's village on the south bank of the Minnesota, above Mendota. Oak Grove band and Good Road's band on the upper bank of the
Minnesota, eight miles above Fort Snelling. Shokpedan, or Little Six, band
near the present town of Shakopee.

In 1854 they were living on a reservation in the valley of the upper Minne-
sota River. The Kaposia band was four miles below the mouth of the Red
Wood River, Shokpedan's band at the mouth of that stream, while those of
Wapatha and Waukouta were nearer the white settlements, and remained here
until after the massacre of 1862, when they were removed to the valley of the
Missouri River.—E. D. N.

[2] Also spelled Accault. La Salle writes that Ako was the leader of the
party.—E. D. N.

Lacs. This fact is mentioned here to show that at this date, this tribe still held possession, and resided on or near this lake. It is further stated that through the influence of the early French traders who first built posts in their country, among whom may be mentioned as most conspicuous the names of Nicholas Perrot and Le Sueur, " the Dakotas began to be led away from the rice grounds of the Mille Lacs region."

Tradition among the Ojibways says otherwise. They deny that the influence of the traders could induce the Mdewakantons to evacuate such a desirable point in their country as Mille Lacs, a spot covered with their permanent earthen[1] wigwams, and the resting place of their forefathers.

Our own experience of the great love and attachment which the red race has ever shown to their ancient village sites, would cause us to doubt this assertion on the part of the Dakotas. It is sooner to be believed that the same force which has caused them to relinquish, step by step, all their former country east of the Mississippi during the course of the past two or three centuries, operated to drive them from this, their strongest hold of olden times.

The manner in which the Ojibways first came into possession of Mille Lacs, is vividly related by their old men, and this event forms a prominent item in the course of their past history. The tradition of this occurrence is briefly as follows, taken by the writer from the lips of one of their most truth-telling sages, who is now a resident of Mille Lacs, and who is the descendant of a long line of noted chiefs.

TRADITION OF THE TAKING OF MILLE LACS BY THE OJIBWAYS.

Five generations ago, shortly after the Ojibways residing on the shores of Lake Superior had commenced to

---

[1] The early French explorers only mention wigwams of bark or skins.
—E. D. N.

obtain fire-arms and ammunition of the old French traders, a firm peace existed between them and the Dakotas, who then resided on the head waters of the Mississippi and the midland country which lay between this river and the Great Lake.

Good-will existed between the two tribes, and the roads to their villages were clear and unobstructed. Peace-parties of the Dakotas visited the wigwams of the Ojibways, and the Ojibways, in like manner, visited the Tepees and earthen lodges of the Dakotas. The good feeling existing between them was such, that intermarriages even took place between them.

It appears, however, impossible, that these two powerful tribes should ever remain long in peace with each other. On this occasion the war-club had lain buried but a few winters, when it was again violently dug up, and the ancient feud raged more fiercely than ever.

Ill-will was first created in the breasts of the two tribes against one another, through a quarrel which happened between an Ojibway and a Dakota gallant, respecting a woman whom they both courted. The woman was a Dakota, and the affair took place at a village of her people. Of her two suitors she preferred the Ojibway, and the rejected gallant, in revenge, took the life of his successful rival. This act, however, did not result in immediate hostilities; it only reminded the warriors of the two tribes that they *had once been enemies ;* it required a more aggravating cause than this to break the ties which several years of good understanding and social intercourse had created between them, and this cause was not long in forthcoming.

There was an old man residing at Fond du Lac of Lake Superior, which place had at this time, already become an important village of the Ojibways. This old man was looked upon by his people with much respect and consideration: though not a chief, he was a great hunter, and

his lodge ever abounded in plenty. He belonged to the
Marten Totem family. He was blessed with four sons, all
of whom were full grown and likely men, " fair to look
upon." They were accustomed to make frequent visits to
the villages of the Dakotas, and they generally returned
laden with presents, for the young women of their tribe
looked on them with wishful and longing eyes.

Shortly after the quarrel about the woman had taken
place, which resulted in the death of an Ojibway, the four
brothers paid the Dakotas one of their usual peaceful visits;
they proceeded to their great town at Mille Lac, which was
but two days from their own villages. During this visit,
one of the brothers was treacherously murdered, and but
three returned with safety to their father's wigwam.

The old man did not even complain when he heard that
their former enemies had sent his son to travel on the
Spirit road ; and shortly after, when his three surviving
sons asked his permission to go again to enter the lodges
of the Dakotas, he told them to go, " for probably," said
he, " they have taken the life of my son through mistake."
The brothers proceeded as before to Mille Lac, and on this
occasion, two of them were again treacherously killed, and
but one returned to the wigwam of his bereaved father.
The fount of the old man's tears still did not open, though
he blacked his face in mourning, and his head hung down
in sorrow.

Once more his sole surviving son requested to pay the
Dakotas a peace visit, that he might look on the graves of
his deceased brethren. His sorrow stricken parent said to
him, " go, my son, for probably they have struck your
brothers through mistake." Day after day rolled over,
till the time came when he had promised to return. The
days, however, kept rolling on, and the young man returned not to cheer the lonely lodge of his father. A full
moon passed over, and still he made not his appearance,

and the old man became convinced that the Dakotas had sent him to join his murdered brethren in the land of Spirits. Now, for the first time, the bereaved father began to weep, the fount of his tears welled forth bitter drops, and he mourned bitterly for his lost children.

" An Ojibway warrior never throws away his tears," and the old man determined to have revenge. For two years he busied himself in making preparations. With the fruits of his hunts he procured ammunition and other materials for a war party. He sent his tobacco and war-club to the remotest villages of his people, detailing his wrong and inviting them to collect by a certain day at Fond du Lac, to go with him in " *search* for his lost children." His summons was promptly and numerously obeyed, and nearly all the men of his tribe residing on the shores of the Great Lake, collected by the appointed time at Fond du Lac. Their scalping knives had long rusted in disuse, and the warriors were eager once more to stain them with the blood of their old enemy.

Having made the customary preparations, and invoked the Great Spirit to their aid, this large war party which the old man had collected, left Fond du Lac, and followed the trail towards Mille Lac, which was then considered the strongest hold of their enemies, and where the blood which they went to revenge had been spilt. The Dakotas occupied the lake in two large villages, one being located on Cormorant point, and the other at the outlet of the lake. A few miles below this last village, they possessed another considerable village on a smaller lake, connected with Mille Lac by a portion of Rum River which run through it. These villages consisted mostly of earthen wigwams such as are found still to be in use among the Arickarees and other tribes residing on the Upper Missouri.

The vanguard of the Ojibways fell on the Dakotas at Cormorant point early in the morning, and such was the extent of the war party, that before the rear had arrived, the battle at this point had already ended by the almost total extermination of its inhabitants; a small remnant only, retired in their canoes to the greater village located at the entry. This, the Ojibways attacked with all their forces; after a brave defence with their bows and barbed arrows, the Dakotas took refuge in their earthen lodges from the more deadly weapons of their enemy.

The only manner by which the Ojibways could harass and dislodge them from these otherwise secure retreats, was to throw small bundles or bags of powder into the aperture made in the top of each, both for the purpose of giving light within, and emitting the smoke of the wigwam fire. The bundles ignited by the fire, spread death and dismay amongst the miserable beings who crowded within. Not having as yet, like the more fortunate Ojibways, been blessed with the presence of white traders, the Dakotas were still ignorant of the nature of gunpowder, and the idea possessing their minds that their enemies were aided by spirits, they gave up the fight in despair and were easily dispatched. But a remnant retired during the darkness of night to their last remaining village on the smaller lake. Here they made their last stand, and the Ojibways following them up, the havoc among their ranks was continued during the whole course of another day.

The next morning the Ojibways wishing to renew the conflict, found the village evacuated by the few who had survived their victorious arms. They had fled during the night down the river in their canoes, and it became a common saying that the former dwellers of Mille Lacs became, by this three days' struggle, swept away for ever from their favorite village sites. The remains of their earthen wigwams are still plainly visible in great numbers on the spots where these events are said to have occurred; they are now mostly covered by forests of maple trees. The Ojibways assert as a proof of this tradition, that whenever they have dug into these mounds, which they occasionally do, they have discovered human bones in great abundance and lying scattered promiscuously in the soil, showing that they had not been regularly buried, but were cut in pieces and scattered about, as Indians always treat those they slay in battle.

It is as well to state here, that some of the old men who relate this tradition, give the name of O-maum-ee to the former dwellers of Mille Lacs, and they further assert that these people were totally exterminated on this occasion. The more intelligent affirm that they were the Ab-oin or Dakotas, who having their principal village on a peninsula, or Min-a-waum, were known in those days by the name of O-maum-ee. This, connected with the fact afforded us by the early French explorers, Hennepin, Du Luth and Le Sueur, that the Mdé wakantons were former dwellers of Mille Lacs, is sufficient to prove the identity of the people whom the Ojibways drove from its possession.

Ojibway tradition further states that the Dakotas who had been driven from Mille Lacs, made another village on Rum River, and that they did not finally leave this region of country[1] till about the year 1770, after their great expedition or war party to the head-waters of the Mississippi, which resulted in the battle of Crow Wing, as will be related in a future chapter.

[1] The Mdé wakanton Sioux used to assert that about the year 1780, they lived in one village, on the banks of the Minnesota, a short distance above Mendota.—E. D. N.

CHAPTER XII.

OCCUPATION OF THE ST. CROIX RIVER COUNTRY BY THE OJIBWAYS.

A peace is effected between the Ojibways and Dakotas by the French traders about the year 1695—The French locate a post among the Dakotas—Ojibways locate a permanent village at Rice Lake—Intermarriages between them and the Dakotas—Origin of the Wolf Totem among the Ojibways and of the Merman Totem among the Dakotas—The feud between them is again renewed—Causes thereof—Battle of Point Prescott—The Dakota captive—Consequences of the new rupture—Peace is renewed between the Rice Lake Ojibways and the St. Croix Lake Dakotas—Ojibways form a village at Yellow Lake—Tale of O-mig-aun-dib—The war becomes general.

AFTER the sanguinary battle which resulted in the total evacuation of Mille Lacs by the Dakotas, the ancient feud between them and the Ojibways raged with great fury, and it is at this period that the latter tribe first began to beat the Dakotas from the Rice Lakes of the St. Croix River region which they had long occupied in conjunction with the Odug-am-ees. The pipe of peace was not again smoked between the two belligerent tribes, till the old French traders had obtained a firm foothold among the Dakotas, and commenced an active trade.

According to the Indian mode of counting time, this event occurred four generations ago, or about the year 1695. It was brought about only through the most strenuous efforts of the French traders who resided among the Ojibways on Lake Superior, and those who had at this time built a post among the Dakotas near the mouth of the St. Croix River.[1]

[1] Bernard de la Harpe writes that in 1695 " Mr. Le Sueur by order of the Count de Frontenac, Governor General of Canada, built a fort on an island in the Mississippi more than 200 leagues above the Illinois, in order to effect a peace between the Sauteurs natives who dwell on the shores of a lake of five

The ill-will between the two tribes had risen to such a pitch that it required every persuasion, and the gift of large presents, to effect a reconciliation. The French, during the course of the bloody warfare between these two powerful tribes, while travelling through their country on their trading and exploring expeditions, had often suffered death indiscriminately with Dakota or Ojibway, at the hands of their blood-seeking war parties.

The interests of the fur trade had also severely suffered, for the warriors of either tribe, neglected their hunts to join in the more favorite pastime of war and bloodshed, and their continually prowling war parties prevented the more peaceful-minded and sedate hunters from seeking the beaver in the regions where they abounded in the greatest plenty.

Peace being once effected, this deplorable state of affairs ceased to exist, and once more these two people hunted on their richest hunting grounds without fear and trembling, and plenty reigned in their lodges. On the St. Croix the two tribes intermingled freely, being more immediately under the supervision of their traders. They encamped together, and intermarriages took place between them. It is at this time that a few lodges of Ojibways first located themselves in a permanent village on the waters of the St. Croix River. They chose Rice Lake, the head of Shell River, which empties into the St. Croix, for their first permanent residence and it remains an important village of their tribe to this day.[1]

The principal chief of this band, belonging to the Awause or Catfish Totem family, is said to have died with-

hundred leagues circumference, one hundred leagues east of the river, and the Scioux on the Upper Mississippi."

Bellin, the Geographer, mentions that this trading post was upon the largest of the islands between Lake Pepin and the mouth of the St. Croix River.—E. D. N.

[1] A. D. 1852.

out male issue, and his only daughter married a Dakota chief who belonged to the Wolf Clan of his tribe. He resided among the Ojibways at Rice Lake during the whole course of the peace, and begat by his Ojibway wife, two sons who afterward became chiefs, and who of course inherited their father's totem of the wolf. In this manner this badge became grafted among the Ojibway list of clans.

At this day, Ojibways of the Wolf Totem are numerous on the St. Croix and at Mille Lac, and they are all descended from this intermarriage, and are therefore tinged with Dakota blood. I-aub-aus, present chief of Rice Lake, Shon-e-yah (Silver), chief of Po-ka-guma on Snake River, and Na-guon-abe (Feathers end), chief of Mille Lacs, are direct descendants from the two sons of the Dakota chief and the Ojibway chieftainess.

In like manner Ojibways of the Merman, or Water-spirit Totem, which is a branch of the Awause, married Dakota women, and begat by them sons, who, residing among the Dakotas, introduced in this tribe the badge of their father's totem, and all of this totem among the Dakotas are of Ojibway extraction, and ever since the period of these intermarriages, at every peace meeting of the two tribes, all persons of the Wolf and Merman Totem, in each tribe, recognize one another as blood relations.

The peace on this occasion lasted for several years, and to some extent they learned to speak each other's language. The intermarriages which had taken place between them, proved the strongest link of good-will between them, but the love of war and bloodshed was so inherent in their nature, and the sense of injuries inflicted on one another for centuries past rankled so deep in the breasts of many in each tribe, that even these ties could not secure a long continuance of this happy state of peace and quiet. From a comparative slight cause, the flames of their old hatred again broke forth with great violence. It originated at a war dance which was being performed by the Dakotas on Lake St. Croix, preparatory to marching against some tribe of their numerous enemies toward the south.

On occasions of this nature, the warriors work themselves by hard dancing, yelling, and various contortions of the body, into a state of mad excitement; every wrong which they have suffered at the hands of their enemies, is brought fresh to their remembrance for the purpose of " making the heart strong."

Under a state of excitement, such as is here described, a distinguished Dakota warrior shot a barbed arrow into the body of an Ojibway who was dancing with the Dakotas, intending to join them on the war trail against their enemies. Some of the old men who relate this tradition, assert that the Ojibway was part of Dakota extraction, and the fierce warrior who shot him, exclaimed as he did so, that " he wished to let out the hated Ojibway blood which flowed in his veins." Others state that he was a full-blood Ojibway who had married a Dakota woman, by whom he had a large family of children; that he resided with her people, and had become incorporated amongst them, joining their war parties against the different tribes with whom they were at enmity.

The ruthless shot did not terminate his life, and after a most painful sickness, the wounded man recovered. He silently brooded over the wrong so wantonly inflicted on him, for the warrior who had injured him was of such high standing in his tribe, that he could not revenge himself on him with impunity. After a time he left the Dakotas and paid a visit to his Ojibway relatives on Lake Superior, who received him into their wigwams with every mark of kindness and regard. He poured into their willing ears the tale of his wrong, and he succeeded in inducing them to raise a war party to march against the Dakota encampment on Lake St. Croix.

While this party was collecting at the Bay of *Shaug-a-waum-ik-ong*, the avenger returned to his home and family amongst the Dakotas, and amused their ears with accounts of his visit to his people's villages. He told them that a large party would soon arrive to smoke the pipe of peace with them. Fully believing these tales, the Dakotas collected their scattered hunters, and sent runners to their different villages to invite their people to come and camp with them, in order to receive the expected peace party of the Ojibways, and join in the amusements which generally ensued whenever they thus met in considerable numbers. The tribe (being the season of the year which they generally passed in leisure and recreation), gathered in large numbers, and pitched their camp on the south shore of Lake St. Croix, near its outlet into the Mississippi.

The centre or main portion of their camp (which stretched for a long distance along the shore of the lake), was located at Point Prescott. A few lodges also stood on the opposite shore of the lake, and at Point Douglas.

The Dakotas, believing the reported peaceable disposition of their former enemies, became careless, and hunted in apparent security ; they did not (as is usual when apprehensive of a sudden attack), send scouts to watch on the surrounding hills for the approach of an enemy, and the Ojibways arrived within a close vicinity of their camp without the least discovery. During the night, the leaders of the war party sent five young men who could speak the Dakota language most fluently, to go and spy the lodges of the enemy, note their situation, and find out their number. The five scouts entered the encampment at different points, and drawing their robes closely over their heads they walked about unsuspected by the young Dakota gallants or *night walkers*, who were out watching the lodge fires to flicker away in embers, in order to enter and in the darkness court their sweet hearts.

After having made the rounds of the almost endless rows of lodges, the scouts returned to their party, and informed their leaders that they had counted three hundred lodges, when they became confused and could count no more. Also, that from the different idioms of their language which they had heard spoken in different sections of the camp, they judged that the distant bands of the Sisseton and Yankton Dakotas were represented therein in considerable numbers; they also told of the general carelessness, and feeling of security which prevailed throughout the camp.

Having obtained this information, the Ojibways being strong in the number of their warriors, prepared themselves for battle, and at the earliest dawn of morning, they marched on the sleeping encampment of the Dakotas. They made their approach by a deep ravine which led through the high bluffs (which here bound the shores of the lake) on to the narrow prairie which skirts the water side, and on which was pitched the leathern lodges of the enemy. It is said that through the dim twilight, the advancing warriors saw a woman step out of the nearest lodge to adjust the door covering which a sudden gust of the rising east wind had thrown up ; she stood as if a sound had caught her ear, and she listened anxiously, looking up the dark ravine, when she again entered her lodge. She must have heard the measured tread of the advancing warriors, but mistook it for the moaning of the rising wind, and the dashing of the waves on the sandy beach.

Once fairly debouched on the narrow prairie, the Ojibways lost no time in extending their wings and enveloping the encampment on the land side. When this movement had been completed in perfect silence, they gradually neared the lodges of their sleeping enemies, and as they arrived within the proper distance, and the dogs of the encampment began to snuff the air and utter their sharp quick yelp, the shrill war whistle was sounded by the leaders, and suddenly the dread and fear-striking war-whoop issued from the lips of hundreds of blood-thirsty warriors. Volley after volley of bullets and arrows were fired, and discharged into the frail and defenceless tepees, and the shrieking and yelling of the inmates as they became thus suddenly startled from their sleep, made the uproar of the attack truly deafening.

Completely taken by surprise, the warriors of the Dakotas fought at a disadvantage; their women and children ran shrieking to the water's side, and hastily jumping into their narrow wooden canoes, they attempted to cross to the opposite shores of the lake. The wind, however, had increased in force, and sweeping down the lake in a fearful gale, it caused the waves to run high, and in many instances the crowded and crank canoes filled with water or upset, launching the fleeing women and children into a watery grave.

After a long and unavailing defence, such of the Dakota warriors as had stood their ground, were obliged to retreat. Thirty of their number are said to have fled under a ledge of rock, where, being entirely surrounded, they were shot down one after another.

This is one of the most successful war parties which the Ojibways tell of. It is said that at each encampment on their return homeward, the scalps which they had taken, being each tied to the end of a stick three or four feet long, were planted close together in a single row, and an arrow shot by a strong arm, from one end of this row of human scalps, fell short of reaching the other extremity.

One of their story tellers, who in his youth had long remained a captive among the Dakotas, states explicitly, that on this occasion, the Ojibways secured three hundred and thirty-five scalps, and many more than this are thought to have perished in the water. But one captive is mentioned as having been taken, and the circumstances of his

capture are such that the fact is always mentioned, in connection with the tale relating the above important event
in their history.

It appears that during the heat of the battle, two young
Ojibway lads who had accompanied their fathers on the
war trail, entered a Dakota lodge which they supposed had
been deserted by the fleeing enemy. They, however, found
it to be occupied by a stout and full-grown Dakota warrior;
he sat in the lodge in an attitude of sorrow, holding his
head between his hands, and his elbows resting on his
raised knees, his unstrung bow and full quiver of arrows
lay at his feet, and his war spear stood planted before him.
He did not even lift his head as the two lads entered, the
youngest of whom immediately rushed on him, and being
unarmed, he attempted to secure him as a captive. The
Dakota took him by the arm and gently pushed him aside.
The brave little lad, however, persisted, and calling on his
older comrade to help him, they both fell on the Dakota
and attempted to secure his arms. He pushed them easily
away, and quietly resumed his former position, and remained thus till a number of Ojibway warriors attracted
by the calls of the young lad, entered the lodge and secured
him captive. He was given to the boy who first assaulted
him as his prisoner.

When asked by an Ojibway who could speak his language,
the reason why he had acted so strangely, he replied that the
evening before, his father had scolded him without cause,
and had heaped shameful epithets on him, under which he
felt that he could not survive, and be a tenant of his lodge.
During the night he had dreamed of living amongst the
Ojibways, and early that morning he was preparing to
leave his people forever and seek for a new home among
their villages, when the attack commenced and he determined to risk the chances of neutrality. He became a
great favorite with the family into whose hands he fell,

and who adopted him as a relative, and when some time afterwards, when he was ruthlessly killed by a cowardly Ojibway, blood was nearly shed on his account, and with great difficulty a fierce family feud prevented from ensuing in consequence.

After the battle of Point Prescott (by which name we may designate the event related in this chapter), it may well be imagined that the war was renewed with great fury by these two powerful tribes, and fights of various magnitude and importance took place along the whole country which lay between them.

Ojibways who had intermarried among the Dakotas, were obliged to make a sudden and secret flight to their former homes, leaving their wives and children. Dakotas were obliged to do likewise, and instances are told where the parting between husband and wife was most grieving to behold.

After the first fury of the renewed feud had somewhat spent itself, it is related that the ties of consanguinity which had existed between the Rice Lake or St. Croix Ojibways, and the Dakotas were such, that peace again was made between them, and though the war raged between their tribes in other parts of their extensive country, they harmed not one another.

When the two sons of the Dakota chief, by the chieftainess of Rice Lake, had grown up to be men, the eldest, named O-mig-aun-dib (or Sore Head), became chief of the Rice Lake band of Ojibways, and he afterwards appointed his younger brother to be chief of a branch of his village, which had at this time located themselves at Yellow Lake. These are the first two permanent villages which the Ojibways made in the St. Croix country. Rice Lake was first settled about a century and a half ago, during the peace brought about by the French traders. Yellow Lake was settled about forty years after. Po-ka-gum-a on Snake

River, and Knife Lake have been the sites of Ojibway villages only within a few years past—within the recollection of Indians still living.[1]

Omig-aun-dib, the chief of Rice Lake, had half brothers among the Dakotas, who after the death of their common father became chiefs over their people; through the influence of these closely related chieftains, peace was long kept up between their respective villages. Ill-will, however, gradually crept in between them, as either party continually lost relatives, in the implacable warfare which was now most continually carried on between other portions of their two tribes. At last they dared no longer to make peace visits to one another's villages, though they still did not join the war parties which marched into the region of country which they respectively occupied.

As a proof of the tenacity with which they held on to one another even amidst the bloodshed which their respective tribes continued to inflict on them, the following tale is related by the descendants of Omig-aun-dib.

After the war between them had again fairly opened, a Dakota war party proceeded to Rice Lake and killed three children who were playing on the sandy shores of the lake, a short distance from the Ojibway village. One of these murdered children belonged to Omig-aun-dib, who was away on his day's hunt at the time they were fallen upon and dispatched.

When, on his return, he had viewed the mangled remains of his child, he did not weep and ask his fellows to aid him in revenging the blow, but he silently buried his child, and embarking the next morning alone in his birch canoe, he proceeded down the river toward the Dakota country.

---

[1] The Snake River Ojibways in 1836 were divided into two bands, and numbered about forty men. One band spent the summer at Lake Po-ka-gum-a; the other, on a small lake twenty miles higher on the river. About this time some of the Ojibways of Yellow Lake, Wisconsin, joined them.—E. D. N.

At Point Douglas he discovered the Dakotas collected together in a large camp; their war party had just arrived with the three children's scalps, and he heard as he neared their village, the drums beating, accompanied with the scalp songs of rejoicing, while young and old in the whole encampment were dancing and yelling in celebration of the exploit, and the discomfiture of their enemies.

Omig-aun-dib paddled his light canoe straight towards the centre of the long rows of lodges which lined the water-side: he had covered his face and body with the black paint of mourning. The prow of his canoe lightly struck the beach, and the eyes of the rejoicing Dakotas became all bent on the stranger who so suddenly made his appearance at their water-side: some ran to see who it could be, and as he became recognized, his name passed like wildfire from lip to lip—the music and dancing suddenly ceased, and the former noisy and happy Dakotas spoke to one another in whispers.

Omig-aun-dib sat quietly in the stern of his canoe smoking his pipe. Soon a long line of elderly men, the chiefs of the village, approached him; he knew his half brothers, and as they recognized him and guessed the cause of the black paint on his body, they raised their voices and wept aloud. No sooner was the example set, than the whole encampment was in tears, and loud was the lamentation which for a few moments issued from lips which, but a moment before, had been rejoicing in the deed of blood.

They took the canoe wherein the bereaved father was still sitting, and lifting it off the ground, they carried it on to the bank where stood their lodges. Buffalo robes, beautifully worked with quills and colored with bright paints, were then brought and spread on the ground from the canoe reaching even to the door of the council lodge, and the Ojibway chieftain was asked to walk thereon and enter the lodge.

During the performance of these different acts he had kept his seat in the canoe calmly smoking his pipe; he now arose, and stepped forth, but as he approached the council lodge, he kicked the robes to one side, saying, " I have not come amongst you, my relatives, to be treated with so much honor and deference. I have come that you may treat me as you have treated my child, that I may follow him to the land of spirits."

These words only made the sorrow of the Dakotas still more poignant; to think that they had killed the child of one who was their relative by blood, and who had never raised his arm against their tribe.

Omig-aun-dib repeated his offer of self-sacrifice in public council, but it was of course refused, and with great difficulty he was at last induced to accept presents as a covering for his child's grave, and a child was given to him to adopt instead of the one which had been killed. With this reparation he returned to his village. . . . .

The breach between the two tribes became widened by almost daily bloody encounters, and the relationship existing between them became at last to be almost forgotten, though to the present day the occasional short terms of peace which have occurred between the two tribes, have generally been first brought about by the mixed bloods of either tribe who could approach one another with greater confidence than those entirely unconnected by blood.

CHAPTER XIII.

THE COUNTRY ABOUT THE SOURCE OF THE MISSISSIPPI.

The adaptation of this region of country as a home for the Indian—The Ojibways first find it in possession of the Dakotas—Bi-aus-wah, an Ojibway war chief, leads a large war party and dispossesses the Dakotas of Sandy Lake—Sandy Lake becomes the first Ojibway village on the Upper Mississippi—Remarks on the earthen mounds which are scattered throughout this region of country—Gi-aucth.in-ne-wug, "men of the olden time," occupy the Upper Mississippi country prior to the Dakotas—Origin of the earthen mounds, as given by the Ojibways.

THE region of country from which the Mississippi derives its source, is covered with innumerable fresh and clear water lakes, connected with one another, and flowing into the "Father of Rivers" through rapid and meandering streams. All these lakes and streams abound with fish of the finest species and flavor. In Leech, Winnepeg, Cass, and other of the larger lakes, the whitefish are found equal in size to the celebrated whitefish in Lake Superior. And so are also the salmon trout which (curious enough) are to be found only in Puk-a-gum-ah and trout lakes. Mus-cal-longe have been found to grow to the great size of from four to six feet in length. Brook trout, sturgeon and catfish are not found in the waters of the Mississippi above the Falls of St. Anthony.

The shores of these beautiful lakes are lined with groves of the tall pine, and the useful maple from which the Indian manufactures sugar. The birch tree also abounds, from which the Ojibway has long been accustomed to procure the covering to his wigwam, and material for the formation of his ingeniously wrought canoe. In many of these lakes which lie clustered together within an area of several hundred miles, the wild rice grows in large quantities and most luxuriantly, affording the Indian an important staple of subsistence.

In former times this region of country abounded in buffalo, moose, deer, and bear, and till within thirty years past, in every one of its many water courses, the lodges of the valuable and industrious beaver were to be found.

Possessing these manifold advantages, this country has always been a favorite home and resort for the wild Indian, and over its whole extent, battle fields are pointed out where different tribes have battled for its possession.

The attention of the Ojibways was early directed to it. They found it in possession of the powerful and wide-spread Dakotas, whom after many years of severe fighting, they eventually forced to seek for new homes farther westward, and they in turn, took possession and have kept to this day the large and beautiful lakes which form the sources of the "Great River."

It is related by their old traditionists, that the boy whose father had died in his stead on the burning fagots of the cruel O-dug-am-ees (as has been related in a former chapter), grew up to be a man. The remembrance of his deep wrong made him a warrior. He never let pass an opportunity of taking revenge and letting his prowess be known among the enemies of his tribe. To him, war not only became a chief business in life, but a pastime, and having adopted the name of his murdered father, Bi-aus-wah, eventually became a noted war-leader and chief, and the first Ojibway pioneer to the country of the Upper Mississippi.

After the death of his father, he proceeded with his relatives to Fond du Lac, where he remained till middle age, and from which place he joined the war parties which marched against the Dakotas at Sandy Lake, on the St. Croix River and in the vicinity of Mille Lac. When he had earned in many a hard-fought battle, the admiration and confidence of his people, he sent his war-club, tobacco, and wampum belt of war, to the far-scattered bands of his tribe, inviting the warriors to collect at Fond du Lac by a certain day, and march with him, to put out the fire of the Dakotas at Sandy Lake.

Men from all the villages of the Ojibway responded to his call, and canoes laden with warriors arrived on the appointed day from Sault Ste. Marie, Grand Portage, La Pointe, and all the camps of the tribe within the area of the Great Lake. It is said that the train of warriors which followed Bi-aus-wah on this occasion, was so long, as they marched in their usual single file, that a person standing on a hill could not see from one extremity to the other. They marched against the Dakotas of Sandy Lake. They found the enemy collected in force, notwithstanding which, they made the attack, and after a severe fight, they (being armed with the murderous weapons of the pale face), ultimately forced them to retreat and evacuate their village.

Some years after, having struck repeated blows on this band of the Dakota tribe, Bi-aus-wah with many wigwams of his people, lit their fires and permanently located their village, first on the islands of the lake, but afterwards at the point which lies nearly opposite the mouth of East Savannah River.

From this central location, they gradually increased their conquests in western, northern, and southern directions, and drawn by the richness of the hunting grounds in this region of country, many families from Lake Superior, of both the northern and southern divisions of the tribe, who had separated two centuries before at Sault Ste. Marie, moved over, and joined this band of hardy pioneers, increasing their strength and causing them to be better able to withstand the powerful Dakotas, and gradually to increase their new possessions. Sandy Lake or Kah-me-tah-wung-a-guma, signifying " lake of the sandy waters," is the site of the first Ojibway village about the head-waters of the Mississippi.

It is from this point that the war parties proceeded, who eventually caused the Dakotas to evacuate their favorite seats at Leech, Winnepeg, Cass, and Red Lakes, and also from Gull Lake, Crow Wing, and the vicinity of Mille Lacs, as will be hereafter related in the regular course of our narrative.

It will not be amiss in this chapter to say a few words respecting the mounds which are everywhere to be met with throughout the entire region of country covered by sources of the Mississippi.

Having read the conflicting opinions of men who have casually passed through the country, and seen these apparent remains of the works of a former race, my attention was early drawn to this subject, and my inquiries among the more aged and intelligent men of the Ojibways have been most minute, and to my mind, satisfactorily answered.

Esh-ke-bug-e-coshe, whom I have already mentioned as the truth-telling and respected chief of the Pillagers, still living, and now in his seventy-eighth year, informs me that in the course of his lifetime he has made numerous war parties and peace visits to different tribes who live on the banks of the Upper Missouri River. He states, that a tribe who are known to the Ojibways by the name of Gi-aucth-in-in-e-wug, signify " men of the olden time," and named by the French, Gros Ventres, claim to have been formerly possessors of the country from which the Mississippi takes its rise. Their old men relate they were forced or driven from this country by the powerful Dakotas, who have in turn given way to the Ojibways, now its present possessors.

The Gros Ventres further stated to the Pillager chief, that their fathers lived in earthen wigwams, and the small remnant who have escaped the scourge of the scalping

knife and smallpox, still live on the banks of the Missouri
in these primitively constructed dwellings.   This is an important fact in the early Indian history of Minnesota, and
the writer has taken every pains to procure every account
and circumstance which might conduce to prove its truth.

It will account at once for the numerous earthen mounds
which are to be found at different points on the Upper
Mississippi, as they may then be safely considered as the
remains of the earthen lodges of these former occupants of
this fair region.

Till of late years the Kniste-no and Assineboins were
accustomed to send their war parties against the Gros
Ventres and Arickarees, and the Ojibways were often
induced to join them.   They forced them to evacuate their
earthen villages which were located on the east banks
of the Missouri, and to select new homes further west,
placing thereby this great river between them and their
more powerful enemies.

But since the smallpox has swept them nearly all away,
these allied tribes have taken pity on them, and they
occasionally pay them peace visits, and even fight in their
defence.   In this manner a direct communication has arisen
between the Ojibways and these remnants of far western
tribes, which has been the means of saving from total oblivion many of their ancient traditions, and amongst the
number, the fact of their former occupation of the great
basin from which the Mississippi derives its sources.

Esh-ke-bug-e-coshe, who has often visited them in his
younger days, terms them "relatives;" he describes their
earthen wigwams, and says that they are more neat and
cleanly than other Indians, from the fact of daily washing
their bodies and using a certain kind of clay to whiten
their skins.   He says also, that formerly they used to raise
small quantities of tobacco, the leaf of which, as obtained
from them, was considered of great value, and for which

their fellow Indians paid large prices. Peace parties of the Knistenos and Ojibways often proceeded hundreds of miles to visit their villages, chiefly for the purpose of procuring their much coveted tobacco leaf.

Wa-won-je-quon, the chief of the Red Lake Ojibways, relates that several years since, while on a visit to the earthen wigwams of the Gi-aucth-in-in-e-wug or Gros Ventres, he was informed by their old men, that the smoke of their village once arose in the vicinity of Sandy Lake. They showed him a piece of bark on which was very correctly marked the principal streams and lakes on the Upper Mississippi, and pointed him out, as the site of their former village, the entry of East Savannah River into the St. Louis, where the remains of their earthen lodges, now covered by a forest of trees, are still discernible.

Groups of these mounds are to be seen on all the principal lakes in the Upper Mississippi country. At Pukwah Rice Lake, near Sandy Lake, is a group numbering seventy of these mounds, now covered by a thick grove of maple trees. At the mouth of Pine River, which empties into the Mississippi above Crow Wing, there is a group of nineteen, in which bones have been discovered by the Ojibways.

At Gull Lake many of these mounds have also been seen by the writer. At one place there are two standing side by side, each over one hundred feet long and four feet high, and on the top of one stands a high pine tree which looks to be centuries old.

The numerous mounds on the shore of Mille Lacs are accounted for in Ojibway tradition, as the remains of the former earthen lodges of the Dakotas, whom their ancestors drove from this lake.

The mounds which are thickly scattered throughout the St. Croix and Chippeway River region, are said by the Ojibways to be the remains of the former wigwams of their old enemies, the Odugamees.

In the vicinity of some of these mounds on Chippeway River, the writer has distinguished gardens and fields regularly laid out, in which even the rows of corn hills were still plainly discernible, clearly proving that the mounds scattered over this portion of country are not of such ancient origin as some speculative writers would have us believe.

The old men of the Ojibways affirm that nearly all the tribes of the red man who lived in an open prairie country, before the introduction of fire-arms among them, were accustomed to live in earthen wigwams as a protection and defence against the attacks of their enemies.[1]

Truly may it be said of all these Indians tribes, that their hand has been against every one, and every one's hand against them. They have lived in "fear and trembling" of one another, and oft has the sudden midnight attack extinguished for ever the fires of their wigwams. And for greater security against these sudden attacks, and continual state of warfare, first originated the earthen remains, over which now the white man's plow peacefully furrows.

From human bones being occasionally discovered in these mounds, most writers have been led to suppose them as the graves or burial places of distinguished chiefs.

The Indians account for them by saying that these former

---

[1] Alexander Henry, a partner of the Northwest Company of Montreal, in 1806, visited the Gros Ventres at the junction of the Knife and Missouri Rivers. From a copy of his MS. Journal, owned by the writer of this note, the following is extracted. " These people, like their neighbors [Mandans], have the custom of washing morning and evening, and wallowing in the mud and clay which here answers the purpose of soap. . . . . . The huts are constructed as those of their neighbors, with this difference, the ground is dug out about four feet below the surface of the earth, which is much deeper than the others. . . . . . The inside of the huts are commonly kept clean, and day and night the young men are watching and sleeping upon the roofs. The tops of their huts are particularly level, large, and spacious, about fifty feet in circumference, and so supported by firm, stout, and principal posts which support the square pieces of timber, as to sustain the weight of fifty men."— E. D. N.

earthen wigwams were seldom evacuated without a struggle, which generally ended in the massacre of the inmates, and the bones now discovered buried within them are the remains of these former occupants.

The few mounds in which have been discovered human bones regularly deposited, in a position facing the west, may probably be considered as burial mounds; though this, too, may be accounted for, from the fact that of later years the Indians have occasionally buried their dead within these mounds, though this may not be considered as a prevalent custom, as they treat all remains of this nature with great respect, as objects consecrated to the memory of by-gone people and by-gone times.

The Ojibways assert in behalf of their tribe, that they have never been forced to live in earthen wigwams as a defence against their enemies, and none of the mounds which are thickly scattered over the country which they at present occupy west of Lake Superior, originate from or are the work of their ancestors. The country in which they have lived for the past five centuries is covered with dense forests, and plentifully supplied with large lakes, on the bosom of which lay islands, where in times of danger they could always pitch their light wigwams in comparative safety.

CHAPTER XIV.

PROGRESS OF THE OJIBWAYS ON THE UPPER MISSISSIPPI.

The Ojibways force the Dakotas from Cass and Winnepeg lakes—Dakotas concentre their forces at Leech Lake—They make a last effort to beat back the
Ojibways—Their great war party is divided into three divisions—One division
proceeds against Rainy Lake—One against Sandy Lake—And one against
Pembina—They are beaten back—Dakotas retire from Leech Lake—Ojibways take possession—Size and natural advantages of Leech Lake—Dangers
of the first Ojibway pioneers on the Upper Mississippi—They hunt in a body
under the guidance of their chief Bi-aus-wah—Fitful terms of peace with
the Dakotas—Bi-aus-wah puts an end by treaty to the practice of torturing
captives—The Ojibway hunters pay yearly visits to the French trading posts
on Lake Superior—The more northern bands join the Kenistenos on their
trading visits to the British towards Hudson Bay.

THE band or village of the Ojibways, who had dispos-
sessed the Dakotas of Sandy Lake, under the guidance of
their chief Bi-aus-wah, continued to receive accessions to
their ranks from the shores of Lake Superior, and continued
to gain ground on the Dakotas, till they forced them to
evacuate their hunting grounds and village sites on Cass
and Winnepeg lakes, and to concentre their forces on the
islands of Leech Lake, of which, for a few years, they managed to keep possession.

Being, however, severely harassed by the persevering
encroachments of the Ojibways, and daily losing the lives
of their hunters from their oft-repeated incursions, and war
parties, the Dakotas at last came to the determination of
making one concentrated tribal effort to check the farther
advance of their invaders, and, if possible, put out forever
the fires which the Ojibways had lit on the waters of the
Upper Mississippi. They called on the different bands of
their common tribe living toward the south and west, to
aid them in their enterprise, and a numerous war party is

said to have been collected at Leech Lake by the Dakotas to carry out the resolution which they had formed.

Instead, however, of concentrating their forces and sweeping the Ojibway villages in detail, they separated into three divisions, with the intention of striking three different sections of the enemy on the same day. One party marched against the village at Sandy Lake, one against the Ojibways at Rainy Lake, and one proceeded northward against a small band of Ojibways who had already reached as far west as Pembina, and who, in connection with the Kenistenos and Assineboins, severely harassed the northern flank of the Leech Lake Dakotas.

The party proceeding against Rainy Lake, met a large war party of Ojibways from that already important and numerous section of the tribe, and a severe battle was fought between them. The Dakotas returned to Leech Lake disheartened from the effects of a severe check, and the loss of many of their bravest warriors.

The second division, proceeding in their war canoes against the Sandy Lake village, met with precisely the same fate. They were paddling down the smooth current of the Mississippi, when one morning they met a canoe containing the advance scouts of a large Ojibway war party, who were on their route to attack their village at Leech Lake; these scouts were immediately attacked, and pursued by the Dakotas into a small lake, where the main body of the Ojibways coming up, both parties landed and fought for half a day on the shores of the lake. This battle is noted from the fact that a Dakota was killed here whose feet were both previously cut half off either by frost or some accident, and the lake where the fight took place is known to this day as " Keesh-ke-sid-a-boin Sah-ga-e-gun" " Lake of the cut-foot Dakota." The belligerent parties both retreated to their respective villages from this point, their bloody propensities being for the time fully cooled down.

The third division. of the Dakotas went northward in the direction of Red River, but not finding any traces of the Ojibways about Pembina, all returned home but ten, who resolutely proceeded into the Kenisteno country, till discovering two isolated wigwams of Ojibway hunters, they attacked and destroyed their inmates with the loss of two of their number. This attack is noted from the circumstance that one of the Dakota warriors who was killed, had been a captive among the Ojibways, and adopted as a son by the famous chief, Bi-aus-wah of Sandy Lake. He was recognized by having in his possession a certain relic of this chieftain, which he had promised to wet with the blood of an enemy, to appease the manes of a departed child in whose stead he had been adopted.

During the same summer in which happened these memorable events in Ojibway history, the Dakotas having been thus severely checked and driven back by their invaders, became hopeless of future success and suddenly evacuated their important position at Leech Lake, and moved westward to the edge of the great western. prairies, about the headwaters of the Minnesota and Red Rivers.

A few hardy hunters, mostly of the Bear and Catfish clans, gradually took possession of their rich hunting grounds, and planting their lodges on the islands of Cass, Winnepeg, and Leech Lakes, they first formed a focus around which gathered families from Rainy Lake, Sandy Lake, and Lake Superior, which now form the important villages or bands of the Ojibway tribe, who occupy these important lakes at the present day.

According to Nicollet, " The circuit of Leech Lake, including its indentations, is not less than 160 miles. It is next in size to Red Lake, which is said to be two hun-

dred miles in circumference.   The former has twenty-seven
tributaries of various sizes.   A solitary river issues from
it, known by the name of Leech Lake River, forming an
important outlet, from one hundred to one hundred and
twenty feet wide, with a depth of from six to ten feet.   It
has a moderate current and flows into the Mississippi,
after a course of from forty-five to fifty miles."

This quotation from a most reliable source, will give to
the reader an idea of the size of Leech Lake, and its great
importance to the Indian can be judged by its numerous
natural resources.   It abounds in wild rice in large quantities, of which the Indian women gather sufficient for the
winter consumption of their families.   The shores of the
lake are covered with maple which yields to the industry
of the hunter's women, each spring, quantities of sap which
they manufacture into sugar.   The waters of the lake
abound in fish of the finest quality, its whitefish equalling
in size and flavor those of Lake Superior, and are easily
caught at all seasons of the year when the lake is free of
ice, in gill-nets made and managed also by the women.

At the time when the Ojibways first took possession of
Leech Lake and the surrounding country, which is covered
with innumerable lakes and water courses, beaver, and
the most valuable species of fur animals abounded in great
plenty, which procured them the much coveted merchandise of the white traders.   The lake itself is said in those
early days to have been, at certain seasons of the year,
literally covered with wild fowl and swan; pelican and
geese raised yearly their brood of young on its numerous
islands.   From this circumstance Goose and Pelican
Islands have derived their names.   The incentives, therefore, which actuated the first Ojibway pioneers to fight so
strenuously for its possession, were many and great, and
soon caused the band who so fearlessly occupied it to be-

come a numerous body, and to be the most noted western vanguard of the Ojibway tribe.

At first, while they were yet feeble in numbers, they planted their lodges on the islands of the lake for greater security against the Dakotas, who for many years after their evacuation often sent their war parties to its shores to view the sites of their former villages, and the graves of their fathers, and, if possible, to shed the blood of those who had forced them from their once loved hunting grounds.

Almost daily, the hardy bands of Ojibways who had now taken possession of the head lakes of the Mississippi, lost the lives of their hunters by the bands of the Dakotas, and they would soon have been annihilated, had not accessions from the eastern sections of their tribe continually added to their strength and numbers. In those days, the hunter moved through the dense forests in fear and trembling. He paddled his light canoe over the calm bosom of a lake or down the rapid current of a river, in search of game to clothe and feed his children, expecting each moment that from behind a tree, an embankment of sand along the lake shore, or a clump of bushes on the river bank, would speed the bullet or arrow which would lay him low in death. Often as the tired hunter has been calmly slumbering by the dying embers of his lodge fire, surrounded by the sleeping forms of his wife and helpless babes, has he been aroused by the sharp yell of his enemies as they rushed on his camp to extinguish his fire forever. On such occasions the morning sun has shone on the mangled and scalped remains of the hunter and his family.

These scenes, which my pen so poorly delineates, have been of almost daily occurrence till within a few years past, along the whole border which has been the arena of the bloody feud between the Dakotas and Ojibways.

For greater security against the sudden attacks of their enemies, the Ojibways on the Upper Mississippi, under the guidance of their wise chieftain Bi-aus-wah, would collect each fall into one common encampment, and thus in a body they would proceed by slow stages where game was most plenty, to make their fall and winter hunts. While collected in force in this manner, the Dakotas seldom dared to attack them, and it often happened that when the great winter camps of either tribe came in contact, fearing the result of a general battle, they would listen to the advice of their wiser chiefs who deprecated the consequences of their cruel warfare, and enter into a short term of peace and good fellowship. On such happy occasions the singular spectacle could be seen, of mortal foes feasting, caressing one another, exchanging presents, and ransoming captives of war.

The calms, however, of a feud of such intensity and long duration as existed between these two combative .tribes, were of short and fitful duration, and generally lasted only as long as the two camps remained in one another's vicinity. The peace was considered holding only by such of either tribe as happened to be present at the first meeting, and smoked from the stem of the peace pipe.

It is said, however, that the Ojibway chieftain Bi-aus-wah tried hard to bring about a lasting peace with the Dakotas after he had secured a firm footing for his people on the rich hunting grounds of the Upper Mississippi. And it is a noted fact that his humane efforts were so far successful as to put an end by distinct treaty, to the custom of torturing captives, which was still practised by the Dakotas. From the time that he effected this mutual understanding with his enemies, this bad practice ceased altogether, and the taking of captives became less frequent.

For many years after Bi-aus-wah first took possession of Sandy Lake, which event may be dated as taking place about the year 1730, his village remained without a trader, and it was a practice with his bands, as had been before with the tribe when congregated at Shaug-a-waum-ik-ong, to make visits each spring to the nearest French posts on Lake Superior, Grand Portage, and Sault Ste. Marie, to procure in return for their rich packs of fur, clothing, trinkets, fire-arms, and ammunition, and above all, the baneful fire-water which they had already learned to love dearly.

The band who lived at Rainy Lake, and those who had already pierced as far north as Pembina and Red Lake, often joined the Kenisteno and Assineboins on their yearly journeys towards Hudson's Bay for the same purpose ; the English in this direction having early opened the trade, and actively opposed the French who came by the routes of the Great Lakes and Mississippi River.

CHAPTER XV.

OCCUPATION OF THE WISCONSIN AND CHIPPEWA RIVER VALLEYS BY THE OJIBWAYS.

The Ojibways of La Pointe send hunting parties into the midland country lying between the Mississippi and Lake Superior—First permanent residents at Lac Coutereille—Cause of the " three brothers" braving the attacks of their enemies—Lac Coutereille becomes an important Ojibway village—Families branch off who take possession of Lac Shatac, Red Cedar, and Long Lakes, and Puk-wa-wanuh on Chippeway River—The Ojibway pioneers to the headwaters of the Wisconsin—They form their village at Lac du Flambeau—Branches of this band occupy the Wisconsin River and Pelican Lakes—Present descendants of the Lac Coutereille pioneers—Origin of the name Lac Coutereille.

THAT portion of the present State of Wisconsin, comprising the valleys of the Chippeway and Wisconsin rivers, and the country watered by their numerous tributaries, have been occupied by a large section of the Ojibway tribe, for the past century. The beautiful inland lakes from which they head, have been for this length of time the sites of their villages.

After the Ojibways had driven the Odugamees from this section of country, also from the St. Croix rice lakes and the headwaters of the On-ton-a-gun, incited by the fur trade which had actively commenced at this period, large camps of Ojibway hunters began to explore and take possession of the rich hunting grounds which were comprised in the midland country lying between Lake Superior and the Mississippi. For a number of years, however, these hunters made no permanent stay on any spot throughout this country, because danger lurked behind every bush and every tree from the prowling war parties of the Dakotas and Odugamees. Having made their winter hunts, in the course of which they even reached as far as Lac du

Flambeau and Lac Coutereille, the hunting camps would invariably return each spring to La Pointe (Shaug-a-waum-ik-ong), to join their people in the periodical performance of the sacred rites of the Grand Medawe, and to make their summer visits to the nearest French trading posts to barter away their peltries.

Three generations ago, or about the year 1745, the first Ojibway pioneer hunters, braving the attacks of their enemies, first permanently planted their wigwams on the shores of Lake Coutereille, and formed a focus around which families of their tribe have gathered and generated till, at this day, those who claim this as their central village, number full one thousand souls.

The founders of this village consisted of three brothers belonging to the daring and fearless Bear Clan. On the shores of Lac Coutereille (Ottaway Lake), during the course of a winter hunt, they lost one of their children, and as they returned dust to dust, in the silent grave, they buried the seed which caused them, as it were, to grow emplanted on the soil, like a tree, to shade it from the rude gaze of strangers, and watch it against the ravenous visits of wild beasts.

There was a charm about that silent little grave, which caused the mourning parents to brave all dangers, and isolated from their fellows, they passed the spring and summer in its vicinity, and eventually made the spot where it stood the site of a permanent village. Their numbers increased every year, till at last, being followed by their traders, who made Lac Coutereille their inland depot, parties of hunters branched off, and pressing back the Dakotas, they took possession and finally formed new villages at Lac Shatac, Red Cedar and Long Lakes, and at Puk-wa-wanuh on the Chippeway River.

About the time the Odugamees were eventually driven from the Wisconsin River and forced westward to the Mississippi, the Ojibways took possession of the head-waters of this river. The pioneer chieftain of this extensive district of country, was named Sha-da-wish, a son of the great chief of the Crane family, who received a gold medal during the French convocation at Sault Ste. Marie in 1671. From this scion of the family, have directly descended the noted Keesh-ke-mun, Waub-ish-gaug-aug-e (White Crow), and the present ruling chief of this section of the tribe, Ah-mous (Little Bee). From a second son of the same ancient chieftain, named A-ke-gui-ow, are descended the branch of the Crane family residing at La Pointe, of whom the late deceased Tug-waug-aun-e was head and chief during his lifetime.

The French early designated that portion of the tribe who occupied the head-waters of the Wisconsin, as the Lac du Flambeau band, from the circumstance of their locating their central village or summer residence, at the lake known by this name. The Ojibways term it Waus-wag-im-ing (Lake of Torches), from the custom of spearing fish by torch-light, early practised by the hunters of their tribe who first took possession of it.

Before eventually permanently locating their village at this lake, the Ojibways, under their leader, Sha-da-wish, made protracted stands at Trout Lake and Turtle Portage, and it was not till the times of his successor and son, Keesh-ke-mun, that this band proceeded as far west as Lac du Flambeau, for a permanent residence. From this important point there has branched off families who now occupy the country on the Wisconsin River as far down as the Yellow banks, near the mouth of Fox River, and families who occupy the Pelican Lakes in the direction of Lake Michigan.

Within the past century there has spread over this region of country, including the Chippeway River and St. Croix district, from natural increase and accessions from Lake Superior, bands who now number about three thousand souls.

They have encountered inveterate enemies at every step of their advance, and the spots are countless, where they have battled in mortal strife with Dakotas, Odugamees, and Winnebagos. The dangers and vicissitudes of the first pioneers into this section of country were equal to, and of the same character, as beset the onward course of the hardy hunters of the Upper Mississippi.

From the time that the Lac Coutereille and Lac du-Flambeau villages became of sufficient importance, as to assume the privilege of performing the rites of the Me-da-we-win within their own precincts, they were considered actually separated from the common central body and Me-da-we lodge, which had for so many years flourished and concentrated at La Pointe, of Lake Superior, and they became from that time distinct "branches of the same parent tree."

Ka-ka-ke (Hawk), the present war-chief of the Chippe-way River district, is the direct descendant in the third generation of the hunter who lost his child on Lac Cou-tereille, and became the founder of the Ojibway village located on this lake.

Lac Coutereille is named by the Ojibways " Odah-wah-sah-ga-e-gun (Ottaway Lake), from the circumstance that some time over four generations ago, a party of Ojibway hunters discovered on its shores the frozen body of an Ottah-wah, which tribe at this time extended their hunt-ing parties even to this remote point.

CHAPTER XVI.

ENDING OF THE FRENCH SUPREMACY.

The Ojibways aid the French in the war against the British—Mamong-e-sada
leads a party of their warriors from La Pointe, who fight under Montcalm at
the taking of Quebec—Origin of the Ojibway name for the English—They
view with regret the evacuation of their country by the French—Those who
remain amongst them through the ties of marriage, wield an important influence over their conduct—They stand neutral during the strenuous efforts
made by the Algic tribes in opposition to the English—Nature of the hostility evinced by the Ojibways against the British—Speech of Meh-neh-weh-
na to Alexander Henry—Eastern section of the tribe join " Pontiac's war"—
Capture of the fort at Michilimackinac intrusted into their hands—Shrewdness and foresight of the Ojibway chieftain—British commandant refuses to
listen to hints of danger—Game of Baugudoway—Manner in which the fort
was taken—Testimony of Alexander Henry—His capture and ransom—
Troops massacred.

WE have now brought forward the history of the
different sections of the Ojibway tribe, to the time when
the French nation were forced to strike their colors and
cede their possessions in America (comprising the great
chain of lakes), into the hands of the British Empire.

The time during which these two powerful nations battled for the supremacy on the American continent, is an
important era in the history of the Algic tribes who occupied a great portion of Canada, and the areas of the great
western lakes.

Induced by their predilection to the French people, the
causes of which we have given in a previous chapter, the
eastern section of the Ojibway tribe residing at Sault Ste.
Marie, Mackinaw, and the shores of Lake Huron, joined
their warriors with the army of the French, and freely
rallied to their support at Detroit, Fort Du Quesne,
Niagara, Montreal, and Quebec. The Ojibways figured in

almost every battle which was fought during these bloody wars, on the side of the French, against the English. A party of the tribe from their central village of La Pointe on Lake Superior, even proceeded nigh two thousand miles to Quebec, under their celebrated war chief Ma-mong-e-se-da, and fought in the ranks of Montcalm on the plains of Abraham, when this ill-fated general and the heroic Wolfe received their death wounds. According to the late noted British interpreter John Baptiste Cadotte, the name by which the Ojibways now know the British, Shaug-un-aush, was derived from the circumstance of their sudden and almost unaccountable appearance, on that memorable morning on the heights of Abraham. It is a little changed from the original word Saug-aush-e which signifies "to appear from the clouds."

With the deepest regret and sorrow, the Ojibways in common with other Algic tribes, at last viewed the final delivery of the Northwestern French forts into the hands of the conquering British. With aching hearts they bade a last farewell to the kind hearted French local commanders, whom they had learned to term "Father," and the jovial hearted "Coureur du Bois" and open-handed "Marchand voyageur," many of whom took their final departure from the Indian country on its cession to Great Britain. The bonds, however, which had been so long riveting between the French and Ojibways were not so easily to be broken.

The main body of the French traders and common voyageurs who had so long remained amongst them, had many of them become united to the Indian race by the ties of marriage; they possessed large families of half-blood children whom the Indians cherished as their own, and in many instances actually opposed their being taken from their midst. These Frenchmen, as a body, possessed an unbounded influence over the tribes amongst whom they resided, and though they did not openly aid and advise them in the strenuous efforts which they continued to make even after the French as a nation had retired from the field, to prevent the occupation of their country by the British, yet their silence and apparent acquiescence conduced greatly to their noble and protracted efforts headed by the great Algic leader Pontiac.

The fact of their love and adherence to the French people cannot be gainsaid, and to more fully illustrate this feeling, as it actuated their conduct even after the great French nation had delivered them over to the dominion of the British, I will refer to the respected authority of Alexander Henry, the first British trader whom the Ojibways tell of having resided with them after the termination of the disastrous war which we are about to notice.

In 1760, the French forts on the northern lakes were given up to the British, and for the time being the northern tribes of Indians apparently acquiesced in the peace which their Great Father, the French King, had made with Great Britain. In the spring of the following year, Mr. Henry, the well-known author of " Travels and Adventures in Canada and the Indian Territories, between the years 1760 and 1766," tells of making a trading voyage from Montreal to Michilimackinac. He came across a large village of Ojibway Indians on the small island of La Cloche in Lake Huron who treated him in the kindest and most friendly manner, till, " *discovering that he was an Englishman*," they told his men that the Michilimackinac Indians would certainly kill him, and that *they* might as well *anticipate* their share of the pillage. They accordingly demanded a part of his goods, which he prudently gave them. He observed afterwards that from the repeated warnings which he daily received, his mind became "oppressed and much troubled," and learning that the "hostility of the Indians was exclusively against the English," this circumstance suggested to him a prospect of security in securing a Canadian disguise, which eventually enabled him to complete his journey.

He arrived at Michilimackinac, where he found his difficulties to increase, and where he fully learned the nature of the feelings which actuated the minds of the Ojibways against the occupation of their country by the English, nor were his apprehensions allayed, till he received a formal visit from the war chief of the eastern section of the tribe, who resided at Michilimackinac. Mr. Henry describes this man as a person of remarkable appearance, of commanding stature, and with a singularly fine countenance.

He entered the room where the traveller was anxiously awaiting the result of his visit, followed by sixty warriors dressed and decorated in the most formal and imposing fashion of war. Not a word was spoken as they came in one by one, seated themselves on the floor at a signal from the chief, and began composedly to fill and smoke their pipes. The Ojibway chieftain meanwhile looking steadfastly at the trader, made various inquiries of his head boatman, a Canadian. He then coolly observed that " the English were brave men and not afraid of death, since they dared to come thus fearlessly among their *enemies*."

When the Indians had finished smoking their pipes, the chief took a few wampum strings in his hand and commenced the following harangue :—

" Englishman ! It is to you that I speak, and I demand your attention !

" Englishman ! You know that the French king is our father. He promised to be such ; and we, in return, promised to be his children. This promise we have kept.

" Englishman ! It is you that have made war with this

our father. You are his enemy; and how then could you have the boldness to venture among us, his children ? You know that his enemies are ours.

" Englishman ! We are informed that our father, the king of France, is old and infirm ; and that being fatigued with making war upon your nation, he is fallen asleep.

" During his sleep, you have taken advantage of him and possessed yourselves of Canada. But his nap is almost at an end. I think I hear him already stirring and inquiring for his children, the Indians :—and when he does awake, what must become of you ? He will destroy you utterly.

" Englishman ! Although you have conquered the French you have not yet conquered us ! We are not your slaves. These lakes and these woods and mountains were left to us by our ancestors. They are our inheritance, and we will part with them to none. Your nation supposes that we, like the white people, cannot live without bread and pork and beef. But you ought to know that he—the Great Spirit and master of life—has provided food for us in these broad lakes and upon these mountains.

" Englishman ! Our father, the king of France, employed our young men to make war on your nation.

" In this warfare, many of them have been killed, and it is our custom to retaliate, until such time as the spirits of the slain are satisfied. Now the spirits of the slain are to be satisfied in either of two ways. The first is by spilling the blood of the nation by whom they fell ; the other, by *covering the bodies of the dead*, and thus allaying the resentment of their relatives. This is done by making presents.

" Englishman ! Your king has never sent us any presents, nor entered into any treaty with us, wherefore he and we are still at war ; and until he does these things, we must consider that we have no other father or friend among the white men than the king of France. But for you, we have taken into consideration that you have ventured your life among us, in expectation that we should not molest you; you do not come armed with an intention to make war. You come in peace, to trade with us and supply us with necessaries of which we are much in want. We shall regard you therefore as a brother, and you may sleep tranquilly without fear of the Chippeways. As a token of our friendship, we present you with this pipe to smoke."

Mih-neh-weh-na, the name of the chieftain who delivered this noble speech, now gave his hand to the Englishman. His sixty warriors followed his example. The pipe, emblem of peace, went round in due order, and after being politely entertained by the anxious trader, from whose heart they had taken a heavy load, they all quietly took their leave.

So many more able writers than myself have given accurate accounts of the memorable events which occurred during this imporant era in American history, that I desist from entering into details of any occurrence, except in which the Ojibways were actually concerned.

For upwards of four years after the French had ceded the country to the British, the allied Algic tribes, after a short lull of quiet and comparative peace, under the masterly guidance of Pontiac, maintained the war against what they considered as the usurpation, by the British, of the hunting grounds which the Great Spirit had given their ancestors.

Such was the force and accuracy of the organization which this celebrated leader had effected among the northern tribes of his fellow red men, that, on the same day, which was the 4th of June, 1763, and the anniversary of the king's birth (which the Indians knew was a day set apart by the English as one of amusement and celebration), they attacked and besieged twelve of the wide-spread western stockaded forts, and succeeded in taking possession of nine. In this alliance, the Ojibways of Lake Huron and Michigan were most active parties, and into their

hands was entrusted by their common leader, the capture
of the British fort at Mackinaw. "That fort," according
to the description of an eminent writer, "standing on the
south side of the strait between lakes Huron and Michigan,
was one of the most important positions on the frontiers.
It was the place of deposit, and point of departure between
the upper and lower countries; the traders always assembled there, on their voyages to and from Montreal. Connected with it, was an area of two acres, inclosed with
cedar wood pickets, and extending on one side so near to
the water's edge, that a western wind always drew the
waves against the foot of the stockade. There were about
thirty houses within the limits, inhabited by about the
same number of families. The only ordinance on the bas-
tions were two small brass pieces. The garrison numbered
between ninety and one hundred."

The important enterprise of the capture of this important and indispensable post, was entrusted into the hands
of Mih-neh-weh-na, the great war chieftain of the Ojibways
of Mackinaw, whom we have already mentioned, and by
the manner in which he superintended and managed the
affair, to a complete and successful issue, he approved himself a worthy lieutenant of the great head and leader of
the war, the Ottawa chieftain Pontiac.

The Ottawas of Lake Michigan being more friendly
disposed to the British, were not called on by the politic
Ojibway chieftain for help in this enterprise, and a knowledge of the secret plan of attack was carefully kept from
them, for fear that they would inform their English friends,
and place them on their guard. In fact, every person of
his own tribe whom he suspected of secret good-will towards any of the new British traders, Min-neh-weh-na
sent away from the scene of the intended attack, with the
admonition that death would be their sure fate, should the

Saugunash be informed of the plan which had been formed to take possession of the fort.

In this manner did he guard with equal foresight and greater success than Pontiac himself, against a premature development of their plans. Had not the loving Indian girl informed the young officer at Fort Detroit of Pontiac's secret plan, that important post, and its inmates, would have shared the same fate as befell the fort at Mackinaw.

Of all the northern tribes who occupied the great lakes, the Ojibways allowed only the Osaugees to participate with them in their secret councils, in which was developed the plan of taking the fort, and these two tribes only were actively engaged in this enterprise.

The fighting men of the Ojibways and Osaugees gradually collected in the vicinity of the fort as the day appointed for the attack approached. They numbered between four and six hundred. An active trade was in the mean time carried on with the British traders, and every means resorted to for the purpose of totally blinding the suspicions which the more humane class of the French population found means to impart to the officers of the fort, respecting the secret animosity of the Indians. These hints were entirely disregarded by Major Etherington, the commandant of the fort, and he even threatened to confine any person who would have the future audacity to whisper these tales of danger into his ears. Everything, therefore, favored the scheme which the Ojibway chieftain had laid to ensnare his confident enemies. On the eve of the great English king's birthday, he informed the British commandant that as the morrow was to be a day of rejoicing, his young men would play the game of ball, or Baug-ah-ud-o-way, for the amusement of the whites, in front of the gate of the fort. In this game the young men of the Osaugee tribe would play against the Ojibways for a large stake. The commandant expressed his pleasure and willingness to the crafty chieftain's proposal, little dreaming that this was to lead to a game of blood, in which those under his charge were to be the victims.

During the whole night the Ojibways were silently busy in making preparations for the morrow's work. They sharpened their knives and tomahawks, and filed short off their guns. In the morning these weapons were entrusted to the care of their women, who, hiding them under the folds of their blankets, were ordered to stand as near as possible to the gate of the fort, as if to witness the game which the men were about to play. Over a hundred on each side of the Ojibways and Osaugees, all chosen men, now sallied forth from their wigwams, painted and ornamented for the occasion, and proceeding to the open green which lay in front of the fort, they made up the stakes for which they were apparently about to play, and planted the posts towards which each party was to strive to take the ball.

This game of Baug-ah-ud-o-way is played with a bat and wooden ball. The bat is about four feet long, terminating at one end into a circular curve, which is netted with leather strings, and forms a cavity where the ball is caught, carried, and if necessary thrown with great force, to treble the distance that it can be thrown by hand. Two posts are planted at the distance of about half a mile. Each party has its particular post, and the game consists in carrying or throwing the ball in the bat to the post of the adversary. At the commencement of the game, the two parties collect midway between the two posts; the ball is thrown up into the air, and the competition for its possession commences in earnest. It is the wildest game extant among the Indians, and is generally played in full feathers and ornaments, and with the greatest excitement and vehemence. The great object is to obtain possession of the ball; and, during the heat of the excitement, no obstacle is allowed to stand in the way of getting at it. Let it fall far out into the deep water, numbers rush madly in and swim for it, each party impeding the efforts of the other in every manner possible. Let it fall into a high inclosure, it is surmounted, or torn down in a moment, and the ball recovered; and were it to fall into the chimney of a house, a jump through the window, or a smash of the door, would be considered of no moment; and the most violent hurts and bruises are incident to the headlong, mad manner in which it is played. It will be seen by this hurried description, that the game was very well adapted to carry out the scheme of the Indians.

On the morning of the 4th of June, after the cannon of the fort had been discharged in commemoration of the king's natal day, the ominous ball was thrown up a short distance in front of the gate of Fort Mackinaw, and the exciting game commenced. The two hundred players, their painted persons streaming with feathers, ribbons, fox and wolf tails, swayed to and fro as the ball was carried backwards and forwards by either party, who for the moment had possession of it. Occasionally a swift and agile runner would catch it in his bat, and making tremendous leaps hither and thither to avoid the attempts of his opponents to knock it out of his bat, or force him to throw it, he would make a sudden dodge past them, and choosing a clear track, run swiftly, urged on by the deafening shouts of his party and the by-standers, towards the stake of his adversaries, till his onward course was stopped by a swifter runner, or an advanced guard of the opposite party.

The game, played as it was, by the young men of two different tribes, became exciting, and the commandant of the fort even took his stand outside of his open gates, to view its progress. His soldiers stood carelessly unarmed, here and there, intermingling with the Indian women, who gradually huddled near the gateway, carrying under their blankets the weapons which were to be used in the approaching work of death.

In the struggle for its possession, the ball at last was gradually carried towards the open gates, and all at once, after having reached a proper distance, an athletic arm caught it up in his bat, and as if by accident threw it within the precincts of the fort. With one deafening yell and impulse, the players rushed forward in a body, as if to regain it, but as they reached their women and entered the gateway, they threw down their wooden bats and grasping the shortened guns, tomahawks, and knives, the massacre commenced, and the bodies of the unsuspecting British soldiers soon lay strewn about, lifeless, horribly mangled, and scalpless. The careless commander was taken captive without a struggle, as he stood outside the fort, viewing the game, which the Ojibway chieftain had got up for his amusement.

The above is the account, much briefened, which I have learned verbally from the old French traders and half-breeds, who learned it from the lips of those who were present and witnessed the bloody transaction. Not a hair on the head of the many Frenchmen who witnessed this scene was hurt by the infuriated savages, and there stands not on record a stronger proof of the love borne them by the tribe engaged in this business than this very fact, for the passions of an Indian warrior, once aroused by a scene of this nature, are not easily appeased, and generally everything kindred in any manner to his foe, falls a victim to satiate his blood-thirsty propensities.

Alexander Henry, one of the few British traders who survived this massacre, gives the most authentic record of this event that has been published, and to his truthful narrative I am indebted for much corroborating testimony, to the more disconnected accounts of the Indians and old traders. A few quotations from his journal will illustrate the affair more fully, and I have no doubt will be acceptable to the reader, as being better told than I can tell it.

After disregarding the friendly cautionary hints of Wa-wat-am, an Ojibway Indian who had adopted him as a brother, but who dared not altogether disclose the plan of attack formed by his people, Mr. Henry resumes his narrative as follows:—

"The morning was sultry. A Chippeway came to tell me that his nation was going to play at Baggatiway with the Sacs or Saukies, another Indian nation, for a high wager. He invited me to witness the sport, adding that the commandant was to be there, and would bet on the side of the Chippeways. In consequence of this information, I went to the commandant and expostulated with him a little, representing that the Indians might possibly have some sinister end in view, but the commandant only smiled at my suspicions. . . .

"I did not go myself to see the match, which was now to be played without the fort, because, there being a canoe prepared to depart on the following day to Montreal, I employed myself in writing letters to my friends; and even when a fellow trader, Mr. Tracy, happened to call on me, saying that another canoe had just arrived from Detroit, and proposing that I should go with him to the beach to inquire the news, it so happened that I still remained to finish my letters, promising to follow Mr. Tracy in the course of a few minutes. Mr. Tracy had not gone more than twenty paces from the door, when I heard an Indian war-cry and a noise of general confusion. Going instantly to my window, I saw a crowd of Indians within the fort, furiously cutting down and scalping every Englishman they found. In particular, I witnessed the fate of Lieut. Jenette.

I had, in the room in which I was, a fowling piece, loaded with swan shot. This I immediately seized, and held it for a few minutes, waiting to hear the drum beat to arms. In this dreadful interval, I saw several of my countrymen fall, and more than one struggling between the knees of an Indian, who, holding him in this manner, scalped him while yet living! At length, disappointed in the hope of seeing resistance made to the enemy, and sensible of course that no effort of my own unassisted arm could avail against four hundred Indians, I thought only of seeking shelter. Amid the slaughter which was raging, I observed many of the Canadian inhabitants of the fort calmly looking on, neither opposing the Indians nor suffering injury. From this circumstance I conceived a hope of finding security in their houses."

After describing the many hair-breadth escapes which befell him at the hands of the savages, Mr. Henry was eventually saved by Wa-wat-am, or Wow-yat-ton (Whirling Eddy), his adopted Ojibway brother, in the following characteristic manner, which we will introduce in his own words, as an apt illustration of Indian custom :—

"Toward noon (7th June), when the great war chief, in company with Wen-ni-way, was seated at the opposite end of the lodge, my friend and brother Wa-wa-tam, suddenly came in. During the four days preceding, I had often wondered what had become of him. In passing by, he gave me his hand, but went immediately toward the great chief, by the side of whom, and Wen-ni-way, he sat himself down. The most uninterrupted silence prevailed. Each smoked his pipe, and this done, Wa-wa-tam arose and left the lodge, saying to me, as he passed, ' Take courage.'

" An hour elapsed, during which several chiefs entered, and preparations appeared to be making for a council. At length Wa-wa-tam re-entered the lodge, followed by his wife, and both loaded with merchandise, which they carried up to the chiefs, and laid in a heap before them. Some moments of silence followed. at the end of

which, Wa-wa-tam pronounced a speech, every word of
which, to me, was of extraordinary interest:—

"'Friends and relations,' he began, 'what is it that I shall
say? You know what I feel. You all have friends and
brothers and children, whom as yourselves you love, and
you, what would you experience, did you, like me, behold
your dearest friend, your brother, in the condition of a
slave—a slave exposed every moment to insult, and to the
menaces of death! This case, as you all know, is mine.
See there,' pointing to myself, 'my friend and brother
among slaves, himself a slave!

"'You all well know, long before the war began, I adopted
him as my brother. From this moment he became one of
my family, so that no change of circumstances could break
the cord which fastened us together. He is my brother—
and because I am your relation, he is therefore your relation
too; and how, being your relation, can he be your slave?

"'On the day on which the war began, you were fearful,
lest, on this very account, I should reveal your secret. You
requested, therefore, that I should leave the fort, and even
cross the lake. I did so, but did it with reluctance. I did
it with reluctance, notwithstanding that you, Mih-neh-weh-
na, who had the command in this enterprise, gave me your
promise that you would protect my friend, delivering him
from all danger, and giving him safely to me.

"'The performance of this promise I now claim. I come
not with empty hands to ask. You, Mih-neh-weh-na, best
know whether or not, as it respects yourself, you have
kept your word. But I bring these goods, to buy off every
claim, which any man among you all may have on my
brother, as his prisoner.'

"Wa-wa-tam having ceased, the pipes were again filled,
and after they were finished, a further period of silence
followed. At the end of this, Mih-neh-weh-na arose and
gave his reply:—

" ' My relation and brother,' said he, ' what you have spoken is the truth. We were acquainted with the friendship which subsisted between yourself and the Englishman, in whose behalf you have now addressed us. We knew the danger of having our secret discovered, and the consequences which must follow. You say truly that we requested you to leave the fort. This we did in regard for you and your family ; for if a discovery of our design had been made, you would have been blamed, whether guilty or not, and you would thus have been involved in difficulties, from which you could not have extricated yourself. It is also true that I promised you to take care of your friend ; and this promise I performed by desiring my son, at the moment of assault, to seek him out, and bring him to my lodge. He went accordingly, but could not find him. The day after I sent him to Langlade's (a French trader), when he was informed that your friend was safe ; and had it not been that the Indians were then drinking the rum which had been found in the fort, he would have brought him home with him, according to my orders. I am very glad to find that your friend has escaped. We accept your present: and you may take him home with you.'

" Wa-wa-tam thanked the assembled chiefs, and taking me by the hand, led me to his lodge, which was at the distance of a few yards only from the prison lodge. My entrance appeared to give joy to the whole family. Food was immediately prepared for me, and I now ate the first hearty meal which I had made since my capture. I found myself one of the family, and but that I had still my fears as to the other Indians, I felt as happy as the situation could allow."

Mr. Henry says further: " Of the English traders that fell into the hands of the Indians at the capture of the fort, Mr. Tracy was the only one who lost his life. Mr. Ezekiel

Solomons, and Mr. Henry Bostwick, were taken by the Ottawas, and, after the peace, carried down to Montreal, and there ransomed. Of ninety troops, about seventy were killed ; the rest, together with those of the posts in the Bay des Puants (Green Bay) and at the river St. Joseph, were also kept in safety by the Ottawas till the peace, and then either freely restored, or ransomed at Montreal. The Ottawas never overcame their disgust at the neglect with which they had been treated in the beginning of the war, by those who afterwards desired their assistance as allies."

That portion of the Ojibways, forming by far the main body of the tribe who occupied the area of Lake Superior, and those bands who had already formed villages on the Upper Mississippi, and on the sources of its principal northeastern tributaries, were not engaged in the bloody transactions which we have described or at most, but a very few of their old warriors, who have now all paid the last debt of nature, were noted as having been present on the occasion of this most important event in Ojibway history.

CHAPTER XVII.

COMMENCEMENT OF BRITISH SUPREMACY.

The Ojibways of Lake Superior do not join the alliance of Pontiac against the British—They are kept in the paths of peace through the influence of a French trader at Sault Ste. Marie—John Baptiste Cadotte—His first introduction into the Ojibway country—He marries a woman of the tribe, and settles at Sault Ste. Marie—His influence—Character of his Indian wife—Testimony of Alex. Henry—Henry proceeds to the Sault in Madame Cadotte's canoe—Kind reception by Mons. Cadotte—A party of Indians seek his life—He is preserved through Cadotte's influence—Sir Wm. Johnson sends a message to the Ste. Marie's Ojibways—They send twenty deputies to the Grand Council at Niagara—Return of peace—Ma-mong-e-se-da is sent from Shaug-a-waum-ik-ong to Sir William Johnson to demand a trader—Brief sketch of this chieftain's life—Henry and Cadotte enter into the fur trade—They work the copper mines—Grant of land at Sault Ste. Marie to Mons. Cadotte.

THAT portion of the Ojibways, forming by far the main body of the tribe, who occupied the area of Lake Superior, and those bands who had already formed distinct villages on the headwaters of the Mississippi and its principal northeastern tributaries, were not engaged in the bloody transaction of the taking of Fort Michilimackinac, or at most, but a few of their old warriors who have all now fallen into their graves, were noted as having been accidentally present on the occasion of this most important event in the history of their tribe.

It is true that the war-club, tobacco, and wampum belt of war had been carried by the messengers of Pontiac and his lieutenant, the Mackinaw chieftain, to La Pointe, and the principal villages of the tribe on Lake Superior, but the Ojibways listened only to the advice and the words of peace of a French trader who resided at Sault Ste. Marie, and from this point (with an influence not even surpassed by that which his contemporary, Sir Wm. Johnson, wielded

over the more eastern tribes), he held sway, and guided
the councils of the Lake Superior Ojibways, even to their
remotest village.

This man did not stand tamely by, as many of his fellow
French traders did, to witness the butchery of British
soldiers and subjects, and see the blood of his fellow whites
ruthlessly and freely flowing at the hands of the misguided
savages. On the contrary, he feared not to take a firm stand
against the war, and made noble and effective efforts to
prevent the deplorable consequences which their opposition
to the British arms, would be sure to entail on the Ojibways. He knew full well that the French nation had
withdrawn forever from their possessions in this country,
and that their national fire, which was promised would
blaze forever with the fire of the Ojibways, was now totally extinguished, and knowing this, he did not foolishly
stimulate, as others did, the sanguinary opposition which
the Indians continued to make against the predominant
Saxon race, by telling them that " the great king of the
French had only fallen into a drowse, but would soon
awaken, and drive the English back into the great salt
water."

On the contrary, he pointed out to the Ojibways, the
utter uselessness and impotence of their efforts; and he
told them that the war would only tend to thin the ranks
of their warriors, causing their women to cover their faces
with the black paint of mourning, and keep them misera-
bly poor, for the want of traders to supply their wants.

It is through the humane advice of this French trader,
and the unbounded influence which he held over the Lake
Superior Ojibways, which prevented them from joining
the alliance of Pontiac, in his war against the English, and
which has thereby saved them from the almost utter annihilation which has befallen every other tribe who have
been induced to fight for one type of the white race against

another, and which enables them at this day to assume the position of the most numerous and important branch of the Algic race, and the largest tribe residing east of the Mississippi.

The name of this man was John Baptiste Cadotte, and he was a son of the Mons. Cadeau who first appeared in the Ojibway country, as early as in 1671, in the train of the French envoy, Sieur du Lusson, when he treated with the delegates of the northwestern Indian tribes at Sault Ste. Marie.

John Baptist Cadotte (as his name was spelt by the British, and has been retained to this day) had, early in life, followed the example of the hardy western adventurers who had already found their way to the sources of the Great Lakes and the Great River, Mississippi. He went as a " Marchand voyageur," and visited the remotest villages of the Ojibways on Lake Superior, to supply their wants in exchange for their valuable beaver skins. He became attached to one of their women, belonging to the great clan of A-waus-e, and married her according to the forms of the Catholic religion, of which he was a firm believer.

At the breaking out of the war between France and Great Britain, which resulted in the ending of the French domination in America, Mons. Cadotte made it his permanent residence at Sault Ste. Marie, from which point he eventually wielded the salutary influence which we have mentioned. He is the only French trader of any importance whom the Ojibways tell of having remained with them, when the French people were forced to leave the Lake Superior country. And it is said that though he made several attempts to leave the Ojibway people in company with his departing countrymen, such was the affection which they bore to himself and his half-breed children, that their chiefs threatened to use force to prevent his departure.

His Ojibway wife appears to have been a woman of great energy and force of character, as she is noted to this day for the influence she held over her relations—the principal chiefs of the tribe; and the hardy, fearless manner, in which, accompanied only by Canadian "Coureurs du bois" to propel her canoes, she made long journeys to distant villages of her people to further the interests of her husband.

She bore him two sons, John Baptiste, and Michel, who afterwards succeeded their father in the trade, and became, with their succeeding children of the same name, so linked with the Ojibways, that I shall be forced often to mention their names in the future course of my narrative, although at the evident risk of laying myself open to the charge of egotism, or making them prominent because they happen to be my direct progenitors.

Alex. Henry, in his straight-forward and truthful narrative, gives full testimony to all which I have said respecting the position and influence of Mons. Cadotte among the Ojibways during the middle of the past century, and not only for the purpose of making known the noble and philanthropic conduct of this man during this trying season in Ojibway history, but also to more fully illustrate to the reader the position and affairs of the tribe during this era, I will take the liberty to introduce a few more paragraphs from his pen. In the spring of the following year after his capture, having passed the winter as an Indian in the hunting camp of his adopted brother Wa-wa-tam, in whose family he was ever kindly treated, he returned to the fort at Michilimackinac, which now contained but two French traders. He says:—

"Eight days had passed in tranquillity, when there arrived a band of Indians from the bay of Sag-u-en-auw (Saginaw.) They had assisted at the siege of Detroit, and came to muster as many recruits for that serviee as they could. For my own part, I was soon informed that, as I was the only Englishman in the place, they proposed to kill me, in order to give their friends a mess of English broth to raise their courage. This intelligence was not of the most agreeable kind, and in consequence of receiving it, I requested my friend to carry me to the Sault de Saint Marie, at which place I knew the Indians to be peaceably inclined, and that M. Cadotte enjoyed a powerful influence over their conduct. They considered M. Cadotte as their chief, and he was not only my friend, but a friend to the English. It was by him that the Chippeways of Lake Superior were prevented from joining Pontiac."

His friend and brother Wa-wa-tam was not slow in exerting himself for his preservation, and leaving Mackinaw during the night, he proceeded with him to Isle aux Outardes, on the route to Sault Sainte Marie. Here Nonen, the wife of Wa-wa-tam, falling sick, they were obliged to remain for some days, in the greatest fear of hostile Indians, who were now daily expected to pass on the route to Missisaukie, or Straits of Niagara, for the purpose of carrying on the war against the British. A return to Mackinaw was to incur certain destruction, and it was with the greatest pleasure that the distressed traveller at last saw a canoe approaching the island, which he knew must be manned by Canadians, by the manner in which the paddles were managed, and the whiteness of the sail. On entering the lodge of his adopted brother, elated with the news of the approach of white men, he says:—

"The family congratulated me on the approach of so fair an opportunity of escape, and my father and brother (for he was alternately each of these) lit his pipe, and presented it to me, saying, ' my son, this may be the last time that ever you and I shall smoke out of the same pipe. I

am sorry to part with you. You know the affection which
I have always borne you, and the dangers to which I have
exposed myself and family, to preserve you from your enemies; and I am happy to find that my efforts promise not
to have been in vain.' At this time a boy came into the
lodge, informing us that the canoe had come from Michilimackinac, and was bound to the Sault de Sainte Marie.
It was manned by three Canadians, and was carrying
home Madame Cadotte, the wife of M. Cadotte, already
mentioned. My hopes of going to Montreal being now
dissipated, I resolved on accompanying Madame Cadotte,
with her permission, to the Sault. On communicating my
wishes to Madame Cadotte, she cheerfully acceded to them.
Madame Cadotte, as I have already mentioned, was an
Indian woman of the Chippeway nation, and she was very
generally respected. . . . Being now no longer in the society of Indians, I put aside their dress, putting on that of
a Canadian: a moleton or blanket coat over my shirt,
and a handkerchief about my head, hats being very little
worn in this country. At daylight on the second morning
of our voyage, we embarked, and presently perceived several canoes behind us. As they approached, we ascertained
them to be the fleet bound for the Missisaki, of which I
had been so long in dread. It amounted to twenty sail.

" On coming up with us, and surrounding our canoe, and
amid general inquiries concerning the news, an Indian
challenged me for an Englishman, and his companions supported him, saying that I looked very like one, but I
affected not to understand any of the questions which they
asked me; and Madame Cadotte assured them that I was
a Canadian, whom she had brought on his first voyage
from Montreal. The following day saw us safely landed
at the Sault, where I experienced a generous welcome from
M. Cadotte. There were thirty warriors at this place, restrained from joining the war only by M. Cadotte's influ-

ence. Here, for five days, I was once more in possession of tranquillity; but on the sixth, a young Indian came into M. Cadotte's, saying that a canoe full of warriors had just arrived from Michilimackinac; that they had inquired for me; and that he believed their intentions to be bad. Nearly at the same time, a message came from the good chief of the village, desiring me to conceal myself, until he should discover the views and temper of the strangers. A garret was the second time my place of refuge; and it was not long before the Indians came to M. Cadotte's. My friend immediately informed Match-i-ki-wish, their chief, who was related to his wife, of the design imputed to them, of mischief against myself. Match-i-ki-wish frankly acknowledged that they had had such a design; but added, that if displeasing to M. Cadotte, it should be abandoned. He then further stated, that their errand was to raise a party of warriors to return with them to Detroit; and that it had been their intention to take me with them.

"In regard to the principal of the two objects thus disclosed, M. Cadotte proceeded to assemble all the chiefs and warriors of the village, and then, after deliberating for some time among themselves, sent for the strangers, to whom both M. Cadotte and the chief of the village addressed a speech. In these speeches, after recurring to the designs confessed to have been entertained against myself, who was now declared to be under the protection of all the chiefs, by whom any insult I might sustain would be avenged, the embassadors were peremptorily told that they might go back as they came, none of the young men of this village being foolish enough to join them.

"A moment after, a report was brought that a canoe had just arrived from Niagara. As this was a place from which every one was anxious to hear news, a message was sent to these fresh strangers, requesting them to come to the council. The strangers came accordingly, and being seated, a long silence ensued. At length, one of them, taking up a belt of wampum, addressed himself thus to the assembly :—

' " My friends and brothers, I am come with this belt from our great father, Sir William Johnson. He desired me to come to you as his embassador, and tell you that he is making a great feast at Fort Niagara : that his kettles are all ready and his fires lit. He invites you to partake of this feast, in common with your friends, the Six Nations, who have all made peace with the English. He advises you to seize this opportunity of doing the same, as you cannot otherwise fail of being destroyed ; for the English are on their march with a great army, which will be joined by different nations of Indians. In a word, before the fall of the leaf, they will be at Michilimackinac, and the Six Nations with them.' "

The tenor of this speech greatly alarmed the Indians throughout the Northwest, and those who fortunately had not embrued their hands too deeply in British blood, were glad to send delegates to the Great Council at Niagara. Among the rest, the Sault Ste. Marie Ojibways sent twenty deputies, with whom Mr. Henry, after one year of captivity and trouble, returned once more to his friends. These deputies, though they went in fear and trembling, were well received at the hands of Sir William Johnson, and they now experienced the good consequences of having listened to the advice of their trader.

During the summer of the same year, 1764, in which the council was held at Niagara, where it is said that twenty-two different tribes were represented, a British force of three thousand men under Gen. Bradstreet proceeded up the lakes as far as Detroit. Under the command of this officer, Alexander Henry had a battalion of Indian allies, among whom were " ninety-six Ojibways of Sault

Ste. Mary," who, however, nearly all deserted before the army reached Fort Erie.

On arrival of this large body of troops at Detroit, a permanent peace was effected with all the northern tribes, including the Ojibways. Pontiac, the head and heart of the bloody Indian war which had now come to an end, was not present at this treaty. His best allies, the tribes of the northern lakes, had deserted him, and he thereafter confined his exertions to the tribes of the Miamis, Shawanoes, and Illinois, towards the south and west. He never overcame his animosity to the Saxon race, and had he not suffered a premature death at the hands of an Indian of the Kaskaskia tribe, he would again have fanned the flames of another sanguinary war. His name and influence extended over all the Algic tribes, and their regret for his loss is fully proved by the manner in which the Ojibways, Pottawaudumies, Ottawas, and Osaugees revenged his death by total extermination of the tribe to which belonged his assassin, and of the Illinois, Cahokias, and Peorias, who rallied to their defence, but a few families were saved from total annihilation.

For two years after the ending of Pontiac's war, the fear of Indian hostility was still so great that the British traders dared not extend their operations to the more remote villages of the Ojibways, and La Pointe, during this time, was destitute of a resident trader. To remedy this great evil, which the Indians, having become accustomed to the commodities of the whites, felt acutely, Ma-mong-e-se-da, the war chief of this village, with a party of his fellows, was deputed to go to Sir Wm. Johnson, to ask that a trader might be sent to reside among them. He is said to have been well received by their British father, who presented him with a broad wampum belt of peace, and gorget. The belt was composed of white and blue beads, denoting purity and the clear blue sky, and this act settled the foundation of a lasting good-will, and was the commencement of an active communication between the British and Ojibways of Lake Superior.

A brief notice may not be considered amiss in this place, of the chief Ma-mong-e-se-da, who acted in this important affair as the representative of his tribe. His father was a member of the Reindeer Clan, and belonged to the northern division of the tribe. He moved from Grand Portage on the north shore of Lake Superior when a young man, to the main village of his tribe at Shaugha-waum-ik-ong. Becoming noted as an active and successful hunter, and having distinguished himself at the battle of Point Prescott, where the Ojibways destroyed so many of their enemies, he married a woman of the La Pointe village, who had been the wife of a Dakota chief of distinction during the late term of peace which the French traders had brought about. The renewal of the war had obliged her to separate from her Dakota husband, and two sons whom she had borne him, one of whom afterwards became a celebrated chief, whose name, Wabasha, has descended down in Dakota and Ojibway traditions to the present times.

Ma-mong-e-se-da (Big Feet), was the offspring of his mother's second marriage with the young hunter of the Reindeer Clan. He became noted as he grew up to be a man, for the fearless manner in which he hunted on the best hunting grounds of the Dakotas, on the lower waters of the Chippeway River, and an incident worthy of note is related as having happened to him during the course of one of his usual fall hunts. His camp on this occasion consisted of several lodges of his own immediate relatives. They had approached near the borders of the Dakota country, in the midland district lying between the Mississippi and Lake Superior, when, one morning, his camp was fired on by a party of Dakota warriors. At the second volley, one of his men being wounded, Ma-mong-e-se-da grasping his gun sallied out, and pronouncing his name loudly in the Dakota tongue, he asked if Wabasha, his brother, was among the assailants. The firing ceased immediately, and after a short pause of silence, a tall figure ornamented with a war dress, his head covered with eagle plumes, stepped forward from the ranks of the Dakotas and presented his hand. It proved to be his half brother Wabasha, and inviting him and his warriors into his lodge, Ma-mong-e-se-da entertained them in the style of a chief.

This chieftain was noted also for the frequency of his visits to Montreal and Quebec, and the great love he bore to the French people, whose cause he warmly espoused against the British. He was at last recognized as a chief, and received a medal and flag at the hands of the French. He actively aided them in their wars with Great Britain, and on one occasion he took a message from Gen. Montcalm to the Lake Superior Ojibways, asking them to come to his aid in Canada. But a small party followed the chieftain on his return to join the French general, in whose ranks he fought at the taking of Quebec in 1759.

After the failure of the Indian opposition to the British arms in 1764, Ma-mong-e-se-da, through the attentions he received at the hands of Sir William Johnson, became a fast friend to the English. After his death he was succeeded by his son Waub-o-jeeg, in his war chieftainship, who became much more noted in Ojibway history than even his father.

The British trader Alexander Henry, notwithstanding the losses and misfortunes which had befallen him at the hands of the Ojibways, again returned into their country immediately after the peace, and joining his more ample means with the greater influence of Mons. Cadotte in partnership, they carried on the fur trade with the Ojibways of Lake Superior, which had for a time been discontinued. They made it their depot at Sault Ste. Marie and from this point they sent outfits to Shaug-a-waum-ik-ong and other points of the great lake. It is even said that Mons. Cadotte, through his influence with the Indians, and knowledge of the former mining localities of the French, being acquainted with rich deposits of copper ore and masses of the virgin metal, he in conjunction with Mr. Henry, carried on mining operations in connection with their trade on the Ontonagon River.

I have learned from some of the old chiefs of the tribe, among whom I may mention Ke-che-wash-keenh, or Great Buffalo, of La Pointe, that soon after the first arrival of the British into their country, the chiefs of the Ojibways at Sault Ste. Marie made a formal grant of a large tract of land, comprising the present site of the town of Ste. Marie, to Mons. Cadotte and his half-breed children. The written grant it appears, through some means fell into the hands of Alexander Henry, after whose death some person brought it back into the Ojibway country, and made inquiries of some of the principal chiefs as to its authenticity. It was shown to Great Buffalo at Sault Ste. Marie, and he described it as being a very old-looking paper, being much torn and patched up, and the writing upon it hardly discernible. Many questions were asked him by the gentleman who had it in possession, respecting the number and where-abouts of Cadotte's descendants. The paper was taken back to Montreal, and has never been heard of since.

CHAPTER XVIII.

GRAND EXPEDITION OF THE DAKOTAS TO THE SOURCES OF THE MISSISSIPPI, AGAINST THE OJIBWAYS.

The Dakotas make a grand tribal effort to drive back the Ojibways—Their warriors collect at St. Anthony Falls—They ascend the Mississippi in canoes —They make the circuit of the Upper Mississippi country—Death of the Ojibway hunter, Waub-u-dow—Death of Minaigwatig with his family at Gauss Lake—Death of three boys at Little Boy Lake—Death of an Ojibway hunter near the Falls of Pokeguma—The Dakotas are discovered by two Ojibway hunters—Chase down the Mississippi—Arrival at Sandy Lake— Drunken carouse of the Ojibways—Death of the Ojibway scout—Dakotas capture thirty women while picking berries—They attack the village of Sandy Lake—They are repulsed and proceed down the river—An Ojibway war party discover their marks, and lie in ambuscade at Crow Wing— Preparations for battle—Three days' fight—Dakotas finally retreat and evacuate Rum River County—Dakota legend.

AFTER having given, in the two preceding chapters, a summary account respecting the affairs of the Ojibways, attendant on the change from the French to the British supremacy, we will once more return to the northwestern vanguard of the tribe, under the chief Bi-aus-wah, whom we left battling with the fierce Dakotas for the possession of the Upper Mississippi country.

As near as can be judged from their mode of computing time, by events, and generations, it is now[1] about eighty five years [1768] since the following events occurred, to that portion of the tribe who had located their village at Sandy Lake, and hunted about the sources of the Great River. The incidents to be related, resulted in a fierce battle between the warriors of the two contending tribes, at the confluence of the Crow Wing River with the Mississippi.

---

[1] A. D. 1852.

The most reliable account of this occurrence which the writer has been enabled to obtain, is that given by Esh-ke-bug-e-coshe, the venerable and respected chief of the northern Ojibways. He is one whose veracity cannot be impeached. He is between seventy and eighty years of age, and the tale having been transmitted to him by his grandfather Waus-e-ko-gub-ig (Bright Forehead), who acted as leader of the Ojibway warriors who fought in this action, his account can be implicitly relied on.

" The M'dé-wak-anton Dakotas, being at last obliged, from the repeated incursions of the Ojibways, to evacuate their grand villages at Mille Lacs and Knife Lake, now located themselves on Rum River. Smarting under the loss of their ancient village sites, and their best hunting grounds and rice lakes, they determined to make one more united and national effort to stem the advance of their troublesome and persevering enemies, and drive them back to the shores of Lake Superior.

Having for some years past been enjoying an active communion with the French traders, they had become supplied with fire-arms, and in this respect they now stood on the same footing with the Ojibways, who had long had the advantage over them, of having been first reached by the whites.

War parties formed at the different villages of the Dakotas, and met by appointment at the Falls of St. Anthony, where the ceremonies preceding the march of Indian warriors into an enemy's country being performed, the party, consisting of from four to five hundred men, embarked in their canoes, and proceeding up the Mississippi, reached, without meeting an enemy, the confluence of the Crow Wing River with the " Father of Rivers."

It was but a short time previous that they had possessed and occupied the country lying on and about the head-waters of the Mississippi, and being thus perfectly familiar with the route and portages from lake to lake, and the usual summer haunts of the Indian hunter, they determined to make the grand circuit by Gull, Leech, Cass, and Winnepegosish Lakes, and descending the Mississippi from its head, pick up the stray hunters and rice-gatherers of their enemy, and attack the village of the western Ojibways at Sandy Lake. Carrying this plan of their campaign into execution, the Dakotas ascended the Crow Wing and Gull Rivers into Gull Lake, from the northern extremity of which they made their first portage. Carrying their canoes about two miles, they again embarked on Lake Sibley; making another portage, they passed into White Fish, or Ud-e-kum-ag Lake, and through a series of lakes into Wab-ud-ow Lake, where they spilt the first Ojibway blood, killing a hunter named Wab-ud-ow (White Gore), from which circumstance the lake is named to this day by the Ojibways. From this place they passed into Gauss Lake, where again they massacred an unfortunate hunter with his wife and children. The tale of this transaction is briefly as follows:—

An Ojibway named Min-ah-ig-want-ig (Drinking Wood), was travelling about in his birch bark canoe, with his family, making his summer hunt. One evening, after dark, he arrived at Gauss Lake, where seeing a long line of fires lighting the shore, and supposing it to be the encampment of a war party of Rainy Lake Ojibways on their way to the Dakota country, he silently but confidently approached the shore to camp with them. On hearing, however, the language of their enemies spoken, he discovered his mistake, and quickly backing out, he entered the mouth of a little creek, and pushing his canoe into a clump of tall grass, or rushes, he and his family passed the night in the canoe, within plain hearing of the loud talking and singing of their enemies.

Towards morning the foolish hunter, placing his paddle

upright behind his back to rest upon, fell asleep. On the first appearance of day, the Dakotas embarked, and one of their canoes passing close to the shore, noticed with an Indian's wariness and sagacity, the mark of a canoe through the grass and weeds at the entry of the little creek. One of the Dakotas arose in his canoe, and seeing the end of the upright paddle sticking up above the tall grass in the creek, he quietly informed his fellows, and the Ojibway, being surrounded, was surprised in his sleep—he and his family killed and scalped, with the exception of one child taken captive.

Much elated, the Dakota war party proceeded on their way, and at Little Boy, or Que-wis-aus Lake, they again attacked and killed three little boys, while engaged in gathering wild rice. Their parents, hearing the noise of the firing incident to the attack, made their escape. From this circumstance, this large and beautiful sheet of water has derived its Ojibway name of Que-wis-aus (Little Boy).

The Dakotas passed into Leech Lake, and crossing over by a short portage into Cass Lake, they commenced their descent of the Mississippi. A short distance above the Falls of Puk-a-gum-ah, they again destroyed an Ojibway hunter and his family. On the banks of the river where this occurrence took place, the Dakotas made marks on the pine trees, which are still discernible to the eye of the traveller. The Ojibways call it Mun-zin-auk-wi-e-gun (tree picture marks).

Some distance below the Falls of Puk-a-gum-ah, they were met and discovered by two Ojibway hunters, in a birch canoe, who turned and fled down the river, warning their fellows as they went. The Dakotas made a warm pursuit, as they wished to attack the village of their enemies at Sandy Lake by surprise. The fleeing hunters, by making short portages across long bends of the river, left their pursuers some distance, and arrived at the Sandy

Lake village during the night, but found a number of the bravest warriors gone on a war party down the Mississippi, and the remainder of the men of their village drinking " fire-water," which had been brought by a number of their fellows, who had just returned from their periodical summer visit to Sault Ste. Marie and Mackinaw. The alarm was given, and the drinking stopped, though many of the older men were already *hors du combat* through the effects of the liquor.   Such as were able, prepared for defence.

One of the young hunters who had arrived to warn the village, having dropped a small looking glass, while crossing a short portage, which is sometimes made from the Mississippi into Sandy Lake, and it being in those days an article rare and much valued among them, he returned early in the morning to look for it.   He went alone in his light birch canoe, but found the portage covered with the Dakotas who had been pursuing them.   Some were crossing in their canoes, while the main body were making their way on foot to attack the Ojibway village by land. On being discovered, a hot pursuit in canoes was made after the young hunter by the Dakotas, and being single in his canoe, they fast gained on him.   Making straight for an island which lies directly in front of the village, the young man landed, pulled his canoe across the island, and again embarking, paddled away for life.   By this manœuvre he gained a little on his pursuers, who were obliged to round the point of an island in their heavier canoes. The Dakotas, however, being full manned, caught up with and dispatched the fleeing hunter before he reached the main shore, and in full sight of the Ojibway village.

In the mean time, the party who were approaching to attack the village by land, discovered a party of Ojibway women, who were picking huckleberries, whom they surrounded and easily captured.   These female captives, most of whom were young and unmarried, numbered thirty.

The Dakotas then attacked the village, but such of the
Ojibways as were sober, and had got over their drunken
frolic, having made their preparations, manfully resisted
the attack, till the drunken warriors, being brought to
their sober senses by being frequently immersed in cold
water by the women, increased the ranks of the defenders,
and after a desperate struggle finally succeeded in causing
the Dakotas to retreat, who returning to their canoes, embarked with their prisoners, and continued their course
down the Mississippi, triumphing in the repeated blows
they had inflicted on their enemies.

They were doomed, however, to run a severe gauntlet
before reaching their villages, and to pay dearly for the
temerity which had led them to proceed so far into the
country which the Ojibways claimed as their own. A
party of sixty Ojibway warriors had, a short time previous,
left their village at Sandy Lake (as has been mentioned),
and under the leadership of Waus-uk-o-gub-ig, a distinguished war-chief, they proceeded down the Mississippi in
their birchen canoes, to the haunts of their enemies. Meeting with no success in their foray after scalps, they left
their canoes in the enemy's country, and were returning
home on foot, when, arriving at Crow Wing, they discovered the late encampment of the Dakotas, who were
making the grand circuit of the northern country.

From the marks thus discovered, the Ojibways became
satisfied that the enemy, who had gone up the Crow Wing
River, would either soon return the same way, or come
down the Mississippi, after having perhaps massacred
their wives and children at Sandy Lake. They determined,
therefore, to await their coming at the confluence of these
rivers, and notwithstanding the apparent strength of their
enemies, to give them battle.

About half a mile below the main mouth of the Crow

Wing, and a few rods above Allan Morrison's present[1] establishment, or trading post, on the east side of the Mississippi, the river makes a curve, and the whole force of the current is thrown against the banks in the bend, which rise almost perpendicular from the water's edge, fifty feet high, and on the brow of which stands a few pine trees. Boats or canoes passing down the river are naturally drawn by the current immediately under this bank ; and, with an eye to these advantages, the Ojibway warriors determined to post themselves here in ambuscade. They dug several holes along this bank, for two or three hundred feet, capable of holding eight or ten men each, in rows, from which, perfectly invisible to their passing enemy, and sheltered from their missiles, they intended to commence the attack.

Satisfied at the immense odds they would have to contend with, they made every preparation. Hunters were sent out to kill and dry meat sufficient to sustain the whole party for several days, and scouts were sent some distance above the river, to watch the first coming of their enemies.

One morning after their preparations had all been completed, one of their scouts, who had been sent about a mile up the Mississippi, and who was watching on the bank for the first appearance of the Dakotas, descended carelessly to the water's edge to drink. While lapping the water with his hand to his lips, looking up the river, he perceived a canoe suddenly turn a point of land above him. Instinctively he threw himself flat on the ground, and gradually crawled unperceived up the bank. When out of sight, on looking back, he saw the whole bosom of the river covered with the war canoes of those for whose coming he had been sent to watch. Seeing that he had not been noticed, he flew back to his comrades, who now prepared fully for the approaching conflict, by putting on their war paints and ornaments of battle.

[1] A. D. 1852.

Directly opposite the main mouth of the Crow Wing, on the spot where the American Fur Company's post is now[1] located, and in plain view of their ambuscade, the Ojibways saw their enemies disembark, and proceed to cook their morning meal. They saw the large group of female prisoners, as they were roughly pushed ashore, and made to build the fires and hang the kettles. Amongst them, doubtless, were their wives, daughters, or sisters. They saw the younger warriors of the enemy form in a ring, and dance, yelling and rejoicing, over the scalps they had taken. They saw all this, and burning with rage, they impatiently awaited the moment when their foes would come within range of their bullets and arrows. With difficulty the leader restrained his younger and more fool-hardy warriors from rushing forth to attack their enemies while engaged in their orgies.

Amongst the captives was an old woman, who at every encampment, had exhorted her fellows not to be cast down in their spirits, for their men who had gone on a war party would certainly, at some place, attack their captors, and in this case they must upset the canoes they were in, and swim for life to the shore from which their friends would make the attack. In this manner did she teach " her grand-children," as she called them, to be prepared for a sudden onslaught.

The Dakotas, having finished their morning meal, and scalp-dancing, once more poured into their canoes. They floated down with the current in a compact mass, holding on to each other's canoes, while filling and lighting their pipes, and passing them from one to another, to be alternately smoked. Above them, dangling from the ends of poles, were the bloody scalps they had taken. In the foremost canoes were the war leaders, and planted before them were the war ensigns of feathers. After smoking out their

[1] A. D. 1852.

pipes, the Jeen-go-dum[1] was uttered by the whole party, with a tremendous noise. The drums commenced beating, accompanied with yells and songs of triumph. Still moving in a compact flotilla, in full rejoicing, the force of the current at length brought them immediately under the deadly ambuscade of their enemies.

The moment had now come which the Ojibways had so long been aching for, and at the sound of their leader's war-whistle, they suddenly let fly a flight of bullets and barbed arrows into the serried ranks of the enemies, picking out for death the most prominent and full plumed figures amongst them. Yelling their fear-striking sas-sak-way, or war-whoop, they sent their deadly missiles like hail amongst their enemies, sending many of their bravest warriors to the land of spirits. The confusion amongst the Dakotas at this sudden and unexpected attack was immense. The captives overturned the canoes they were in, and the rest running against one another, and those in the water struggling to re-embark, and the sudden jumps of those that were wounded, caused many of them to overturn, leaving their owners struggling in the deep current. Many were thus drowned, and as long as they remained within range of their enemies' weapons, the Dakotas suffered severely.

Some dove and swam ashore on the opposite side—then running down the bank of the river, they joined those of their fellows who still floated, about a mile below the place of the attack, where they all landed and collected their upturned canoes, and such of their articles as floated past. Many of their captives made their escape by swimming to their friends. Some were dispatched at the first onset, and the few that still remained in their hands, the Dakotas took and tied to trees, to await the consequences of the

---

[1] The Jeen-go-dum is a peculiar cry, uttered by warriors after killing an enemy.

coming struggle, for, smarting under the loss of their bravest men, and having noticed the comparatively small numbers of the Ojibways, they determined to go back and fight the battle anew, and revenge the death of their relatives.

They bravely made the attack, but the Ojibways were so strongly and securely posted, that they sustained the fight till dark without losing any of their men, while the Dakotas suffered severely, being obliged to fight from open ground, without shelter. The fight lasted till night, when the Dakotas retreated. They encamped where they had landed, and in plain view and hearing of their enemies, who, during the night distinctly heard their lamentations, as they wept for their relatives who had been slain during the day's fight.

In the morning, the Dakotas, burning for vengeance, returned to the attack. Acting with greater caution and wariness, they approached the Ojibway defences by diging counter holes, or making embankments of earth or logs before them, to shield them from their missiles. The ammunition of the contending warriors failing them, the Dakotas dug their hiding holes so close to those of their foes, that large stones were easily thrown from hole to hole. In this manner, a late noted Ojibway chief named We-eshcoob (Sweet), who was then a young man, received a stunning blow on his face, which broke his jawbone. Some of the bravest warriors fought hand to hand with clubs and knives, and the Ojibways lost one of their number, who, fighting rather rashly, was dispatched by a Dakota brave, and scalped.

The Ojibways, however, defended themselves so obstinately, that they eventually forced their enemies to retreat. Having suffered a severe loss, the Dakota warriors returned to their villages, and for fear that the Ojibways would retaliate, by making a similar incursion into their country,

the M'dé-wak-an-ton section of the tribe evacuated the
Rum River country, and moved to the Minnesota River.

DAKOTA LEGEND.

The following Dakota legend connected with the invasion of their tribe to the heads of the Mississippi, of which
we have given the preceding account, was related to the
writer by Waub-o-jeeg (White Fisher), a chief of the Mississippi Ojibways, who being of part Dakota origin, in his
younger days lived more or less with them, and learned to
speak their language. In this manner he picked up many
of their traditions and beliefs, and among the number, the
following simple, but affecting story :—

A young Dakota warrior, eager to gain renown, determined to join the war party which was gathering at his
village at St. Anthony's Falls, and destined to sweep the
Ojibway country, and put out the fires which this tribe
had lighted on the Upper Mississippi. He had just taken
to wife a beautiful girl of his tribe, whom he loved, and
who dearly loved him. She endeavored to dissuade him
from going to war on this occasion. He would not listen
to the soft persuasions, nor allow her loving caresses to
affect his determination, for all the young men of his village were going, and they would laugh at him were he to
remain alone with the women, when there were eagle
plumes and renown to be gained. With tears the young
wife importuned her husband to remain. She told him
that a presentiment weighed on her heart, that he would
never return from this war path.

The young warrior, though he dearly loved his bride,
was resolute in withstanding her persuasions, but to appease
her anxious mind, and her dreams of ill-boding, he
solemnly promised and called on the spirits to hear him,
that he would return to her. Their last parting was sad

and tearful, and she could not even bear to witness the ceremonies attendant on the departure of the warriors from their village. She counted every day of his absence, and as the days increased in number, she daily eagerly looked for his return. The warriors had overstayed the appointed number of days, in which they had promised to return, and they were now hourly expected back to their homes. Their wives and sweethearts decked themselves out in their finery, in anticipation of their coming.

The anxious young wife retired to the water's side early one morning, and sat down on the grassy banks of the flowing Mississippi, to comb and braid her long and beautiful hair. The glassy surface of the bright waters at her feet served her for a mirror. Notwithstanding her former presentiments, she expected the return of her young husband that day, for he had solemnly promised it by the name of the spirits. She prepared, therefore, to appear to him to the best advantage. As she cast her eyes at the current which sluggishly swept past her feet, she noticed a dark object floating beneath the surface of the waters. The circling eddies brought it to her feet, and with a slight scream of surprise, and a cold thrill at her heart, she recognized a human figure. Instinctively she sprang forward, and catching the body by the arm, pulled it partly on shore. As if an ice bolt had been applied to her heart, she knew the features of her young husband. The feathered end of a barbed arrow which had pierced his heart, still stuck from his breast. He had kept his promise—he had returned, indeed, but in death. The young, heart-broken wife, uttering a piercing shriek, fell senseless on the inanimate body. The villagers hearing that despairing cry, ran to the water's side, and at sight of the dead warrior, they received the first intimation of the loss which their warriors had suffered at Crow Wing fight. The young husband had probably been killed while floating down the river in his canoe, at the first fire of the ambushed Ojibways, and the current might naturally have taken his body to the spot where his wife was awaiting his arrival, while his fellows were fighting at Crow Wing, and during their return homeward.

The shattered remains of this grand war party returned the same day. The young wife whose presentiment had thus been most awfully fulfilled, pined away, and wept herself to death. She died happy in the hope and belief of rejoining her young warrior husband, in the happy land of spirits.

CHAPTER XIX.

PROGRESS OF THE OJIBWAYS ON THE UPPER MISSISSIPPI.

Ojibways of Sandy Lake send a war party into the Dakota country—They attack a village on the banks of the Minnesota River—Origin of the Ojibway name of this river— Ke-che-waub-ish-ash leads a party of 120 warriors against the Dakotas—Accidental meeting with a party of the enemy of equal strength at Elk River—Indian fight—The retreating Dakotas are reinforced —Retreat of the Ojibways—They make a firm stand—The Dakotas set the prairie on fire—Final flight of the Ojibways, who take refuge on an island— A second fight on Elk River, " Battle Ground"—Death of the war chief Ke-che-waub-ish-ash—Brief sketch of his life.

IN order to retaliate on the Dakotas the invasion which they had made on the Upper Mississippi, which resulted in the battle of Crow Wing, and the capturing of their women at Sandy Lake, the Ojibways, early the following spring, collected a war party nearly two hundred strong, who, embarking in their birch canoes, paddled down the current of the Mississippi into the country of their enemies. They discovered no signs of the Dakotas in the course of their journey as far down as the mouth of Crow River, within thirty miles of St. Anthony Falls. Here they left their canoes, and proceeding across the country to the Minnesota River, they discovered a village of their enemies situated a short distance from its confluence with the Mississippi. The attack on this village, though severely contested by the Dakotas, was perfectly successful, and the war party returned home with a large number of scalps. The incidents of this fight were told to me by Waub-o-jeeg (White Fisher), a present living sub-chief of the Mississippi Ojibways, whose grandfather No-ka acted as one of the leaders of this party ; but as his accounts are somewhat obscure, and much mixed with the unnatural, I refrain from giving the details.

This incursion to the Dakota country is, however, notable from the fact, that it is the first visit of the kind which the Ojibways of this section tell of their ancestors having made to the Minnesota River. When the warriors left their homes in the north, it was early spring, and the leaves had not yet budded. On arriving at the Minnesota River, however, they were surprised to find spring far advanced, and the leaves on the trees which shaded its waters, in full bloom. From this circumstance they gave it the name of Osh-ke-bug-e-sebe, denoting " New Leaf River," which name it has retained among the Ojibways to the present day.

A few years after the incursion of No-ka to the Minnesota River, the Ojibways again collected a war party of one hundred and twenty men, and under the leadership of Ke-che-waub-ish-ashe (Great Marten) a noted warrior, who acted as the war chief of Bi-aus-wah, they embarked in their canoes, and floated down the Mississippi, which they had now learned to make their chief and favorite war course. On their way down the river, the leader every morning deputed a canoe of scouts to proceed some distance in advance of the main body, to search for signs of the enemy, and runners were sent ahead by land, to follow down each bank of the river, to prevent a surprise of the party from an ambuscade of the enemy. Guarded in this manner from any sudden surprise, the Ojibway warriors quietly floated down with the current of the great river. On this occasion they had reached a point a short distance above the mouth of Elk River, when the scouts in the foremost canoe, as they were silently paddling down, hugging the eastern bank of the Mississippi, immediately below an extensive bottom of forest trees, heard loud talking and laughing in the Dakota language, on the bank just above them. Instantly they turned the bow of their canoe up stream, and swiftly stealing along close to the bank they escaped undiscovered, behind the point of the heavy wooded bottom, we have mentioned. Here they met the main party of their fellows, whose canoes nearly covered the broad bosom of the river for half a mile. The scouts threw up the water with their paddles as a signal for them to make for the eastern bank, and this signal being made from canoe to canoe, the warriors soon leaped ashore and pulling their canoes upon the grassy bank, they waited but to rub on their faces and bodies the war paints, ornament their heads with eagle plumes, and secure on their bodies the pe-na-se-wi-ame, or war medicine sack, they rushed on without order through the wooded bottom, and as they emerged one after another on the open prairie, they saw a long line of Dakota warriors, about equal in numbers to themselves, walking leisurely along, following the war path against their villages.

They were out of bullet range from the edge of the wood, but the Ojibway warriors rushed out on the open prairie towards them, as if to a feast, and " first come was to be best served." Their war whoop was bravely answered back by the Dakotas who now, for the first time, perceived them, and bullet was returned for bullet. The warriors of both parties leaped continually from side to side, to prevent their enemies from taking a sure aim ; and as they stood confronting one another for a few moments on the open prairie, exchanging quick successive volleys, their bodies in continual motion, the plumes on their heads waving to and fro, and uttering their fierce, quick, sharp battle cry, they must have presented a singular and wild appearance. For a short time only, the Dakotas stood the eager onset of the Ojibways. For, seeing warrior after warrior emerging in quick succession from the wood, in a line of half a mile, they began to think that the enemy many times out-

numbered them, and under this impression, dropping their
blankets and other incumbrances, they turned and fled
down the prairie towards the mouth of Elk River. As
they ran, they would occasionally turn and fire back at
their pursuers. And in this manner, a running fight was
kept up for about three miles, when the Dakotas met a
large party of their fellows who had come across from the
Minnesota River to join them in their excursion against
the Ojibways. With this addition, they outnumbered
the Ojibways more than double, and the chase was now
turned the other way.

The Ojibways, hard pressed by the fresh reinforcements
of their enemy, ran up and along the banks of Elk
River, till, becoming wearied by their long run, they
made a firm stand in a grove of oak trees, which skirt a
small prairie near the banks of Elk River. Here the fight
was sustained for a long time, the Ojibways firing from
the shelter of the oak trees, and the Dakotas digging holes
in the ground on the open prairie, and thus gradually
approaching the covert of their enemies. The Ojibways,
however, manfully stood their ground, and the Dakotas
after losing many lives in the attempt to dislodge them,
resorted to a new and singular expedient. A strong south
wind was blowing, and being the spring of the year, before
the green grass had grown to any length, the prairie was
still covered with a thick coating of the last year's dry
grass. To this the Dakotas set fire, and it blowing
immediately against the Ojibways, the raging flames
very soon caused them to leave their covert, and seek
for safety in flight. It required the utmost endeavors of
their best runners to keep ahead of the flames, and those
who had been wounded during the course of the previous
conflict, were soon caught and devoured by the raging
element.

The Ojibways fled panting for breath, in the dense smoke of the burning prairie, towards the Mississippi, and jumping into its waters, they eventually took refuge on an island. It is said that the froth hung in wide flakes from the lips of the tired warriors as they reached this, their last covert. The Dakotas followed them closely in the wake of the murderous fire which they had lit, but they dare not attack them on the island, where they had sought refuge, and from this point, after one of the most terrible combats which is told of them in their traditions, both parties returned to their respective villages.

The Ojibways acknowledge to have lost eight of their warriors at the hands of the Dakotas, and three caught and consumed by the flames. They claim having made a much greater havoc in the ranks of their enemies, especially during the time they fought from the secure shelter of the oak grove. And as the Dakotas have always acknowledged them as being the better shots during battle, it is not at all unlikely that they suffered a severe loss in killed and wounded on this occasion.

On the following year it happened that the Ojibways, to the number of sixty, again proceeded down the Mississippi on a war party, and on the very spot where the preceding year they had accidentally met the Dakotas, they again met them in greater force than ever.   From all accounts which I have gathered, the enemy, on this occasion, numbered full four hundred warriors, but the hardy Ojibways, again under the guidance of their brave war-chief, Big Marten, although they first discovered the enemy, refused to retreat, and the camps remained in sight of each other's fires during the first night of their meeting. The Ojibways, however, prepared for the coming battle. They dug holes two or three feet deep in the ground, large enough to hold one and two men, from which they intended to withstand

the attack which the Dakotas, through their great superiority of numbers, were expected to make on the following day.

Early the ensuing morning the enemy possessed themselves of a wood which lay within bullet range of the Ojibway defences, and the fight actively commenced. Each
party fighting from behind secure shelters, the battle was
kept up the whole day without much loss to either side.
It was only on occasions when an enemy was seen to fall,
that the bravest warriors would rush from their coverts, to
secure the scalp, and the opposite party as eager to prevent
their man from being thus mutilated, would rally about
his body, and the conflict between the bravest warriors
would be, for a few moments, hand to hand, and deadly.

On an occasion of this nature, the Ojibways, towards
evening, lost their brave leader, the " Big Marten," who
was foremost in every charge, and fighting but little from
behind a covert, he had been, during the day, the most
prominent mark of the Dakota bullets. At night the
enemy retreated, but camped again within sight of the Ojibways, who, discouraged at the loss of their brave war-chief,
made a silent retreat during the darkness of the night, and
returned to their village at Sandy Lake.

From the circumstance of two battles having been
fought in such quick succession on the point of land between the Elk and Mississippi Rivers, this spot has been
named by the Ojibways, Me-gaud-e-win-ing, or " Battle
Ground."

Ke-che-waub-ish-ash, who fell lamented by his tribe at
the last of these two fights, belonged, as his name denotes,
to the Clan of the Marten. He was a contemporary of Bi-
aus-wah, and the right-hand man of this noted chief. He
was the war-chief of the Upper Mississippi, and tradition
says, that his arm, above all others, conduced to drive the
Dakotas from the country covered by the sources of the

great river. While Bi-aus-wah acted as the civil and peace chief, Ke-che-waub-ish-ash influenced the warriors, and when the war was raging between his people and the Dakotas, into his hands its direct management was entrusted. He figured in every important engagement which we have mentioned as taking place between the Sandy Lake Ojibways and their enemies. He was noted for great hardihood and bravery, and he fell at the last, deeply lamented by his people, at Elk River fight, covered with wounds received in a hundred fights. He is one of the few whose name will long be remembered in Ojibway tradition.

CHAPTER XX.

CLOSING OF THE WAR BETWEEN THE OJIBWAYS AND ODUGAMIES.

The Odugamies, after partially regaining their former numbers, make their
last tribal effort against the Ojibways—Battle of St. Croix Falls—Tradition
of this event, as told by the Ojibways—Waub-o-jeeg collects a war party at
La Pointe—He proceeds at the head of 300 men into the Dakota country—
Failure of the Sandy Lake warriors to keep their appointment—Landing of
the Ojibways at the head of the St. Croix Falls—They discover the allied
Odugamies and Dakotas landing at the foot of the Falls—Preparations for
battle—Ojibways and Odugamies engage—Odugamies are beaten, and
Dakotas rally to their rescue—Ojibways are forced to retreat, but are reinforced by 60 warriors from Sandy Lake—Disastrous flight and loss of their
enemies—Waub-o-jeeg loses his brother, and is himself wounded—Remnants of the Odugamies ask to be incorporated with the Osaugees—Their
prayer is granted—Waub-o-jeeg—A sketch of his life.

THE Odugamies (Foxes), who had been forced by the
Ojibways during the French domination to retire from the
Wisconsin and Fox Rivers to the Mississippi, had, under
the guardianship of the Osaugees, partially regained their
former strength and numbers; and, still smarting from the
repeated and powerful blows which their fathers had
received at the hands of the Ojibways about eighty years
ago, they made their last grand tribal effort to revenge
their wrongs and regain a portion of their former country.

They ascended in war canoes the current of the broad
Mississippi, and prevailing on their former allies, the
Dakotas, to join them, together they proceeded up the
St. Croix. While crossing their canoes over the portage
at the Falls of this river, they encountered a war party of
Ojibways, and here, among the rocks and boulders of the
St. Croix, the Odugamies fought their last tribal battle.

The account which the old men of the Ojibways give of
this important event is briefly as follows: Waub-o-jeeg

(White Fisher), the son of Ma-mong-e-se-da, had succeeded on his father's death, to the war chieftainship of the Lake Superior Ojibways. He was a brave and a wise man, who had already become famous for the success of every party which he joined, or led, against the hereditary enemies of his tribe. On this occasion, he sent his club of war, tobacco, and wampum, to all the scattered bands of the Ojibways, to collect a war party to proceed against the Dakota villages on the St. Croix and Mississippi, who had lately very much annoyed their hunting camps in this district. Warriors from the Falls of St. Marie, Grand Island, Kuk-ke-wa-on-an-ing (L'Ance), the Wisconsin and Grand Portage, obeyed his call, and at the head of three hundred men Waub-o-jeeg started from La Pointe, Shaug-a-waum-ik-ong.

In their light birch-bark canoes, they ascended the left branch of the Mush-kee-se-be or "Bad River," to its head, and made a portage of ten miles in length to Long Lake, a beautiful sheet of clear water which lies on the dividing summit between the Mississippi and Lake Superior. Making three more short portages from lake to lake, they at last embarked on the Num-a-kaug-un branch of the St. Croix, and having now entered the dangerous country of their enemies, the wise leader proceeded slowly, keeping scouts continually ahead, to prevent surprise from an ambuscade. It took him six days to descend to the mouth of Snake River, where he expected to meet a party of warriors from the Sandy Lake and Mille Lac villages. He had sent them his war club and tobacco, with word that "at a given time he would be on the waters of the St. Croix searching for their enemies," and they had sent tobacco and word in return, that "sixty of their warriors would join him on a certain day at the meeting of the waters of the Snake and St. Croix Rivers." On arriving at the spot designated, Waub-o-jeeg discovered no signs of the promised party, but still confident in his numbers, he continued on his course down stream.

The Ojibways arrived at the head of the St. Croix Falls (a distance of two hundred and fifty miles from their starting point), early in the morning, and while preparing to take their bark canoes over the rugged portage, or carrying place, the scouts who had been sent in advance, returned with the information that a very large war party of Odugamies and Dakotas were landing at the foot of the falls, apparently with the intention of crossing over their wooden canoes. Now, commenced the hurry and excitement of approaching battle. The "novices," or those of the party who were on their first war path, were forcibly driven back into the water by the elder warriors, there to wash off the black paint which denoted their condition of initiates into the mysteries of war. This customary procedure on the eve of an attack or battle, being performed, the warriors grasped their medicine bags, and hurriedly adorned their faces and naked bodies with war paint, those that earned them planted the eagle plumes on their headdress, which denoted enemies they had slain or scalps taken, and the pe-na-se-wi-am, holding the charms of supposed invulnerability, were attached to different portions of their head-dress, armlets, or belts.

During this busy scene of preparation for the coming contest, the war leader called on the Great Spirit with a loud voice for protection to his followers and success against their enemies. Then addressing his fellows, his clear voice rang among the rocks and mingled with the noise of the waterfall, as he urged them to fight like men, be strong of heart, at the same time advising them to be careful of their lives, that their relatives might not weep in mourning for their loss. Having finished these customary preparations, the Ojibways, grasping their arms, proceeded to find their enemies. The scouts of their opponents had already discovered them, and the two parties, as if by mutual agreement, met in the middle of the portage. The battle which ensued was the most chivalric which is told of in their traditions. The Odugamies, after seeing the comparatively small number of the Ojibways, and over confident in the prowess of their own more numerous warriors, are said to have requested their allies, the Dakotas, to stand quietly by, to witness how quickly they would gather the scalps of the Ojibways.

This request was granted, and the Dakotas retired to an adjacent eminence, and calmly filling their pipes, they viewed the conflict as though perfectly unconcerned. The fight between the warriors of the two contending tribes, is said to have been fiercely contested, and embellished with many daring acts of personal valor. The voices of the war chiefs resounded above the rattle of musketry and yells of their warriors, as they urged them to stand their ground, and not turn their backs in flight. In fact the nature of the ground on which they fought was such, that retreat was almost impracticable for either party. It was a mere rugged neck of rock, cut up into deep ravines, through which the deep and rapid current of the river forces a narrow passage, and at either end of the portage a sudden embarkation into their frail canoes could not safely be effected in face of an enemy. There is a wood around the portage on the land side, inclosing the neck of rock over which it leads, and only through this could the beaten party safely retreat. Waub-o-jeeg, early in the fight secured this important point, by sending thither a number of his warriors.

About midday, after fighting with great desperation, the Odugamies began to give ground, and they were at last forced to turn and flee in confusion. They would probably have been killed and driven into the river to a man, had not their allies, the Dakotas, arose from their seats at this juncture, and yelling their war-whoop, rushed to the rescue of their discomfited allies. The Ojibways resisted their new enemies manfully, and it was not till their ammunition had entirely failed, that they in turn showed their backs in flight. But few would tell the sad tale of defeat and the death of brave men, had not the party of sixty warriors from Sandy Lake, who were to have joined them at the mouth of Snake River, arrived at this opportune moment, and landed at the head of the portage. Eager for the fight, and fresh on the field, the band rushed forward and withstood the onset of the Odugamies and Dakotas, till their friends could rally again to the battle.

After a short but severe contest, the warriors of the two allied tribes were forced to flee, and the slaughter in their ranks is said to have been great. Many were driven over the rocks into the boiling floods below, there to find a watery grave. Others, in attempting to jump into their narrow wooden canoes, were capsized into the rapids. Every crevice in the cliffs where the battle had been fought, contained a dead or wounded enemy. The Ojibways suffered a severe loss in the death of a large number of their bravest warriors. The brother of Waub-o-jeeg was numbered among the dead, and the war-chief himself carried on his person the marks of the sanguinary fight, in a wound on his breast. But a few of the Odugamies escaped, and from this time they forever gave up the contest with the victorious Ojibways. They retired to the south, far away from the reach of the war-club, which had so often made them to weep, and now so nearly exterminated their warriors.

The old Ojibway chief, "Great Buffalo," of La Pointe, says that the fire of the Odugamies was, by this last stroke, nearly extinguished, and they were reduced to fifteen lodges. A second time they went weeping to the village of the Osaugees, who had intermarried with them to a considerable extent, and begged to be incorporated in their tribe, and to live under their powerful protection. They offered to be their cutters of wood and carriers of water, and filled with compassion at their broken numbers and tears of sorrow, the Osaugees, who are a family of the Algic stock, at last, for the first time, formally received them into their tribe, and it is only from this period that the fire of these two tribes (whose names are so linked together in modern history), can be truly said as having become one and undivided.

The old men of the Ojibways assert that the Odugamies speak a distant language,[1] and do not really belong to the Algonquin council fires, and it is only since their close intercourse with the Osaugees that the Algonquin language has become in use among them. I am aware that this assertion is directly contrary to the results of Mr. School-craft's researches, who places the Odugamies as one of the most prominent tribes of the Algics. Never having had the advantage of comparing the peculiar dialect of this tribe with the Ojibway, I am consequently not prepared to deliver a direct opinion. Their warfare with the Oduga-mies has been of such long standing and so sanguinary, that the Ojibways may naturally consider them as much a dis-tinct race from themselves, as the Dakotas or Winnebagoes, the last of whom, in time of peace, they are accustomed to denominate as "younger brothers," which circumstance, however, should not mislead us into the belief that they consider them as being really a kindred tribe in any closer degree than their being respective families of the red race in general.

[1] A French memoir on the Indians between Lake Erie and the Mississippi River, prepared in 1718, and which appears as Paris, Doc. vii. in N. Y. Col. Doc. vol. ix., contains this statement : " The Foxes are eighteen leagues from the Sacs, they number five hundred men, abound in women and children, are as indus-trious as they can be, and have a different language from the Outaouaes. An Outaouae interpreter would be of no use with the Foxes."—E. D. N.

As I shall not probably again have occasion to mention, in the further course of my narrative, the name of the distinguished war-chief who led the Ojibways in the battle of St. Croix Falls, which so effectually put a final stop to their old war with the Odugamies, I will here present to the reader a brief account of his short but brilliant career.

Mr. Schoolcraft, in one of his valuable works on the red race, has given an elaborate notice of the life of this noted chieftain, and as he doubtless obtained his information from his direct descendants, nearly thirty years since, when he acted in the official capacity of United States agent among the Ojibways, and when the acts of Waub-o-jeeg were still comparatively new in the traditions of his tribe, the account which he has given can be implicitly relied on, and very little, if anything, can be added to it.

We glean from this, that Waub-o-jeeg was born about the year 1747. He early gave indications of courage, and, Mr. Schoolcraft relates this anecdote, that on the occasion which we have mentioned in a previous chapter, when his father, Ma-mong-e-se-da, turned a sudden attack of the Dakotas on his camp into a peace visit, by calling out for his half-brother, the Dakota chief, Wabasha—Waub-o-jeeg, then a mere boy, posted himself with a war-club close to the door of his father's lodge, and as his tall Dakota uncle entered, he gave him a blow. Wabasha, pleased with the little brave, took him in his arms, caressed him, and predicted that he would become a brave man, and prove an inveterate enemy of the Dakotas. Mr. Schoolcraft continues his biographical notice of Waub-o-jeeg as follows:—

"The border warfare in which the father of the infant warrior was constantly engaged, early initiated him in the arts and ceremonies pertaining to war. With the eager interest and love of novelty of the young, he listened to their war songs and war stories, and longed for the time when he would be old enough to join these parties, and also make himself a name among warriors. While quite a youth, he volunteered to go out with a party, and soon gave convincing proof of his courage. He also early learned the arts of hunting the deer, the bear, the moose, and all the smaller animals common to the country; and in these pursuits he took the ordinary lessons of Indian young men in abstinence, suffering, danger, and endurance of fatigue. In this manner his nerves were knit and formed for activity, and his mind stored with those lessons of caution which are the result of local experience in the forest. He possessed a tall and commanding person, with a full, black, piercing eye, and the usual features of his countrymen. He had a clear and full-toned voice, and spoke his native language with grace and fluency. To these attractions he united an early reputation for bravery and skill in the chase, and at the age of twenty-two, he was already a war leader."

Expeditions of one Indian tribe against another require the utmost caution, skill, and secrecy. There are a hundred things to give information to such a party, or influence its action, which are unknown to civilized nations. The breaking of a twig, the slightest impression of a foot-print, and other like circumstances, determine a halt, a retreat, or an advance. The most scrupulous attention is also paid to the signs of the heavens, the flight of birds, and above all to the dreams and predictions of the jos-so-keed, priest or prophet, who accompanies them, and who is intrusted with the sacred sack. The theory upon which all these parties are conducted, is secrecy and stratagem; to steal upon the enemy unawares; to lay in ambush, or decoy; to kill, and to avoid as much as possible the hazard of being killed. An intimate geographical knowledge of the country is also required by a successful war leader, and such a man piques himself not only upon knowing every prominent stream, hill, valley, wood, or rock, but the particular productions, mineral and vegetable, of the scene of operations. When it is considered that this species of knowledge, shrewdness, and sagacity is possessed on both sides, and that the nations at war watch each other as a lynx for its prey, it may be conceived that many of these border war parties are either light skirmishes, sudden on-rushes, or utter failures. It is seldom that a close, well-contested, long-continued hand battle is fought. To kill a few men, tear off their scalps in haste, and retreat with these trophies, is a brave and honorable trait with them, and may be boasted of in their triumphal dances and war-like festivities.

" To glean the details of these movements would be to acquire the modern history of the tribe, which induced me to direct my inquiries to the subject; but the lapse of even forty or fifty years, had shorn traditions of most of these details, and often left the memory of results only. The Chippeways told me that this chief had led them seven times to successful battle against the Sioux and Outagamies, and that he had been wounded thrice—once in the thigh, once in the right shoulder, and a third time in the side and breast, being a glancing shot. His war party consisted either of volunteers, who had joined his standard at the war dance, or of auxiliaries, who had accepted his messages of wampum and tobacco, and came forward in a body to the appointed place of rendezvous. These parties varied greatly in number. His first party consisted of but forty men; his greatest and most renowned of three hundred, who were mustered from the villages on the shores of the lake, as far east as St. Mary's Falls."

This last party is the one which Waub-o-jeeg led in the battle of the St. Croix, an account of which Mr. Schoolcraft proceeded to give. Respecting the details of this important occurrence, however, it appears that he has received but meagre information, as he finishes it in a single paragraph.

He does not mention the sixty warriors from Sandy Lake, who decided the fate of the battle, and which swelled the ranks of Waub-o-jeeg to three hundred and sixty warriors. The tradition of this event is still clearly related by the Ojibways of the Mississippi, they having learned it from the lips of their fathers who were present at the battle.

After giving in verse the plaintive lament of Waub-o-jeeg for the warriors who fell at St. Croix Falls, Mr. Schoolcraft, who, through his long official connection with the Ojibways, obtained an accurate knowledge of their general customs and mode of passing the different seasons of the year, continues in his forcible and lucid style to give a faithful picture of Indian life:

"It is the custom of these tribes to go to war in the spring and summer, which are not only comparatively seasons of leisure with them, but it is at these seasons that they are concealed and protected by the foliage of the forest, and can approach the enemy unseen. At these annual returns of warmth and vegetation, they also engage in festivities and dances, during which the events and exploits of past years are sung and recited: and while they derive fresh courage and stimulus to renewed exertion, the young, who are listeners, learn to emulate their fathers, and take their earliest lessons in the art of war.

"Nothing is done in the summer months in the way of hunting. The small furred animals are changing their pelt, which is out of season. The doe retires with her fawns from the plains and open grounds, into thick woods. It is the general season of reproduction, and the red man, for a time, intermits his war on the animal creation, to resume it against man. As the autumn approaches, he prepares for his fall hunts, by retiring from the outskirts of the settlements and from the open lakes, shores, and streams, which have been the scenes of his summer festivities, and proceeds, after a short preparatory hunt, to his wintering grounds. This round of hunting, festivity, and war, fills up the year; all the tribes conform in these general customs. There are no war parties raised in the winter. This season is exclusively devoted to procuring the means of their subsistence and clothing, by seeking the valuable skins which are to purchase their clothing and their ammunition, traps, and arms.

"The hunting grounds of the chief, whose life we are considering, extended along the southern shores of Lake Superior, from the Montreal River, to the inlet of the Wis-a-co-da, or Burnt Wood River of Fond du Lac. If he ascended the one, he usually made the wide circuit indicated, and came out at the other. He often penetrated by a central route up the Mas-ki-go, or Bad River. This is a region still abounding, but less so than formerly, in the bear, moose, beaver, otter, marten, and muskrat. Among the smaller animals are also to be noticed the mink, lynx, hare, porcupine, and partridge, and towards its southern and western limit, the Virginia deer.

"In this ample area, the La Pointe, or Chagoimegon, Indians hunted. It is a rule of the chase, that each hunter has a portion of the country assigned to him, on which he alone may hunt; and there are conventional laws which decide all questions of right and priority in starting and killing game. In these questions, the chief exercises a proper authority, and it is thus in the power of one of these forest governors and magistrates, when they happen to be men of sound sense, judgment, and manly independence, to make themselves felt and known, and to become true benefactors to their tribes. And such chiefs create an impression upon their followers, and leave a reputation behind them, which is of more value than their achievements in war.

"Waub-o-jeeg excelled in both characters; he was equally popular as a civil ruler and war-chief; and while he administered justice to his people, he was an expert hunter, and made due and ample provision for his family. He usually gleaned, in a season, by his traps and carbine, four packs of mixed furs, the avails of which were ample to provide clothing for all the members of his lodge circle, as well as to renew his supply of ammunition and other essential articles.

" On one occasion he had a singular contest with a moose. He had gone out one morning early, to set his traps. He had set about forty, and was returning to his lodge, when he unexpectedly encountered a large moose in his path, which manifested a disposition to attack him. Being unarmed, and having nothing but a knife and small hatchet which he carried to make his traps, he tried to avoid it, but the animal came towards him in a furious manner. He took shelter behind a tree, shifting his position from tree to tree retreating. At length, as he fled, he picked up a pole, and quickly untying his moccasin strings, he bound his knife to the end of the pole. He then placed himself in a favorable position behind a tree, and when the moose came up, stabbed him several times in the throat and breast. At last the animal, exhausted with the loss of blood, fell. He then dispatched him, and cut out his tongue to carry home to his lodge, as a trophy of victory. When they went back to the spot for the carcase, they found the snow trampled down in a wide circle, and copiously sprinkled with blood, which gave it the appearance of a battle-field. It proved to be a male of uncommon size.

" The domestic history of a native chief can seldom be obtained. In the present instance, the facts that follow may be regarded with interest, as having been obtained from residents of Chagoi-me-gon, or from his descendants. He did not take a wife until about the age of thirty, and he then married a widow, by whom he had one son. He had obtained early notoriety as a warrior, which perhaps absorbed his attention. What causes there were to render this union unsatisfactory, or whether there were any, is not known; but after the lapse of two years, he married a girl of fourteen, of the Totem of the Bear, by whom he had a family of six children. He is represented as of a temper and manners affectionate and forbearing. He evinced thoughtfulness and diligence in the management of his affairs, and the order and disposition of his lodge. When the hunting season was over, he employed his leisure moments in adding to the comforts of his lodge. His lodge was of an oblong shape, ten fathoms long, and made by setting two rows of posts firmly in the ground, and sheathing the sides and roof with the smooth bark of the birch. From the centre rose a post crowned with the carved figure of an owl, which he had probably selected as a bird of good omen, for it was neither his own nor his wife's totem. The figure was so placed that it turned with the wind, and answered the purpose of a weather-cock.

"In person, Waub-o-jeeg was tall, being six feet six inches, erect in carriage, and of slender make. He possessed a commanding countenance, united to ease and dignity of manners. He was a ready and fluent speaker, and conducted personally the negotiations with the Fox and Sioux nations. It was perhaps twenty years after the battle on the St. Croix, which established the Chippeway boundary in that quarter, and while his children were still young, that there came to his village in the capacity of a trader, a young gentleman of a respectable family in the north of Ireland, who formed an exalted notion of his character, bearing, and war-like exploits. This visit, and his consequent residence on the lake during the winter, became an important era to the chief, and has linked his name and memory with numerous persons in civilized life. Mr. Johnston asked the northern chief for his youngest daughter.

'Englishman,' he replied, 'my daughter is yet young, and you cannot take her, as white men have too often taken our daughters. It will be time enough to think of complying with your request when you return again to this lake in the summer. My daughter is my favorite child, and I cannot part with her, unless you will promise to acknowledge her by such ceremonies as white men use. You must ever keep her, and never forsake her.' On this basis a union was formed, it may be said, between the Erse and Algonquin races, and it was faithfully adhered to till his death, a period of thirty-seven years.

" Waub-o-jeeg had impaired his health in the numerous war parties which he conducted across the wide summit which separated his hunting grounds from the Mississippi Valley. A slender frame under a life of incessant exertion, brought on a premature decay. Consumption revealed itself at a comparatively early age, and he fell before this insidious disease in a few years, at the early age of about forty-five. He died in 1793, at his native village of Chagoimegon."

Waub-o-jeeg will long live in the traditions of the annals of his tribe. His descendants of mixed blood, by his youngest daughter, who married Mr. Johnston, are now numerous and widespread, being connected with some of the first families in the northwest. Mr. Schoolcraft himself, who is so well known by his numerous valuable works on the red race, married a daughter of this union, who was educated in Ireland. She proved, during the comparatively short period that her life was spared to him, an amiable and loving wife.

CHAPTER XXI.

ORIGIN OF THE DISTINCTIVE NAME OF PILLAGERS APPLIED TO
THE LEECH LAKE BAND OF OJIBWAYS; AND ERA OF THE
SMALLPOX.

General remarks on the character of the Leech Lake Ojibways—Their gradual
increase—Origin of their present distinctive name—Their camp is visited by
a trader from the Lower Mississippi, in the summer of 1781—His inability,
through sickness, to trade—Indians commence to take his goods on credit—
A pillage ensues—Whisky found—The trader is forced to leave, and dies at
Sauk Rapids—The Pillagers send a delegation to Mackinaw to atone for
their conduct—They receive presents from the British—On distribution of
the presents at Fond du Lac they fall sick of the smallpox—Common saying
against the British—Account of the real manner in which the smallpox
came to be introduced among them—War party of Assineboines, Kenistenos,
and Ojibways to the Missouri—Attack on a village of dead enemies—They
catch the infection—The Kenisteno village is depopulated—Course of the
contagion—Loss of lives among the allied tribes.

In the year 1781, the large band of the Ojibways, who
had taken possession of Leech Lake (one of the principal
sources of the Mississippi), became for the first time known
by the distinctive appellation of " Pillagers," Muk-im-dua-
win-in-e-wug (men who take by force).[1]   They had become
noted at this time (and it is a character which they have
retained ever since), as being the bravest band of the tribe.
Being obliged, continually, to fight with the Dakotas for
the country over which they hunted, every man capable of
bearing arms became a warrior and had seen actual service.
They were consequently filled with a daring and indepen-
dent spirit, and no act was so wild, but that they were
ready and disposed to achieve it.

This band was formed mostly of the noted clans of the
Bear, and A-waus-e or Catfish, and at the time which we
are now considering, they probably numbered about one

[1] Henry found " Pillagers" in 1775 at Lake of the Woods.—E. D. N.

hundred warriors. In 1832, Mr. Schoolcraft estimates
their total number of souls at eight hundred. In 1836
Mr. Nicollet estimates them as numbering one thousand,
and in 1851, according to their payment census list, they
number twelve hundred and fifty souls, and their chief
estimates the men who are capable of bearing arms at
about three hundred. These, it will be remembered,
include only the band who make Leech Lake their home,
or summer residence; and it is only these that are known
by the distinctive name of Pillagers. The large bands
residing at the present day at Red, Cass, and Winnepeg
lakes, and on Pembina River, are known by the general
term of Northern Ojibways.

Notwithstanding the never failing yearly drain which
their warfare with the Dakotas have made in their ranks,
yet still, from a natural increase, the healthfulness of the
country they occupy, and gradual accessions from other
villages, this band have increased in numbers and strength,
till they now form a most respectable section of the Ojibway tribe. The manner in which they obtained the
significant name by which they are now generally known,
is told by their old men as follows:—

During the summer of the year which we have designated, the Leech Lake band had moved down towards the
well stocked hunting grounds of the Dakotas, and encamped at the entry of a small creek which empties into
the Crow Wing River, about ten miles above its confluence
with the Mississippi. While making the usual preparations for the performance of their grand medawe rite, a
large canoe arrived from the Lower Mississippi, manned
by white men, and laden with merchandise. The trader
who had, for the first time, come to this far off point of the
great river, had started from a great distance below on its
waters, for the purpose of trading with the Ojibways. He
arrived at their camp very sick, and was not able to enter

immediately into the barter for which the Indians were eager. Some of his goods having got wet by rain, were untied by his men, and exposed to the sun to dry. The temptation to the almost naked Indians, who had not seen a trader for a long time, was too great to be easily overcome, and being on the eve of their grand festival rite, when they are accustomed to display all the finery of which they are possessed, caused them doubly to covet the merchandise of the sick trader. They possessed plenty of furs, which they offered repeatedly to exchange, but the trader's men refused to enter into a trade till their master was sufficiently recovered to oversee it. There was no preconcerted plan, or even intention of pillage, when the rifling of the trader's effects actually commenced.

A number of young men, women, and children, were standing around, admiring the goods which had been exposed to dry, and longing for possession, as much as an avaricious white man for a pile of yellow gold, when a forward young warrior approached a roll of cloth, and after feeling, and remarking on its texture, his itching fingers at last tore off a piece sufficient to make him a breech clout, at the same time he remarked, that he had beaver skins in his lodge, and when the trader got well, he would pay his demands. The trader's men stood dumb, and making no effort to prevent the young pillager from carrying off the cloth, others becoming bold followed his example, and tearing off pieces of calico for shirts, cloth for blankets, the goods spread out to dry soon disappeared at a very uncertain credit.

The young pillagers taking their trophies to the lodges, the excitement in the village became general, as each person became determined to possess a share of the trader's remaining bales. The crediting of the goods was now changed to an actual pillage, and the only anxiety evinced by the Indians, men, women, and children, was, who would secure the greatest quantity. A keg of fire water being discovered in the course of the ransacking the sick trader's outfit, added greatly to the excitement and lawlessness of the scene, and the men soon becoming unmanageable and dangerous, the rifled trader was obliged quickly to embark in his empty canoe, and leave the inhospitable camp of the Ojibways to save his life. It is said that he died of the sickness from which he was suffering, at Sauk Rapids, on his way down the Mississippi.

From this circumstance, this band of the Ojibways became known amongst their fellows (who generally very much deprecated this foolish act), by the name of Pillagers, and the creek on which the scene we have described was enacted, is known to this day as Pillage Creek.

At this time the Upper Mississippi bands had no regular trader to winter among them, and they were obliged to make visits each summer to La Pointe, Sault Ste. Marie, and Mackinaw, to procure the necessaries which their intercourse with the whites had learned them to stand in absolute need, such as clothing, arms, and ammunition, and to *want*, such as fire water. The few traders who had occasionally paid them visits, during this period in their history, had come from the direction of Lake Superior, and the trader who was pillaged, is the first they tell of having come from the Lower Mississippi.

The conduct of the Pillagers in this affair, was generally censured by their more peaceful fellows as foolish and impolitic, as it would tend to prevent traders from coming amongst them for fear of meeting with the same treatment. To make up, therefore, for their misconduct, as well as to avert the evil consequences that might arise from it, the Pillagers on the ensuing spring, gathered a number of packs of beaver skins and sent a delegation headed by one of their principal men to the British fort at Mackinaw, to appease the ill-will of the whites, by returning an ample consideration for the goods which they had pillaged. The British commandant of the fort received the packs of beaver, and in return he assured the Pillagers of his good will and friendship towards them, and strengthened his words by giving their leader a medal, flag, coat, and bale of goods, at the same time requesting that he would not unfurl his flag, nor distribute his goods, until he arrived into his own country.

With this injunction, the Pillager chief complied, till he landed at Fond du Lac, where, anxious to display the great consequence to which the medal and presents of the British had raised him in his own estimation, he formally called his followers to a council, and putting on his chief's coat, and unfurling his flag, he untied his bale of goods, and freely distributed to his fellows. Shortly after, he was taken suddenly sick, and retiring to the woods, he expired by himself, as the discovery of his remains afterwards indicated. All of those who had received a portion of the goods also fell sick, one after another, and died. The sickness became general, and spreading to different villages, its fearful ravages took off a large number of the tribe. It proved to be the smallpox, and many of the Ojibways believed, and it is a common saying to this day, that the white men purposely inflicted it on them by secreting bad medicine in the bale of goods, in punishment for the pillage which the Leech Lake band had committed on one of their traders.

This was a serious charge, and in order to ascertain if it was really entertained by the more enlightened and thinking portions of the tribe, I have made particular inquiries, and flatter myself that I have obtained from the intelligent old chief of the Pillagers, a truthful account of the manner in which the smallpox was, on this occasion, actually introduced among the Ojibways.

A war party of Kenistenos, Assineboines, and Ojibways, was once formed at the great Kenisteno village, which was at this time located on Dead River, near its outlet into the Red River of the North. They proceeded westward to the waters of the Ke-che-pe-gan-o, or Missouri River, till they came to a large village of the Gi-aucth-in-ne-wug (Gros Ventres), which they surrounded and attacked. Through some cause which they could not at first account for, the resistance made to their attack was feeble. This they soon overcame, and the warriors rushing forward to secure their scalps, discovered the lodges filled with dead bodies, and they could not withstand the stench arising therefrom. The party retreated, after securing the scalps of those whom they had killed, among which was the scalp of an old man who must have been a giant in size, as his scalp is said to have been as large as a beaver skin. On their return home, for five successive nights, this scalp, which had been attached to a short stick being planted erect in the ground, was found in the morning to lean towards the west. This simple occurrence aroused the superstitious fears of the party, and when, on the fourth day, one of their number died, they threw away the fearful scalp, and proceeded homeward with quickened speed. Every day, however, their numbers decreased, as they fell sick and died.   Out of the party, which must have numbered a considerable body of warriors, but four survived to return home to their village at Dead River. They brought with them the fatal disease that soon depopulated this great village, which is said to have covered a large extent of ground, and the circumstance of the great mortality which ensued on this occasion at this spot, in the ranks of the Kenisteno and Assineboine, has given the river the name which it now bears Ne-bo, or Death River. In trying to run away from the fatal epidemic, the Ojibways of this village spread the contagion to Rainy Lake, which village also it almost depopulated. From thence by the route of Pigeon River it reached Lake Superior at Grand Portage, and proceeded up the lake to Fond du Lac, where its ravages were also severely felt, and where the Pillager party on their return from Mackinaw caught the infection, and taking it to Sandy Lake, but a few of their number lived to reach their homes at Leech Lake, where it is said to have stopped, after having somewhat lessened the number of the Pillagers. The large village of Sandy Lake suffered severely, and it is said that its inhabitants became reduced to but seven wigwams.

The loss of lives occasioned by this disease in the tribes of the allied Kenistenos and Assineboines, amounted to several thousands. And the loss among the Ojibways, as near as can be computed from their accounts at the present day, amounted to not less than fifteen hundred, or two thousand. It did not, luckily, spread generally, over the country occupied by the tribe, and its ravages were felt almost exclusively in the section and villages which have been designated.

CHAPTER XXII.

CONTINUED PROGRESS OF THE OJIBWAYS ON THE UPPER MISSIS-
SIPPI DURING THE END OF THE EIGHTEENTH CENTURY.

The Pillagers and Sandy Lake bands concentre their forces, and make their
fall and winter hunts in the vicinity of Crow Wing and Long Prairie—The
manner in which they employ themselves during different seasons of the
year—Game abounds on the Dakota hunting grounds about Crow Wing—
Fruits of one day's chase of the Ojibway hunter *No-ka*—Noka River is
named after him—Pillagers and Sandy Lake bands rendezvous at Gull
Lake—They proceed by slow marches towards Long Prairie—Meetings with
the Dakotas—A temporary peace is affected, that either party may hunt in
security—Manner of affecting a peace—Interchanges of good feeling and
adopted relationship—The peace is often treacherously broken—Wa-son-
aun-e-qua, or a tale of Indian revenge.

As beaver, and the larger animals, such as buffalo, elk,
deer, and bear, decreased in the immediate vicinity of Leech
and Sandy Lakes, the hardy bands of Ojibways who had
taken possession of these beautiful sheets of water, were
obliged to search further into the surrounding country for
the game which formed the staple of life. It became
customary for these two pioneer bands to meet by appointment, every fall of the year, at Gull Lake, or at the confluence of the Crow Wing with the Mississippi; and from
thence to move in one collected camp into the more plentifully supplied hunting grounds of the Dakotas.

The camp, consisting of between fifty and a hundred
light birch bark wigwams, moved by short stages from
spot to spot, according to the pleasure of the chiefs, or as
game was found to abound in the greatest plenty. This
mode of hunting was kept up from the first fall of snow
at the commencement of winter, to the month of February,
when the bands again separated, and moved back slowly
to their respective village sites, to busy themselves with

the manufacture of sugar, amidst the thick groves of the valuable maple which was to be found skirting the lakes of which they had taken possession. As a general fact the women only occupied themselves in the sugar bushes, while the men scattered about in small bands, to hunt the furred animals whose pelts at this season of the year were considered to be most valuable. When sugar-making was over and the ice and snow had once more disappeared before the warmth of a spring sun, the scattered wigwams of the different bands would once more collect at their village sites, and the time for recreation, ball-playing, racing, courtship, and war, had once more arrived. If no trader had passed the winter amongst them, many of the hunters would start off in their birch canoes to visit the trading posts on the Great Lakes, to barter their pelts for new supplies of clothing, ammunition, tobacco, and fire-water.

If any one had lately lost relatives, naturally, or at the hands of the Dakotas, now was the proper time to think of revenge; and it is generally at this season of the year that war parties of the red men prowled all over the north-western country, searching to shed each other's blood.

According to invariable custom, the Ojibway mourns for a lost relative of near kin, for the space of one year; but there are two modes by which he can, at any time, wipe the paint of mourning from his face. The first is through the medium of the Meda, or grand medicine, which, to an Indian, is a costly ordeal. The next is to go to war, and either to kill or scalp an enemy, or besmear a relic of the deceased in an enemy's blood. This custom is one of their grand stimulants to war, and the writer considers it as more fruitful of war parties, than the more commonly believed motive of satiating revenge, or the love of renown.

The spring of the year is also the favorite time for the performance of the sacred grand Meda-we rites. The person wishing to become an initiate into the secrets of this religion, which the old men affirm the Great Spirit gave to the red race, prepares himself during the whole winter for the approaching ceremony. He collects and dries choice meats ; with the choicest pelts he procures of the traders, articles for sacrifice, and when spring arrives, having chosen his four initiators from the wise old men of his village, he places these articles, with tobacco, at their disposal, and the ceremonies commence. For four nights, the medicine drums of the initiators resound throughout the village, and their songs and prayers are addressed to the master of life. The day that the ceremony is performed, is one of jubilee to the inhabitants of the village. Each one dons the best clothing he or she possesses, and they vie with one another in the paints and ornaments with which they adorn their persons, to appear to the best advantage within the sacred lodge.

It is at this season of the year also, in which, while the old men are attending to their religious rites, and the lovers of glory and renown are silently treading the war path, the young men amuse themselves in playing their favorite and beautiful game of *baug-ah-ud-o-way*, which has been described in a former chapter, as the game with which the Ojibways and Sauks captured Fort Michilimacinac in the year 1763.

The women also, at this season of the year, have their amusements. The summer is the season of rest for these usual drudges of the wild and lordly red hunters. Their time, during this season, is generally spent in making their lodge coverings and mats for use during the coming winter, and in picking and drying berries. Their hard work, however, again commences in the autumn, when the wild rice which abounds in many of the northern inland lakes, becomes ripe and fit to gather. Then, for a month or more, they are busied in laying in their winter's supply.

When the rice-gathering is over, the autumn is far advanced, and by the time each family has secreted their rice and other property with which they do not wish to be encumbered during the coming winter's march, they move once more in a body to the usual rendezvous at Gull Lake, or Crow Wing, to search for meat on the dangerous hunting grounds of their enemies. In those days which we now speak of, game of the larger species was very plentiful in this region of country, where now the poor Ojibway, depending on his hunt for a living, would literally starve to death.

As an illustration of the kind and abundance of animals which then covered the country, it is stated that an Ojibway hunter named No-ka, the grandfather of the Chief White Fisher, killed in one day's hunt, starting from the mouth of Crow Wing River, sixteen elk, four buffalo, five deer, three bear, one lynx, and one porcupine. There was a trader wintering at the time at Crow Wing, and for his winter's supply of meat, No-ka presented him with the fruits of this day's hunt. This occurred about sixty-five years ago, when traders had become more common to the Ojibways of the Upper Mississippi. It is from this old warrior and stalwart hunter, who fearlessly passed his summers on the string of lakes which form the head of the No-ka River, which empties into the Mississippi nearly opposite the present site of Fort Ripley, that the name of this stream is derived.

Long Prairie, the present site of the Winnebago agency, was at this time the favorite winter resort of those bands of the Dakota tribe now known as the Warpeton and Sisseton. It was in the forests surrounding this isolated prairie, that herds of the buffalo and elk took shelter from the bleak cold winds which at this season of the year blew over the vast western prairies where they were accustomed to feed in summer; and here, the Dakotas, in concentrated camps of over a hundred lodges, followed them to their haunts, and while they preyed on them towards the west, the guns of the Ojibways were often heard doing likewise towards the east. The hunters of the two hostile camps prowled after their game in "fear and trembling," and it often happened that a scalp lock adorned the belt of the hunter, on his return at evening from his day's chase.

The chiefs of the two camps, and the older warriors deeply deprecated this state of affairs, as it resulted only in the perpetual " fear and trembling" of their wives and children, and caused hunger and want often to prevail in camp, even when living in the midst of plenty. Efforts were made to bring about a peaceable meeting between the two camps, which were at least crowned with success, and it soon became customary, let the war rage ever so furiously during all other seasons. The pipe of peace was smoked each winter at the meeting of the two grand hostile hunting camps, and for weeks they would interchange friendly visits, and pursue the chase in one another's vicinity, without fear of harm or molestation.

The Ojibways assert, that when the two camps first neared each other in the fore part of winter, and the guns of the enemy whom they had fought all summer, and whose scalps probably still graced their lodge poles, were heard booming in the distance, towards Long Prairie, they were generally the first to make advances for a temporary peace, or as they term it in their euphonious language, to create *pin-dig-o-daud-e-win* (signifying, "to enter one another's lodges"). Their grudge against the Dakotas was never so deep seated and strong as that which this tribe indulged against them, probably from the fact that their losses in their implacable warfare, included not their ancient village sites, and the resting places of their ancestors.

No sooner, therefore, than the guns of the Dakotas announced their vicinity, than the war chiefs of the Ojibway camp would collect their warriors, and well armed, and prepared for battle if necessary, but taking with them the sacred peace pipe, they would proceed at once to find the enemies' camp. Arrived in sight, they would place the bearer of the peace pipe, and the banner carriers in front, and march fearlessly into the camp of the Dakotas, prepared to act according to the manner of their reception. The Dakotas, surrounded by their women and children, whose safety was dear to them, though probably their hearts were filled with gall and thoughts of vengeance, never refused on these occasions to run out of their lodges and salute the Ojibways with the firing of guns, and in great ceremony to smoke from the stem of their proffered peace pipe. During these first and sudden salutations, it is told that bullets often whizzed close by the ears of the Ojibways, as if their new friends were shooting to try how near they could come to the mark without actually hitting. When the peace party has been few in numbers, and the camp of the enemy large, it has been only through the most strenuous efforts of the wiser warriors, that blood has not been shed. The first excitement once over, and the peace pipe smoked, the Dakotas, smoothing down their angry looks, would invite the Ojibways into their lodges, and feast them with the best they possessed.

In this manner were the returns of temporary peace effected between these two warlike people. And when once the " good road" had been broken in this manner, interchanges of friendly visits would become common, and it often happened that during the winter's intercourse of the two camps, a Dakota chief or warrior taking a fancy to an Ojibway, would exchange presents with him, and adopt him as a brother.   This the Ojibways would also do. These adopted ties of relationship were most generally contracted by such as had lost relations in the course of their feud, and who, in this manner, sought to fill the void which death had made in the ranks of his dearest friends.

These ties, temporary and slight as they may seem, were much regarded by these people, and it has often happened in the course of their ever renewed warfare, that Ojibway and Dakota has saved the life of an adopted brother in times of trouble, of massacre, and battle ; and whenever these ties have been disregarded or grossly violated, the occurrence is told in their lodge tales, in terms to teach the rising generation never to do likewise.

In the course of their history, there are many instances in which these temporary lulls of peace have been suddenly broken by some one or more foolish young men of either tribe, taking advantage of the security in which their former enemy temporarily reposed, and taking the life of some stray hunter.   The most important of these instances and those to which the direct consequences have accrued, will be related in the future course of our narrative.

Illustrative of the manner in which these peace lulls were generally broken, and of the strong propensity existing in the Indian character for revenge, I will here introduce a tale which I obtained from the lips of Esh-ke-bug-e-coshe, the chief of the Pillagers :

INDIAN REVENGE.

Esh-ke-bug-e-coshe, the present living chief of the Pillagers,[1] relates of his deceased father, whose name was Wa-son-aun-e-qua (signifying, " Yellow Hair"), that he was not a chief by hereditary descent, but that he gained a gradual ascendency over the minds of the fearless Pillagers, through

---

[1] A. D. 1852.

his supreme knowledge of medicine, especially such as destroyed life. He possessed a most vindictive and revengeful temper. Injury was never inflicted on him, but he retaliated twofold; and it is said that persons who fell beneath his displeasure, lost their lives in a sudden and unaccountable manner. His people feared him; and he came to be treated with the greatest respect and first consideration. It happened one winter, that the allied camps of the Pillagers and Sandy Lake band met the camp of the Dakotas at Long Prairie, and as it had become usual, a temporary peace was effected. During the friendly intercourse which ensued between the two tribes, a Dakota warrior of some note, belonging to the War-pe-ton band, gave presents to *Yellow Hair*, and requested to be termed his brother. The presents were accepted, and these two warriors of hostile tribes treated one another as brethren, during the course of the whole winter. *Yellow Hair* had partly learned to speak the language of his adopted brother, having formerly taken to wife, a Dakota captive woman, and he now learned to speak it with greater ease and fluency. A lasting peace was discussed between the elders of the two camps, and a mutual understanding was made between them to meet in peace during the summer, at certain points on the Mississippi River.

As the time for making sugar approached, the camps of the two tribes separated, in peace and good-will, and they moved slowly back, each to their village. It happened that *Yellow Hair* remained behind the main camp of his people, for the purpose of hunting a few days longer in the vicinity of Long Prairie. His camp, consisting of four lodges, was located on the woody shores of a little lake, which lay partly embosomed in a deep forest, while one end barely peeped out on the smooth and open prairie.

On the ice of this lake, the boys of the four lodges were accustomed to go out and play, throwing before them their

shosh-e-mans, or little snow slides, and as no fear of an
enemy prevailed in the breasts of their parents, they were
allowed to go thither, whenever they listed. One morning,
after *Yellow Hair* had started on his usual day's hunt, and
the mother of his children was attending to her within-
door duties, a plaintive moaning was heard at the door of
the lodge, and the mother, rushing forth, beheld the out-
stretched form of her oldest boy, painfully crawling homewards through the snow, bleeding and scalpless! The
Dakotas had done it! The anguish cry of the mother soon
gathered the inmates of the surrounding lodges to her side,
and with streaming eyes the women lifted the wounded
and mutilated boy into the parents' wigwam—then rushing to the lake on the bloody track which marked his
course homewards, they beheld their children, three in
number, lying dead and mangled, where the tomahawks of
the Dakotas had struck them down.

The Ojibway hunter returned at evening from his day's
chase, in time to witness the last death struggle of his
murdered boy, his eldest son. He listened to the bloody
tale in silence—no tear dimmed his eye, for the feelings
which harrowed his heart could not be satisfied with such
a vent. The stem of his pipe seldom left his strongly
compressed lips the whole of that night, and the vehemence with which he smoked was the only outward sign
he gave of his emotions.

Early in the morning, the camp was raised, and they
moved in the direction of Leech Lake, taking with them
the corpses of the murdered children. When he had
reached the village site of his people, and placed the body
of his boy in its last resting place, Yellow Hair, with five
comrades, returned on his trail to seek the murderers of
his child. At Crow Wing they found the Sandy Lake
Ojibways still collected, moving but slowly towards their
village. It was not difficult for their fellows to divine

their errand, for the treacherous massacre of their children was the common topic on every one's lips. It was, however, supposed that the bloody deed had been perpetrated by the prairie Dakotas, who had not been present at the peace meetings which had taken place during the winter between the hunting camps of the Ojibways and Warpeton, or lower Dakotas.

Under this impression, the chiefs of the Sandy Lake camp, invited Yellow Hair and his five followers to council, and endeavored by every argument, to dissuade them from following the war-path, as they felt anxious to keep up the peace with the Dakotas. Arguments and speeches, however, appeared to produce no effect, and as a last resort, presents were given them sufficient, in Indian custom and parlance, to "cover the graves of their dead children." The determination of Yellow Hair, was, however, inflexible, but as he perceived that his movements would be watched, he at last silently accepted the presents, and left the camp on his homeward track, pretending to have given up his bloody designs. When arrived at a sufficient distance from the camp to prevent an early discovery of the new trail he was about to make, he left the beaten road, and turning back, he avoided the camp, and proceeded towards Long Prairie. From this place he followed up the return trail of the Dakota hunting camp, hoping to catch up with, and wreak his vengeance on them, before they reached their villages. Arrived at Sauk Lake, he discovered a small trail to branch off from the main and deeply beaten path which he had been following. This he followed, and he soon discovered that those who moved on it consisted of but two lodges, and every one of their old encampments, which the eager warriors passed, proved to them that they were fast nearing their prey.

On the head waters of Crow River, nearly two hundred miles from the point of his departure, Yellow Hair at last caught up with the two lodges of his enemies. At the first peep of dawn in the morning, the Dakotas were startled from their quiet slumbers by the fear-striking Ojibway war-whoop, and as the men arose to grasp their arms, and the women and children jumped up in affright, the bullets of the enemy fell amongst them, causing wounds and death. After the first moments of surprise, the men of the Dakotas returned the fire of the enemy, and for many minutes the fight raged hotly. An interval in the incessant firing at last took place, and the voice of a Dakota, apparently wounded, called out to the Ojibways, "Alas! why is it that I die? I thought my road was clear before and behind me, and that the skies were cloudless above me. My mind dwelt only on good, and blood was not in my thoughts."

Yellow Hair recognized the voice of the warrior who had agreed to be his adopted brother during the late peace between their respective tribes. He understood his words, but his wrong was great, and his heart had become as hard as flint. He answered: " My brother, I too thought that the skies were cloudless above me, and I lived without fear; but a wolf came and destroyed my young; he tracked from the country of the Dakotas. My brother, for this you die !"

" My brother, I knew it not," answered the Dakota— " it was none of my people, but the wolves of the prairies."

The Ojibway warrior now quietly filled and lit his pipe, and while he smoked, the silence was only broken by the groans of the wounded, and the suppressed wail of bereaved mothers. Having finished his smoke, he laid aside his pipe, and once more he called out to the Dakotas :

" My brother, have you still in your lodge a child who will take the place of my lost one, whom your wolves have devoured ? I have come a great distance to behold once

more my young *as I once beheld him*, and I return not on
my tracks till I am satisfied!"

The Dakotas, thinking that he wished for a captive to
adopt instead of his deceased child, and happy to escape
certain destruction at such a cheap sacrifice, took one of
the surviving children, a little girl, and decking it with
such finery and ornaments as they possessed, they sent her
out to the covert of the Ojibway warrior. The innocent
little girl came forward, but no sooner was she within
reach of the avenger, than he grasped her by the hair of
the head and loudly exclaiming—" I sent for thee that I
might do with you as your people did to my child. I
wish to behold thee as I once beheld him," he deliberately
scalped her alive, and sent her shrieking back to her
agonized parents.

After this cold-blooded act, the fight was renewed with
great fury. Yellow Hair rushed desperately forward, and
by main force he pulled down one of the Dakota lodges. As
he did so, the wounded warrior, his former adopted brother,
discharged his gun at his breast, which the active and
wary Ojibway adroitly dodging, the contents killed one of
his comrades who had followed him close at his back. Not
a being in that Dakota lodge survived; the other, being
bravely defended, was left standing; and Yellow Hair,
with his four surviving companions, returned homeward,
their vengeance fully glutted, and having committed a deed
which ever after became the topic of the lodge circles of
their people.

CHAPTER XXIII.

ATTACK OF A WAR PARTY OF DAKOTAS ON A FRENCH TRADING
HOUSE, ON THE UPPER MISSISSIPPI, IN THE YEAR 1783.

A French trader whom the Ojibways name " the Blacksmith" builds a cabin,
and winters at the mouth of Pena River, which empties into the Crow Wing
—He is attacked by two hundred Dakotas—The Dakotas, being armed
mostly with bows and arrows, are finally repulsed with loss—Two Frenchmen are wounded.

ESH-KE-BUG-E-COSHE, the old chieftain of the Pillagers,
who is now[1] beyond his seventieth year, relates that when
he was a small boy, not yet able to handle a gun, he was
present at a trading house located at the confluence of Pat-
ridge, or Pe-na River, with the Crow Wing, when it was
attacked by a large war party of Dakotas. The different
circumstances of this transaction appear still fresh and
clear in the old man's memory, and as he is one of the few
Indian story tellers who is not accustomed to exaggerate,
and in whose accounts perfect reliance can be placed, I
have thought the tale worthy of insertion here, from notes
carefully taken at the time I first heard the old chief relate
it, as an important incident in the course of his adventurous and checkered life.

The trading house had been built late in the fall by a
French trader whom the Indians designated with the name
of Ah-wish-to-yah, meaning, a Blacksmith. He had ven-
turously pitched his winter's quarters in the heart of the
best hunting grounds on lands at that time still claimed
by the Dakotas, but on which the Pillagers were now
accustomed to make their fall and winter hunts, undeterred
by the fear of their enemies, with whom they continually

[1] A. D. 1852.

came in deadly contact, while engaged in the pursuit of the game whose fur procured them the merchandise of the whites.

Being located in a dangerous neighborhood, the trader had erected a rude fence, or barrier of logs, around his dwelling, and the cluster of Indian wigwams containing the women and children of his hunters, which stood a few rods from his door, were also surrounded with felled trees and brush, as a defence against the sudden midnight attack which at any moment they might expect from the Dakotas. Ten hunters had left their families at the camp some days previous, to go and trap beaver which abounded in the vicinity. One night, long before they were expected back, they startled the inmates of the wigwams and trading house from their quiet slumbers, by their sudden arrival. They reported the approach of two hundred Dakotas, who would doubtless attack the party, as they had ever proved enemies to the whites who traded with the Ojibways, and supplied them with the guns and ammunition which made them such able opponents, and who thus gave them the means and power of possessing their best hunting grounds.

The ten hunters had, the day previous to their sudden arrival at the camp, discovered the trail of the enemy, over which the peculiar odor of their tobacco smoke still lingered, discernible to the keen sense of the hunter's nostrils, denoting that the party had but just passed on the trail. The course of the Dakotas led directly towards a small hunting camp which was perfectly defenceless, and which contained the relatives of the ten hunters, who determined, if possible, to save them from certain destruction. In order to effect their purpose, they concluded to turn the course of the war party towards the trading house, where from behind the defences, they hoped to beat them off, while at the same time the report of their guns would warn the scattered hunters in the vicinity, of danger, and collect them to their succor. In order to effect this plan, the ten hunters made a circuit and heading the Dakotas during the night, while encamped, they crossed their course at right angles, and proceeded straight towards the trading house, judging that in the morning, when the war party fell across their tracks (as they would certainly do), they would eagerly follow them up. The hunters had marched all night, and were consequently several hours in advance of the enemy. These hours were employed by the trader and his people in strengthening the barriers around the house. The trees and logs were hauled by main force from around the wigwams, and piled on the defences, and the women, with the children (among whom was the narrator), were invited to take shelter within the house.

The Indian hunters, together with the trader and several " coureurs du bois," numbered nearly twenty men, capable of bearing arms in defence of the post, against a party judged, by the depth and size of their trail, to number two hundred warriors.

The preparations of the Ojibways and their white allies had hardly been completed, when the enemy made their appearance, on the opposite banks of the river. They leisurely made their usual preparations for battle by adorning their persons with paints, feathers, and ornaments; and relying on their numbers, they bravely crossed the stream on the ice, and commenced the attack on the trading house by discharging clouds of barbed arrows, accompanied with a terrific yelling of the war-whoop. Their comparatively harmless missiles were promptly answered with death-winged bullets, by the trader and his hunters, and such of the Dakotas as approached too near the wooden wall, suffered for their temerity.

The western, or prairie, Dakotas had not as yet generally

become possessed of the fatal fire-arm, and on this occasion, in the whole party of two hundred warriors, they hardly numbered half a dozen guns. They fought with the bow and arrow, and in this consisted the safety and salvation of the twenty Ojibway hunters and Frenchmen who fought against such immense odds, and who, being all supplied with fire-arms, easily kept off their numerous assailants.

The only manner in which they were annoyed was by the enemy's shooting their arrows into the air in such a manner as to fall directly into the inclosure, on the heads of its defenders. The more timid were thus forced to retreat into the house for shelter, as for many minutes, the barbed arrows fell as thick as snowflakes, and two of the hunters being severely wounded, were disabled from further fighting.

Having exhausted their arrows without materially lessening the destructive fire of the Ojibways and Frenchmen, the Dakotas having lost a number of their men, finally retreated, first dragging away their dead, whom they threw into holes made in the ice, to prevent their being scalped.

Shortly after their departure, the hunters in the vicinity of the trading house, who had heard the firing attendant on the late fight, arrived one after another to the scene of action, till, at sunset, forty men had collected, all eager for pursuing the retreating enemy. The trader, however, humanely dissuaded them from the enterprise, and as they had lost no lives in the late attack, they were the more easily persuaded to forego their intent.

CHAPTER XXIV.

THE SOURCES OF THE MISSISSIPPI BECOME OPEN TO THE ENTERPRISE OF THE FUR TRADE, 1792.

John Baptiste Cadotte—His early career as an Indian trader—He organizes a large trading expedition to explore the sources of the Mississippi—He winters on Leaf River and is attacked by the Dakotas—Peace effected and he visits the camp of his enemies to trade—Treachery of the Dakotas—A division of Cadotte's party winter at Prairie Portage, on Red River, and another at Pembina—Trouble with the Dakotas at Prairie Portage—Return of the Expedition by way of Rainy Lake and Pigeon River—Arrival at Grand Portage—Northwest Fur Company proceed to occupy the Upper Mississippi country—They locate a depot at Fond du Lac—They build stockaded posts at Sandy Lake and at Leech Lake—Occupation of Red Lake by the Ojibways dated from this Expedition—Death of Negro Tom.

THE great Basin covered with innumerable lakes and streams, from which the Mississippi, flowing into the Gulf of Mexico, and Red River, flowing into Hudson's Bay, take their rise, was first fully opened to the enterprise of the old northwestern fur traders, by John Baptiste Cadotte, a son of the Mons. Cadotte, who is so often mentioned in the earliest era of the white man's intercourse with the Ojibways, and who figures so prominently in the simple but truthful narrative of Alexander Henry.

John Baptiste Cadotte received a college education at Montreal. He was among the first individuals whose European, or white blood, became intermixed with the blood of the Ojibways. On leaving college, he became possessed of forty thousand francs which had been bequeathed to him by his father, and with this sum as a capital, he immediately launched into the northwestern fur trade. He wintered on the Bay of Shag-a-waum-ik-ong, and made large returns of beaver skins to the market at Montreal. His careless and spendthrift habits, however, and open-handedness and generosity to his Indian relatives, soon caused him to run through with his capital and profits of his trade. Unable to raise an equipment on his own account, he applied for help to Alexander Henry, who had traded in partnership with his deceased father, and who still, from his establishment at Montreal, continued in the fur trade. Henry provided him with a large equipment for an expedition, which Cadotte proposed to make to the headwaters of the Mississippi, where beaver were reported to abound in great plenty.

The ferocity of the Naud-o-wa-se, or Dakotas, who still kept possession of this region of country, battling stoutly for it against the persevering pressure of the Ojibway hunters, was the theme of every lip at Montreal, Mackinaw, and Sault Ste. Marie, and deterred many an enterprising trader from proceeding to winter on these dangerous grounds. The few enterprising men who had risked these dangers from time to time, had been attacked by the Dakotas, and the pillage of the sick trader by the Ojibways, which has given the distinctive name of Pillagers to an important division of this tribe, also contributed greatly to shut up this, then almost unknown, region of country to the enterprise of the fur trader.

Cadotte, noted for courage and fearlessness, easily formed a large party, consisting of traders, "coureurs du bois," trappers, and a few Iroquois Indians, who had assumed the habits and learned to perform the labor, of Canadian "voyageurs," to accompany him on an expedition to these dangerous regions. Besides his own immediate engagees and servitors, the party consisted of the trader Reyaulm and his men; Pickette, Roberts, and Bell, with their men fully equipped for trading and trapping. Altogether they numbered sixty men, among whom was also a younger brother of Cadotte, named Michel, who managed an outfit on his own account.

This large party started from Sault Ste. Marie late in the summer, in large birch bark canoes, of over a ton burthen each, which were then denominated "Canoe du maitre," and made expressly for the fur trade, they being comparatively light and easily carried across portages on the shoulders of the "coureurs du bois." Cadotte coasted along the southern shores of Lake Superior, and proceeded to Fond du Lac, its extreme head. He entered the St. Louis River, and packing their canoes and equipments over the nine-mile, or "grand portage," which leads around the tremendous rapids and falls on this river, they poled up its rapid current, and proceeded by the old or prairie portage route, into Sandy Lake.. From this point, my informants differ as to which route the party took. Some state, that they ascended the Mississippi to Leech Lake, crossed over to Cass Lake by a short portage, proceeded to Red Lake, thence into Red River, up which stream they proceeded a short distance and finally located their winter quarters at "Prairie portage," where they were met by two traders who had come by the Grand Portage, or Rainy Lake route, one of whom was Cameron, noted as being among the earliest pioneers into these then remote northwestern regions. This is the account as given by Mr. Bruce, a half-breed Ojibway who was born at Grand Portage on Lake Superior, and is now seventy-eight years of age, still possessing a perfect and surprising memory. He was a young man at the time of this celebrated expedition, and wintered the same year of its occurrence, as an engagee, at a small trading post on Great Lake, Winnipeg, and made, on a small outfit, the enormous returns of forty-eight packs of beaver skins, showing the great abundance of this valuable animal in those times, in these northern regions.

Madame Cadotte, relict of Michel Cadotte, who is mentioned as having joined this party, and who is now nearly ninety years of age, relates that she, with many other women of the party, were left to winter at Fond du Lac, as their husbands were going into a dangerous region, and did not wish to be encumbered with women. Her son, Michel Cadotte, Jr., now living at La Pointe, and aged sixty-one years, was then in his cradle. This old woman's memory is still good, and she gives the following account of the progress and adventures of the party after they reached Sandy Lake:—

They proceeded down the Mississippi to the forks or entry of Crow Wing River, which they ascended, and cold weather overtaking them at the mouth of Leaf River, which empties into the Crow Wing, and discovering here numerous signs of beaver, and it, also, being as far as they dare proceed into the country of the fierce and warlike Dakotas, Mons. Cadotte located his winter quarters, and set his men immediately to work in erecting log huts sufficient to hold his whole party and his winter supplies. The country was then covered with game, such as buffalo, elk, bear, and deer, and the hunters soon collected a sufficient quantity of meat for their winter's consumption. Signs of the vicinity of the much dreaded Dakotas being discovered, Cadotte ordered a log fence or wall to be thrown up around his cabins for a defence against any attack which these people, on whose hunting grounds he was encroaching, might think proper to make on him.

In those days, Leech Lake was considered as the extreme northwestern frontier of the Ojibway country, and but a few hardy and fearless hunters, who had already earned the name of Pillagers, remained permanently located on the islands of the lake, for greater security against the oft-repeated attacks and incursions of their enemies. Happy to hunt on the rich hunting grounds of the Dakotas, under the protection of such a large party of white traders, the Pillager and Sandy Lake hunters moved in their wake, and lay scattered about in different winter camps, in the vicinity of their winter quarters, carrying on, with the different traders, an active barter of furs for their merchandise.

When all the preparations for passing the winter comfortably and safely had been completed, the trappers were sent out in small parties, to pursue their winter's avocation, wherever they discovered the wigwams of the industrious but fated beaver to abound in the greatest plenty. Cadotte, was left with but few men at the winter quarters, when early one morning a large party of Dakota warriors made their appearance, arrayed and painted for battle. They approached the wall which surrounded the log cabins, leaping from side to side and yelling their war-whoop, and when arrived within bullet range they discharged a cloud of arrows, and such few as were armed with guns fired upon the white man's defences. Two of Cadotte's men were slightly wounded from the repeated discharges and volleys of the enemy, yet he desisted from returning their fire, and commanded his exasperated men not to fight. His numbers being feeble, he could not be certain as to the result of a battle, and at the same time being anxious to conciliate and be at peace with the Dakotas, for the sake of their trade, he determined to make a trial to disarm their enmity. He ordered the British flag to be planted on his defences, and hoping that his assailants might understand its import, he hung out a white flag on a pole. His hopes were not disappointed, for as soon as the flags were fully displayed, the enemy ceased firing, and after a short consultation among themselves, a number of their warriors cautiously approached the defences which surrounded the traders' cabins.

Mons. Cadotte, standing in his gateway, informed them, through a "coureur du bois" named Rasle, who could speak the Dakota tongue, that " he had not come into their country to make war on them, but to supply them with necessaries in exchange for their furs." The Dakotas replied to the effect, that, considering them to be a party of Ojibways interloping on their best hunting grounds, they had collected their warriors to destroy them ; but as they had now discovered them to be white men, with whom they wished to be friends, they would shake hands with them, and smoke with them from the same pipe, intimating that they wished to enter within his dwelling.

Cadotte, who possessed a perfect knowledge of Indian character, perceived at once the necessity of complying with their request, for the purpose of proving to them that he confided in their words, and to show to them that he feared them not. He therefore opened his gate, and allowed the chiefs and principal men to fill his cabin, where he held a short council with them, while his men vigilantly guarded the defences, and keenly watched the movements of the numerous Dakota warriors, who stood outside. He gave the Dakotas presents of tobacco and ammunition, and he distributed amongst them meat sufficient for a meal. In return, they welcomed him with apparent cordiality to their country, and invited him to go back with them to their winter camp, where they told of possessing many beaver skins.

Cadotte, placing confidence in their expressions of goodwill, determined to accept their invitation. Most of his men, who were hunting in the vicinity of his trading house, had now arrived, having heard the report of the Dakota guns, as they made their attack in the morning. The Indians, only, kept aloof for fear of the enemy.

He selected thirty of his best men, well-armed, and giving them packs of goods to carry, at their head, he accompanied the Dakotas back to their camp, which they reached at the distance of one day's march. They found the camp to number over one hundred lodges, formed of leather. They were well received, and entertained with the choicest portions of the buffalo, elk, and bear meat, which abounded in every lodge. Cadotte was himself installed in the chief's more extensive lodge, where the whole night long he carried on an active trade, as one after the other, warriors, hunters, and women, entered to exchange their furs for such articles as they needed, or such trinkets as struck their fancy. He soon collected as many packs of beaver and other fur as his men could well carry away. Notwithstanding his brisk trade, many of the goods still remained on his hands, and Cadotte could not help but notice the covetous looks which the chief and his warriors cast on these as he ordered his men to bale them into packs in order to carry away.

In the morning, after the Dakotas had again feasted and smoked with them, the trader prepared to depart. The Dakota chief insisted on accompanying him a part of the way with a guard of his warriors, as a mark of honor and respect, and Cadotte, unable to resist his importunities, at last accepted the offer of his company, and together they left the camp. The Dakotas, nearly equal in number to themselves, led the van, and in this order they travelled, occasionally making short halts to smoke and rest, till they reached about half the distance to their trading house, when, just as they were about to enter a heavy clump of trees and thickets, through which winded their path, the Dakota chief and his men suddenly stopped, sat down on the roadside, and prepared to fill their pipes, requesting their white brothers to take their turn and go ahead, while

they, being light, would take a smoke, and soon catch up
with them.

Mons. Cadotte, perfectly unsuspicious, followed the wishes
of the chief, and at the head of his men, he was leading
off, when his interpreter, Rasle, approached and remarked
to him, that he suspected treachery. He had noticed
in the morning when they started to leave the camp, that
all the men but those who accompanied them, had disappeared, and also that they had been holding secret councils
in different lodges during the whole night. Rasle further
intimated that the heavy clump of trees through which
they were about to pass, being the only spot on the route
adapted to an ambuscade, he suspected that men, who had
so early made their disappearance from the camp, had been
sent ahead to here lay in wait and surprise them, while
the chief, with his pretended guard, would attack in the
rear, as his present movement and request for them to go
ahead plainly indicated. The truth of these suspicions
flashed through Cadotte's mind, and being of an impulsive
nature, he instantly ordered his men to throw down their
packs, and prepare for instant action. Then suddenly approaching the chief, who was now quietly smoking his
pipe, he cocked his gun, and presented it to his breast, telling Rasle to say to him, that " he saw through his treachery, and that he would be the first to suffer death, unless
he ordered his warriors to give up their arms, and also
cleared the path he was travelling, of the men whom he
had sent ahead to waylay him."

The chief at first stoutly denied the charge, but when
he saw Cadotte's men forcibly take the arms out of the
hands of his chosen warriors, whom they outnumbered, he
burst into tears, and begged for his life, and the lives of
his men. This being assured in case the ambuscade
amongst the trees ahead would disperse, the chief sent one
of his disarmed warriors thither, and a few moments after,

a large body of painted warriors emerged from the wood, and quietly marched off in single file across the wide prairie towards their camp. The treacherous chief, with his guard, were taken by Cadotte to his post, and kept as hostages, till he could collect and warn his scattered trappers and Pillager hunters, against feeling too secure, in the idea that a firm peace had been effected with the Dakotas. When this had been effected, the post more fully manned, and every man been put on his guard, the chieftain with his men were allowed to go home, once more loaded with tobacco and presents, in hopes that his people would appreciate the kindness and forbearance of their white neighbors.

Mons. Cadotte's party remained at this post all winter, and they received no more molestation from the Dakotas, who did not thereafter even make their appearance in the vicinity of their hunting range. In the spring, after the snow had disappeared, and the ice melted on the lakes and rivers, these adventurers evacuated their winter quarters, and proceeding up Leaf River in their canoes, they made a portage into Otter Tail Lake, and descended from thence down the Red River.

The variance in the different accounts which have been given to me of this expedition, lies mostly in different spots being mentioned where the party are said to have wintered, and different routes having been taken to reach these spots. I am disposed to account for these disagreements, in the accounts of persons whose memory and veracity cannot well be questioned, by assuming the ground that the party, consisting of several different traders, each with his own equipment of supplies and men, must have separated at Sandy Lake, and while one party proceeded (as has been mentioned) up the Mississippi to Red Lake, and wintering at Prairie Portage, and at Pembina, the other party under Cadotte in person, took their course down the Mississippi, and underwent the adventures which we have related.

It is stated, that at Prairie Portage, after the traders had all again collected in the spring, the Dakotas in large numbers made demonstrations to fall upon and pillage them, and the only manner in which the whites succeeded in intimidating them to forego their designs, was to heap their remaining powder kegs into a pile in the centre of their camp, and threatening to set fire to them the moment the Dakotas attempted to pillage. At Pembina the party were obliged to make new canoes of elk and buffalo hides, the seams of which, thickly covered with tallow, made them nearly as water-tight as birch canoes. In these they descended the current of the Red River, and returned to Lake Superior by the Great Lake Winnipeg, a northern route. At Rainy Lake they made birch-bark canoes, in which, late in the summer, they reached Grand Portage, the principal northwestern depot of the Northwest Company. The accounts which they gave of the country which they had explored, induced this rich company immediately to extend their operations throughout its whole extent, and this portion of their trade became known as the Fond du Lac department. The depot, or collecting point, was built at Fond du Lac, near the entry of the St. Louis River, and this post, or "Fort," was surrounded with strong cedar pickets. The remains of this old establishment are still plainly visible. In 1796, the Northwest Company built a stockaded post at Sandy Lake, and soon after, they located another at Leech Lake. These were the immediate results of Cadotte's expedition, and from that period, now sixty years ago, the Ojibways of the Upper Mississippi River have been constantly supplied with resident traders, and their former periodical visits to Sault Ste. Marie and Mackinaw ceased almost entirely.

Wa-won-je-gnon, the aged and intelligent chief of the
Red Lake band of the Ojibways, states, that from this expedition can be dated the settlement of Red Lake by the
Ojibways. He also states that the traders on this occasion,
made a minute exploration of the lake and sounded the
depth of its waters. In the deepest portions they discovered it to be but eight fathoms.

There is living at Red Lake an aged Indian, whose
name is Bow-it-ig-o-win-in, signifying "Sault Ste. Marie
man," who first came into the country as an engagé to
Mons. Cadotte during this voyage, and has remained in it
ever since, having married and raised a family of children.
So far as I can learn, this old Indian is now the only sur-
vivor of the sixty men who are said to have formed the
party. An incident is currently related among the northern Ojibways, which is said to have happened while Cadotte's party were wintering on Leaf River. Mr. Bell,
one of the traders or clerks associated with him, kept in
his employ a gigantic negro, whose name was "Tom." Mr.
Bell himself was a small and feebly constituted man, but
of very irritable disposition, especially when under the
influence of liquor. One evening he quarrelled with his
negro Tom, and both being somewhat intoxicated, they
grappled in mortal strife. The huge negro easily threw
his master on the floor, and pressing him forcibly down, he
unmercifully and dreadfully beat him with his fists. Mr.
Bell's Indian wife was sitting by a table making moccasins,
and held in her hand a penknife which she was occasionally
using. Seeing the hopeless situation of her husband, she
ran to his rescue, and stabbed the negro with her penknife
till she killed him.

CHAPTER XXV.

JOHN BAPTISTE CADOTTE.

He becomes connected with the Northwest Fur Company—He takes charge of
the Fond du Lac Department on shares—An incident at Grand Portage—A
"coureur du bois" is killed by an Indian at Lake Shatac—Cadotte takes
the matter in hand—The murderer is delivered into his hands—He is tried
by a jury of clerks and sentenced to death—Manner of his execution—His
punishment has a salutary effect on the Ojibways.

JOHN BAPTISTE CADOTTE returned to Montreal from his
northwestern expedition, and soon expended in dissipation
the profits on the large return of furs he had made. He
became, moreover, so deeply indebted to Alexander Henry,
who continued to supply his wants, that at last his credit
with this gentleman became impaired, and he was obliged
once more to exert himself towards gaining a livelihood.
His expedition to the sources of the Mississippi had rendered him known as a man of great fearlessness and hardihood, and his abilities as a clerk and Indian trader were
such that it was no difficult matter for him, when so disposed, to find employment.   The Northwest Fur Company
secured his services at once, and he applied himself with
so much vigor and energy towards advancing their interests, that he soon obtained the esteem and fullest confidence of all the principal partners of this rich and prosperous firm.

At a dinner given by Mr. Alex. Henry, at Montreal, to
the several partners of the Northwest Company, among
whom was Sir Alexander McKenzie, Cadotte's name being mentioned in the course of conversation, this gentleman,
who was then the principal northern agent of the firm,
took occasion to speak of him in the highest terms, prais-
ing the courage and fearlessness with which he had pierced

amongst the more wild and unruly tribes of the north-western Indians, and the great tact which he used in obtaining the love and confidence of the Ojibways.

Mr. Henry, perceiving that Cadotte possessed the confidence of his employers, and that his services were held by them in great value, took occasion to make the proposition to Sir Alex. McKenzie, of selling him Mons. Cadotte's indebtedness at a liberal discount. McKenzie informed him that he had discovered Cadotte to be a man extremely careless in his expenditures, and who made it a point to live up fully to his means, whatever amount those means might be, and that it would be extremely difficult to collect from him such an amount of debt as Mr. Henry proposed to transfer against him, and also that he could not assume or buy it, without a consultation with the other partners of the company. Further urging on the part of Mr. Henry at last induced Mr. McKenzie to buy up Mons. Cadotte's debt on his own private account. He paid but three hundred pounds, being less than half of its actual amount. This arrangement was kept secret from Mons. Cadotte, as the partner concerned knew him to be a man of impulsive feelings, and it was uncertain in what light he would consider such a discount being made on his credit, which reflected so strongly on his honor, on which he was known to pride himself. In order to give him an opportunity of retrieving his fortunes, and paying his debts, the North-west Fur Company proposed to give him the entire Fond du Lac department on shares. They agreed to give him such an equipment as he wanted, and this important division of their trade was to be entirely under his management and control.

Mons. Cadotte accepted this fair offer, as it gave him a broad field for the full development of his capacities, and an excellent opportunity to replenish his empty purse. The Fond du Lac department comprised all the country about the sources of the Mississippi, the St. Croix, and Chippeway rivers. The depot was located at Fond du Lac, about two miles within the entry of the St. Louis River, in what is now the State of Wisconsin. A stockaded post had been built the previous year at Sandy Lake, and smaller posts were located at Leech Lake, on the St. Croix and at Lac Coutereille.

Mons. Cadotte procured his outfit of goods for all these posts, at the grand northern depot of the Northwest Company located at Grand Portage, near the mouth of Pigeon River, and within the limits of what is now known as Minnesota Territory. He had busily employed himself all one morning, in loading his canoes, with his outfit of goods, and starting them on ahead towards Fond du Lac, intending to catch up with them in his lighter canoe at the evening encampment, when the following incident occurred, which, to the day of his death the old trader ever spoke of with the deepest emotion.

His canoes had all been sent ahead, and now appeared like mere specks on the bosom of the calm lake towards their destination, and he was preparing to embark himself, in his *canoe a liege* fully manned, when the book-keeper of the post, coming down to his canoe for a parting shake of the hand, informed him that while he had been engaged in sending off his men and outfit, Sir Alexander McKenzie and other gentlemen of the company had been holding a council with the Indians, and attempting to explain to them the reasons and necessity for evacuating their depot at Grand Portage, which was located within the United States lines, and building a new establishment within the British boundaries, at a spot now known as Fort William.[1]

---

[1] Alexander Henry, a nephew of the Henry, who traded in 1775 on the shores of Lake Superior, on the 3d of July, 1802, found brick kilns burning at Kamanistiquia, in charge of R. McKenzie, for the erection of the new post Fort William, in compliment to William McGillivary.—Neill's *History of Minnesota*, fifth edition, 1883, p. 882.

The Indians could not, or would not, understand the necessity of this movement, as they claimed the country as their own, and felt as though they had a right to locate their traders wherever they pleased. They could not be made to understand or acknowledge the right which Great Britain and the United States assumed, in dividing between them the lands which had been left to them by their ancestors, and of which they held actual possession. The bookkeeper further informed Mons. Cadotte that the gentlemen of the company were in considerable trouble for want of an efficient interpreter, to explain these matters to the satisfaction of the Indians, and they would have called on him for his services, but were fearful of retarding his movements, and as he was his own master, they could not command him. On hearing this, Mons. Cadotte (who already bore the name of being the best Ojibway interpreter in the northwest), immediately stepped out of his canoe, and walking up to the council room, he offered to act as interpreter between McKenzie and the Indians. His timely and voluntary offer was gladly accepted, and he soon explained the difficult and intricate question of right, which so troubled the minds of the Ojibways, to the entire satisfaction of all parties ; and as he once more proceeded to embark in his canoe, which lay at the water-side, waiting for him, the gentlemen of the fur company escorted him to the beach, and as Sir Alex. McKenzie shook his hand at parting, he presented him with a sealed paper, with the remark that it was in payment of the service which he had just now voluntarily rendered them.

When arrived at some distance out on the lake, Mons. Cadotte opened the paper, and was surprised to discover it to be a clear quittance of all his indebtedness to Alexander Henry, which had always been a trouble on his mind, and which he had not been made aware had been bought up by his employers. On the impulse of the moment he ordered his canoe turned about, in order that he might go and express his gratitude to the generous McKenzie, but on second thought he proceeded on his journey, imbued with a firm determination to repay this mark of kindness by attending closely to his business, and endeavoring to make such returns of furs in the spring, as would cause the company not to regret the generosity with which they had treated him. He succeeded to his fullest satisfaction, and the Northwest Company, together with himself, reaped this year immense profits from the Fond du Lac department.

It was while Mons. Cadotte had charge of this department, that an occurrence happened, which may be considered as an item in the history of the Ojibways, and which fully demonstrates the strong influence which the traders of the northwest had already obtained over their minds and conduct, and also the fearlessness with which the pioneer, whom we have made the subject of this chapter, executed justice in the very midst of thousands of the wild and warlike Ojibway hunters.

A Canadian " coureur du bois," employed at the Lac Coutereille post, which was under the immediate charge of a clerk named Mons. Coutouse, was murdered by an Indian on Lac Shatac during the winter. This was a crime which the Ojibways had seldom committed, and Mons. Cadotte, knowing fully the character of the Indians with whom he was dealing, at once became satisfied that a prompt and severe example was necessary, in order that such a deed might not again be committed, and that the Ojibways might learn to have a proper respect for the lives of white men. He took the matter especially in hand, and immediately sent a messenger to Lac Coutereille to inform the Indians that the murderer must be brought to Fond du Lac and delivered into his hands, and should they refuse to comply with his demand, he notified them that no more traders should go amongst them, and their supplies of tobacco, guns, ammunition, and clothing should be entirely stopped.

The war-chief of Lac Coutereille, named Ke-dug-a-be-shew, or "Speckled Lynx," a man of great influence amongst his people, and a firm friend to the white man, seized the offender, and in the spring of the year, when the inland traders returned to the depot at Fond du Lac, with their collection of furs, he went with them, and delivered the murderer into the hands of Mons. Cadotte. The rumor of this event had spread to the different villages of the Ojibways, and an unusual large number of the tribe collected with the return of their different traders, around the post at Fond du Lac, induced mostly from curiosity to witness the punishment which the whites would inflict on one who had spilt their blood.

When all his clerks and men had arrived from their different wintering posts, Mons. Cadotte formed his principal clerks into a council, or jury, to try the Indian murderer. His guilt was fully proved, and the sentence which was passed on him was, that he should suffer death in the same manner as he had inflicted death on his victim—with the stab of a knife. Mons. Coutouse, whose " coureur du bois" had been killed, requested to be the executioner of this sentence.

The relatives of the Indian assembled in council, after having been informed of the fate which their brother was condemned to suffer. They sent for Mons. Cadotte and his principal clerks, and solemnly offered, according to their custom, to buy the life of the culprit with packs of beaver skins. Cadotte himself, who is said to have naturally possessed a kind and charitable heart, became softened by their touching appeals, and expressed a disposition to accept their proposition, but the clerks and especially the " coureur du bois," whose comrade had been killed, were so excited and determined on vengeance, that the offer of the Indians was rejected.

On the morrow after the trial, the execution took place. Mons. Cadotte led the condemned man from the room where he had been confined, and leading him out into the open air, he pointed to the sun, and gave him the first intimation of his approaching death, by bidding him to look well at that bright luminary, for it was the last time he should behold it, for the man whom he had murdered was calling him to the land of spirits. He then delivered him into the hands of his clerks; the gate was thrown open, and the prisoner was led outside of the post, into the presence of a vast concourse of his people who had assembled to witness his punishment. The fetters were knocked from his wrists, and at a given signal, Coutouse, the executioner, who stood by with his right arm bared to the elbow, and holding an Indian scalping knife, suddenly stabbed him in the back. As he quickly withdrew the knife, a stream of blood spirted up and bespattered the gateway, and the Indian, yelling a last war-whoop, leaped forward, but as he started to run, a clerk named Landré again buried a dirk in his side. The Indian, though fearfully and mortally wounded, ran with surprising swiftness to the water-side, and for a few rods he continued his course along the sandy beach, when he suddenly leaped up, staggered and fell. Two women, holding each a child in her arms—the Indian wives of John Baptiste and Michel Cadotte, who had often plead in vain to their husbands for his life, were the first who approached the body of the dying Indian, and amidst the deep silence of the stricken spectators, these compassionate women bent over him, and with weeping eyes, watched his last feeble death struggle. The wife of Michel, who is still living[1] at an advanced age, often speaks of this occurrence in her early life, and never without a voice trembling with the deepest emotion.

[1] A. D. 1852.

The traders, being uncertain how the Indians would regard this summary mode of punishment, and possessing at the time the double advantage of concentrated numbers and security within the walls of the stockaded post, determined to try their temper to the utmost, before they again scattered throughout their country in small parties, where, if disposed to retaliate, the Indians could easily cut them off in detail.

Mons. Cadotte was himself so closely related to the tribe, and knew the strength of his influence so well, that he felt no apprehension of these general consequences; but, to satisfy his men, as well as to discover if the near relatives of the executed Indian indulged revengeful feelings, he presented a quantity of "eau de vie" to the Indians, knowing that in their intoxication they would reveal any hard feelings or vengeful purposes for the late act, should they actually indulge them.

The Indian camp was that night drowned in a drunken revel, but not a word of displeasure or hatred did they utter against the traders, and their future conduct proved that it was a salutary and good example, for it caused the life of a white man to be ever after held sacred.

CHAPTER XXVI.

PROGRESS OF THE OJIBWAYS ON THE WISCONSIN AND CHIPPEWAY RIVERS.

Remarks—Numbers of the Lac Coutereille and Lac du Flambeau bands—
Their mode of gaining subsistance—They attribute their gradual westward
advance to the example of their pioneer traders—Michel Cadotte—In 1784
he winters on the Num-a-ka-gun—He winters on the Chippeway within
range of the Dakotas—He again winters on the Chippeway, and experiences
trouble from the Indians—He winters on the Chippeway below Vermilion
Falls—Two Canadians are drowned in the Rapids—Danger from the Dakotas
—Peace is happily effected—Credit due to Cadotte and La Rocque—Warfare between Ojibways and Dakotas—War party and death of " Big Ojibway"—Prairie Rice Lake—The Indian fight on its shores—A family of Ojibways are massacred by the Dakotas—Bravery and revenge of the father—
Exploit of Le-bud-ee—New villages are formed at Lac Shatac, Puk-wa-i-
wah, Pelican Lakes and Wisconsin—Ojibways come in contact with the
Winnebagoes.

WE have now arrived at a period in the history of the
Ojibways, which is within the remembrance of aged chiefs,
half-breeds, and traders still living amongst them ; and we
can promise our readers that but few occurrences will
hereafter be related, but the accounts of which have been
obtained by the writer from the lips of eye-witnesses, and
actual actors therein.

From this period, his labors in procuring reliable information have been light, in comparison to the trouble of
sifting and procuring corroborative testimony from various
sources, the traditions which have been orally transmitted
from father to son, for generations past. The greatest
trouble will now consist in choosing from the mass of
information which the writer has been collecting during
several years past, such portions as may truly be considered
as historical and worthy of presenting to the world. The

important tribe of whom we treat in these pages, is divided
into several distinctly marked divisions, occupying different sections of their extensive country, and we have been
obliged to skip from one section to another, that we might
relate events which have happened to each, in the order of
time.

In this chapter we will again return to the Lac Coutereille and Lac du Flambeau divisions, whom we left, in a
previous chapter, in possession of the sources of the Wisconsin and Chippeway rivers—two large tributaries of
the Mississippi.

In the latter part of the eighteenth century these two
bands already numbered one thousand souls. They had
located their villages on the beautiful lakes which form the
head waters of these rivers, and to some extent they practised the arts of agriculture, raising large quantities of corn
and potatoes, the seed for which had been introduced
amongst them by their traders on Lake Superior. They
also collected each autumn large quantities of wild rice,
which abounded in many of their lakes and streams. As
game became scarce in the vicinity of their villages, they
moved in large hunting camps towards the Mississippi,
and on the richer hunting grounds of the Dakotas they
reaped rich harvests of meat and furs.

The older and more intelligent men of these bands attribute to this day their steady westward advance, and final
possession of the country nearly to the Mississippi, through
following the example and footsteps of their first and old
pioneer trader, Michel Cadotte, a younger brother of J. B.
Cadotte, mentioned in previous chapters.

The memory of this man, the marks of whose wintering
posts are pointed out to this day throughout every portion
of the Ojibway country, is still dear to the hearts of the
few old chiefs and hunters who lived cotemporary with
him, and received the benefits of his unbounded charitable

disposition. Full of courage and untiring enterprise, he is mentioned to this day as having not only placed the weapons into the hands of the Ojibways which enabled them to conquer their enemies, but led them each winter westward and further westward into the rich hunting grounds of the Dakotas, until they learned to consider the country as their own, and caused their enemies to fall back after many a bloody fight west of the " Great River."

He is mentioned as the first trader who wintered amongst the bands who had taken possession of the sources of the Chippeway River. As early as the year 1784, he wintered on the Num-a-ka-gun River, a branch of the St. Croix. The remains of his old post are pointed out a short distance below the portage, which leads towards Lac Coutereille. From this position he secured the trade of both the St. Croix and Chippeway River divisions. From a small outfit of goods which he had procured from the British traders at Michilimackinac, he collected forty packs of beaver skins, with which he returned in the spring by way of La Pointe. A few years after, he wintered on Chippeway River, at a spot known to the Ojibways as Puk-a-wah-on-aun, a short distance above the mouth of Man-e-to-wish River. This region of country was then claimed by the Dakotas, and the enterprise of locating thereon was attended with great danger. Beaver, elk, deer, and bear, were, however, so plenty, that the Indians were induced, though in " fear and trembling," to follow their fearless trader. The Lac Coutereille band in a body floated down the Chippeway River, and pitched their camp by the side of his trading house, and word having been sent to the Lac du Flambeau band, they also, in a body, floated down the Man-e-to-wish, and the two camps joining together, rendered them too strong to fear an attack from their enemies.

Having been very successful in his winter's trade, Cadotte again returned the following autumn, intending to pass another winter at his former post. He sent word as before to the Lac du Flambeau band of his purpose and as he passed Lac Coutereille the hunters of this village followed him down the Chippeway River. It was the custom of the traders in those days to take with them to different wintering posts small quantities of " eau de vie," which, when their hunters had all assembled around them, they made a present of to the principal chiefs, for their people to have a grand frolic.

To the inland bands, this great indulgence came around but once a year, and they looked forward to it with the greatest longing. On receiving their liquor, the chief would generally appoint several of his warriors as masters of the approaching debauch. They would first go around, and collecting the guns, axes, knives and other weapons which a drunken man might be apt to use, if at hand, they would hide them away, and act during the frolic as guardians and mediators between such as possessed bad tempers and quarrelled with one another over their cups. When the camp had once more returned to their sober senses, these several warriors would, in their turn, have their frolic.

On this occasion, when Michel Cadotte had arrived and camped at his old post, the chief of the Lac Coutereille village called on him, and formally demanded the usual present of fire-water given at the opening of the fall hunts. The trader refused to comply with his request, on the ground that the Lac du Flambeau band had not yet arrived, but being daily expected, he would wait till they had camped together, before he gave them their usual present of liquor. The chief went off apparently satisfied, but having waited two whole days in vain for the expected band, his longings for a dram were such that he again

paid Mons. Cadotte a visit, and this time he peremptorily
demanded the fire-water, using the most threatening language in hopes of intimidating him to do as he wished.
The trader, however, firmly refused, and the Indian finally
left the lodge in a great rage. His camp lay on the opposite side of the river, about two hundred yards across. He
embarked in his canoe, and paddled over, all the time
uttering the most abusive and threatening language. Arriving at his water's side, he leaped ashore, and running to
his lodge for his gun, he again ran out, and commenced
firing at Mons. Cadotte's lodge. He had discharged his
gun three times (nearly killing the wife of the trader),
when the war-chief of his band ran to him, and wresting
the gun out of his hands, he was on the point of breaking
the stock over his head, when other Indians interfered.
Many of his own people were so enraged at this foolish act
of their civil chief, that his life would have been taken,
had not Cadotte himself interfered to save him.

When the Lac du Flambeau band (whose chief was a
man of decided character, and an uncle of the trader's wife),
arrived on the Chippeway River, a few miles below the
scene of this occurrence, they were so exasperated that
they refused to come up and camp with the Lac Coutereille band, but sent messengers to invite Mons. Cadotte to
come and locate himself for the winter in their midst.
The trader, to punish the chief who had treated him so
badly, though he now showed the deepest contrition,
accepted the invitation of his Lac du Flambeau relatives,
and proceeding some distance down the river, he wintered
with them at the mouth of Jump River.

The following autumn, Michel Cadotte again returned
to the Chippeway River, and this time he proceeded with
his Indian hunters to the outskirts of the prairies which
stretch up this river for about eighty miles above its confluence with the Mississippi. In descending the upper

falls on this river in their canoes, he lost two of his " coureurs du bois," who were upset in the rapids and drawn
into a whirlpool. His post, during this winter, was located
in such a dangerous neighborhood to the Dakotas, that he
built a wall of logs around his shanty, while his hunters
did the same around their camp.

During the winter the Dakotas gradually approached
them in a large camp, and Cadotte, to prevent his hunters
from leaving him, determined to try if a temporary peace
could not be effected between them. He collected about
one hundred men, and, supplying them with plenty of ammunition, he proceeded at their head to the Dakota camp,
which lay about half a day's march down the river. The
Dakotas materially outnumbered them, and they showed
every disposition for a fight, as the Ojibways made their
appearance with a white flag and pipe of peace. It happened that they, too, had their trader with them, an old
pioneer, named La Roque, the father of the respected old
gentleman of this name who still[1] resides at the foot of
Lake Pepin, and who is well known to all the old settlers
on the Upper Mississippi.

The efforts of this man, in conjunction with Mons. Cadotte, effected on this occasion a temporary peace between
the two hostile parties, and they passed the remainder of
the winter in feasting and hunting with one another.
From this time may be dated the terms of temporary
peace, which almost each winter these two camps, being
nearly equal in numbers, made with one another, in order
that they might pursue their hunts in security. Like
other bands of their tribes, however, notwithstanding the
winter's peace, they appeared to consider it an unavoidable
duty to pass the summer in destroying one another.

The warfare which this division of the Ojibways waged
with the Dakotas of the Wabasha and Red Wing villages,

[1] A. D. 1852.

was as bloody and unremitting as the feud which was being carried on by the St. Croix and Upper Mississippi divisions of their tribe with the Kaposia, Warpeton, and Sisseton Dakotas. The country of their present occupation is covered with spots where the warriors of either tribe have met in mortal strife. Almost every bend on Chippeway and Menominee rivers has been the scene of a fight, surprise, or bloody massacre, and one of their chiefs remarked with truth when asked to sell his lands, that " the country was strewn with the bones of their fathers, and enriched with their blood."

From the time we have mentioned, when Cadotte wintered on the outskirts of the western prairies, the Ojibways may be considered as having taken actual possession of the valuable hunting region stretching from Lake Superior nearly three hundred miles to the lower Falls of the Chippeway River, within two days' march of the Mississippi.

Through the efforts and influence of their early traders, peace was occasionally effected. John Baptiste and Michel Cadotte on the part of the Ojibways, and Mons. La Roque on the part of the Dakotas, are mentioned, and deserve much credit, as often having arrested the blow of the war-club, and changing what would have been scenes of bloodshed and death to those of peace and rejoicing. These terms of peace were generally short and transient, and seldom lasted the full length of a year. For no sooner than spring and summer again came around, the time of pastime and recreation for the red hunters, than a longing desire seized the warriors for blood and renown, or revenge for old injuries, or to wipe away the paint of mourning for the death of some near relative. The villagers of either tribe never considered the pleasures of the general summer season as complete, without the enjoyment of dancing and singing merrily around the scalp lock of an enemy.

Were accounts of all the acts of treachery after a formal peace, the fights, massacres, and surprises which have occurred during the past century between these two war-like divisions of the Ojibway and Dakotas to be collected and written, they would fill a large volume. In our present work we have space only to give a few characteristic instances, illustrating the nature of the warfare they have waged with one another. Scenes or events, where acts of unusual courage and bravery have been performed by any of their warriors, are long remembered in the tribe, and are related with great minuteness in their winter evening lodge gatherings, for the amusement and benefit of the rising generation.

The following circumstance is one of this nature, which deserves record in the annals of these warlike people:—

One summer about the year 1795, a noted war-chief of Lac Coutereille named " The Big Ojibway," having recently lost some near relatives at the hands of the Dakotas, raised a small war party consisting of twenty-three men, and proceeded at their head towards the West, to revenge the blow on their enemies. They reached the mouth of the Chippeway River without meeting with any fresh signs of the Dakotas. Arriving on the banks of the Mississippi, however, they beheld long rows of lodges on the opposite shore, and from the beating of drums and dancing, which they could hear and perceive was being performed by their enemies, they judged that they were preparing to go to war.

Under this impression, the Ojibway war party laid an ambush at a spot peculiarly adapted for the purpose, by a thick forest of trees which grew to the very banks of the Chippeway River. Scouts were placed at the entry of this stream, directly opposite the Dakota encampment, to watch the departure of the expected war party. Early the next morning the Dakotas were seen to embark in their wooden canoes, to the number of about two hundred men, and proceed up the current of the Chippeway. The watchful scouts, after being fully satisfied of the course the enemy was about to take, ran to their leader, and informed him of all that which they had observed.

The numbers of the Dakotas made it an act of almost certain self-destruction for the small Ojibway party to attack them, and the more prudent and fearful advised their chief to make a quiet retreat. His determination, however, was fixed, and bidding such as feared death to depart and leave him, he prepared himself for the coming conflict. Not one of his little party left his side, and they awaited in silence the moment that the enemy would pass by their place of ambush. Soon the Dakotas made their appearance, singing their war-songs, and paddling their canoes slowly up the rapid current of the river.

Arriving opposite the unsuspected ambuscade of the Ojibways, a volley was suddenly fired amongst them, killing three of their most prominent warriors, and wounding many others. The Ojibways waited not to reload their guns, but springing up, they ran for their lives, in hopes that in the first confusion of their sudden attack, the Dakotas would not immediately pursue, and thus give them a chance for escape. They were, however, disappointed, for their enemy lost no time in leaping ashore and following their footsteps. The Ojibway leader was a large, portly man, and unable to run for any distance. He soon fell in the rear, and though the yells of the Dakotas were plainly heard apparently fast gaining on them, his little party refused his entreaties to leave him to his fate. At last he stopped altogether, and addressing his warriors, he bade them to leave him, and save their lives, for he had not brought them there to leave their bones to whiten the prairie. For his part, he knew that he must die. His guardian spirit had foretold it to him in a dream, but in the mean time he would stand between them and their pursuers, that they might return in safety to their people.

His comrades reluctantly left him, and to a man they arrived at their homes in safety. The Dakotas, at a peace party, afterwards told of the last brave struggle of the "Big Ojibway." They found him seated in a clump of tall grass, on a small prairie, calmly smoking his pipe. The van of the Dakotas stopped suddenly at seeing him, and commenced leaping from side to side to distract his aim, as they expected him to fire in their midst: but the Ojibway warrior appearing to take no notice of them, they ceased their dodging, and awaited the arrival of the whole party, being uncertain in what light to consider the conduct of their fearless and stoical enemy, and fearful that it was some ruse to decoy them into an ambush of a larger party of the enemy, than had yet appeared.

When the Dakotas had all assembled, they gradually and cautiously surrounded the warrior, and when they had discovered the fact of his being entirely alone, they commenced firing at him. At the first volley the brave man fell forward as if dead, and the Dakotas in a body ran forward to secure his scalp. As they reached him, he suddenly sprang up, and shooting down the foremost warrior, he rushed among the thickest ranks, and dispatched another with the stock of his gun; then drawing his knife, he continued to fight till pierced by many spear points and barbed arrows, he fell on his knees. Still, his blood welling from many a gaping wound, he yelled his war-whoop, and fairly kept his numerous enemies at bay, till, weakened by loss of blood and continued wounds, the bravest of the Dakotas grappled with him, and seizing his scalp lock, severed with his knife the head from his body. It is said that during the whole fight, the Ojibway warrior had laughed at his enemies, and his face, after the head had been separated from his body, was still wreathed in a smile.

Such a high notion did the Dakotas entertain of his bravery, that they cut out his heart, which, being cut into small pieces, was swallowed by their warriors raw, in the belief that it would make them equally " strong hearted." The length of time which the " Big Ojibway" had retarded the pursuit of the Dakotas, enabled his little war party to make their escape, and they always attributed their salva' tion on this trying occasion to the manly courage and self sacrifice of their chief, whose name will long be remem bered in the traditions of his people.

In the year 1798, a handful of Ojibway warriors fought a severe battle with a large party of Dakotas, at' Prairie Rice Lake. As this lake has been the scene of several engagements between these two tribes, a brief description of its position, size, and advantages will not be considered amiss. On Mons. Nicollet's map, it is named Mille Lacs, and empties its waters into Red Cedar, a tributary of Chippeway River. Mr. Nicollet, who has given us a map which may be considered as generally correct, must, how·· ever, have been misinformed in the name, and somewhat in the position of this lake. It has always been known to the Ojibways by the name of Mush-ko-da-mun-o-min-e-kan, meaning Prairie Rice Lake, and to the French as Lac la Folle. During a two years' residence (in 1840–41) in the vicinity of this lake, and especially during a tour which the writer made through this district of country, in the summer of 1850, circumstances happened which made him fully acquainted with this lake, and the country surrounding it.

It is situated about forty miles directly north of the lower rapids on Chippeway River, where the extensive establishment known as Chippeway Mills is now[1] located.

[1] A. D. 1852.

Its entire length is about eight miles, but averages less than a quarter of a mile in width. A clear, rapid stream connects it with another lake of nearly equal size, known to the Indians as Sha-da-sag-i-e-gan, or Pelican Lake, and from thence discharges their superfluous waters into the Red Cedar, or Me-nom-in-ee River. A portage of only two miles in length connects Prairie Rice Lake with this river, and the foot of the portage, or the spot where it strikes the river, is twenty miles above its outlet into it. The lake being miry-bottomed, and shallow, is almost entirely covered with wild rice, and so thick and luxuriant does it grow, that the Indians are often obliged to cut passage ways through it for their bark canoes. From the manner in which they gather the rice, and the quantity which a family generally collects during the harvesting season, this lake alone would supply a body of two thousand Indians.

In the fall of 1850, when the writer passed through it, he found it occupied by fifty wigwams of the Ojibways, numbering over five hundred souls. They were busily employed in gathering the rice, camping separately in spots where it grew in the greatest thickness and abundance. The country surrounding the lake is sparsely covered with pine trees, through which fires appear to have occasionally run, burning the smaller trees and thickets, and giving the country a prairie-like appearance, which has given it the Indian name which it at present bears. One single island about four acres in size, and covered with a grove of beautiful elm trees, lies on the bosom of this picturesque lake. In times of danger, the Ojibway " rice makers" have often pitched their wigwams on it for greater security.

From the earliest period of their occupation of the Chippeway River country, the most fearless of the Ojibways came thither each fall of the year, to collect a portion of the abundant rice crop, notwithstanding its close vicinity

to the Dakota villages, and notwithstanding they lost lives
from their sudden attacks almost yearly.

In the year which has been mentioned, several wigwams
of the Lac Coutereille band, under the guidance of the
war-chief, " Yellow Head," collected at Prairie Rice Lake,
to gather wild rice, and as usual in those days of danger,
they located themselves on the island.   Early one morning
the chief called the men of the camp into his lodge, to take
a social smoke, when he informed them that he had been
visited during the night by his guardian spirit in a dream,
and he knew that the Dakotas must be lurking near.   He
bade them not to go on their usual day's hunt, and sent
two young men to go and scout the shores of the lake, to
discover some fresh signs of the enemy.   The scouts, embarking in a canoe, immediately started on their errand.
They had not arrived more than half a mile from the camp,
when, approaching the shore, they were fired at by an ambuscade of the enemy.   One was killed, and the other,
though severely wounded, succeeded, amid volleys of
bullets, in pushing his canoe out of their reach.

The men of the Ojibways, hearing the firing, all that
were able to bear arms grasped their weapons, and to the
number of twenty-five, many of whom were old men and
mere boys, embarked in their canoes, and paddled towards
the scene of action, to join the fight.   The Dakotas, perceiving this movement, sent a body of their warriors to lie
in ambush at the spot where they supposed the Ojibways
would attempt a landing.   The women of the camp, however, seeing the enemy collecting in large numbers to
intercept their men, halloed to them, and informing them
of the ambuscade, the Ojibways turned about, and landed
on the main shore, immediately opposite the island.   Intending to attack the Dakotas by land, they sent the canoes
back by some women who had come with them for the
purpose.   Yellow Head, then heading the party, led them

through a thicket of underbrush towards the point where the enemy were still firing at the scouts.

In passing through these thickets, Yellow Head discovered a Dakota women, holding in her arms a young boy, about two years old, covered with a profuse quantity of wampum and silver ornaments. She was the wife, and the child a son, of a noted Dakota war-chief who had been lately killed by the Ojibways, and she had followed the war party of her people, raised to revenge his death, in order to initiate her little son, and wipe the paint of mourning from her face. In expectation of a fight, the Dakotas had bade her to hide in these thickets, little thinking that they would be the first victims whose scalps would grace the belts of the Ojibways. Yellow Head, on perceiving the woman and child, yelled his fierce war-whoop, and rushing up to her he snatched the boy from her arms, and throwing him with all his force behind him, he bade his aged father (who was following his footsteps) to despatch it. He then pursued the woman, who had arisen, and now fled with great swiftness towards her friends, uttering piercing shrieks for help. The Dakotas, having heard the Ojibway war-yell, and now hearing the cries of their woman, ran, to the number of near one hundred men, to her rescue. A younger warrior of the Ojibways had passed his war-chief, and though seeing the advance of the enemy, he followed up the chase, till, catching up with her, he stabbed her in the back, and was stooping over her body to cut off her head, when his chief called on him to fly, for the Dakotas were on him. Not a moment too soon did the young warrior obey this call, for the spears of the enemy almost reached his back as he turned to fly, and being laden with the bloody head, which he would not drop, the foremost of the Dakotas fast gained on him ; but not till he felt the end of a spear point entering his back did he call on his chief to turn and help him.

Yellow Head, who was noted for his great courage, instantly obeyed the call, and throwing himself behind a pine tree, he shot down the Dakota who had caught up with him, and was almost despatching his comrade. The fallen warrior was dressed in a white shirt, wore a silver medal on his breast, and silver ornaments on his arms. He carried nothing but a spear in his hand, denoting him to be a chief, and the leader of the Dakota war party. He was the uncle of the boy who had just been dispatched, which accounts for the eagerness with which he pursued the Ojibway warrior, keeping so close to his back that his warriors dared not discharge their fire-arms, for fear of hitting him.

The moment the Dakota leader fell, his fellows took cover behind the trees, and Yellow Head, having saved his comrade, who now stood panting by his side, called on his people, " if they were men, to turn and follow his example." But ten out of the twenty-five were brave enough to obey his call, and these, taking cover behind trees and bushes, fought by his side all day. Though the Dakotas ten times outnumbered them, the Ojibways caused them to retreat at nightfall, leaving seven of their warriors dead on the field. The Ojibways lost but three men, besides the scout who had been killed by the ambuscade. Some days after the fight, the Ojibways discovered a number of bodies which the enemy, to conceal their loss, had hid in a swamp adjacent to the battle-field.

The Dakotas, in their occasional " peace makings" with the Ojibways, have generally accorded to them the art of being the best fighters in a thicket or forest, while they claim an equal superiority on the open prairie, being swifter of foot, and better dodgers. The Ojibways claim, also, that they fight with cooler courage than the Dakotas, and that they never throw away their ammunition ; and from the general results of their numerous rencontres, it must be conceded that they are far the best shots. These things are mentioned to account for the numerous instances where a determined few have committed such havoc in the ranks of the enemy, as almost to surpass belief.

On another occasion, a single lodge of Ojibways located on the shores of Prairie Rice Lake, was attacked by a party of two hundred Dakotas, and all its inmates massacred. The head of the family, a man noted in the wars of those times for great courage, happened to be away, spearing fish, when his family were murdered. Hearing the firing, he ran to their rescue, but arrived only to witness the ashes of his lodge, and the mangled remains of his wife and children. Determined on revenge or death, singly he pursued the enemy, and having caught up with them, he sustained the unequal fight till his ammunition gave out, when, having seen several of the enemy fall under his aim, he turned, and though nearly surrounded, he made his escape. Shortly after, he returned to the field of the fight, and discovered five Dakotas whom he had killed, left by their friends in a sitting posture, facing the west. Having scalped them, he returned, without kin, but loaded with honor, to the village of his people.

About the same time (between fifty and sixty years ago), another family were massacred by the Dakotas at this lake. Le-bud-ee, a son of the old man who was killed on this occasion, raised a small war party during the ensuing winter, and attacked a large lodge of the enemy on Hay River. There were eight men of the Dakotas in the lodge, who returned the fire of the Ojibways very briskly. Becoming desperate at their obstinate defence, Le-bud-ee, followed by one of his bravest comrades, rushed madly forward, and cutting open the leathern covering of the lodge, they entered into a hand to hand conflict with such of the Dakotas as still remained alive. Le-bud-ee's comrade was killed in the act of entering the lodge, while he himself jumped in, despatched a warrior with his knife, and had taken two women captive, before the remainder of his party had fairly arrived to his help. This action is related by the Ojibways as one of great courage, as they seldom, in their warfare, come to a hand to hand conflict.

At a peace-making, following soon after this last event, the two captives of Le-bud-ee were returned to the Dakotas.

Many more instances similar in nature to these which have been related in this chapter, might be given to swell the annual record of bloodshed in which the division of the Ojibway tribe under our present consideration were engaged in, during this period of their history, but it is deemed that enough have been presented to illustrate their mode of living, and warfare, and the dangers which daily assailed them in becoming possessed of the country over which their children now claim unquestioned right, over any other tribe of their fellow red men.

In this chapter we have brought down the annals, or history of this section of the Ojibways, to within a half century of the present time.

The grand or principal villages at Lac Coutereille and Lac du Flambeau, had commenced to shoot forth new branches or communities, who located their wigwams on some of the many beautiful lakes and streams which swell the waters of the Chippeway and Wisconsin. Lac Shatac early became a separate village. So also, Ke-che-puk-wa-i-wah, a reservoir or lake through which the Chippeway River passes.

From Lac du Flambeau, a large community branched off down the Wisconsin, who sometimes came in deadly contact with the Winnebagoes, who occupied the country about the Fox River, and who sometimes joined the war parties of their relatives, the Dakotas, against the Ojibways. This custom they followed but seldom, and never openly, as being literally surrounded by tribes of the Algic stock, they always feared to enter into an open war with any of their branches or relatives.

Another considerable band located themselves at Suk-a-aug-un-ing towards Green Bay. They are now known as the Pelican Lake band. In 1848 this band numbered over two hundred souls. They have since been nearly cut off by the smallpox, and other diseases introduced among them by the white population, which has spread over this portion of their former country.

CHAPTER XXVII.

OJIBWAYS OF THE WISCONSIN AND CHIPPEWAY RIVERS.

System of governmental polity among the Chippeway and Wisconsin River villages—Descendants of Ke-che-ne-zy-auh—The ascendancy of the Crane Totem family—Keesh-ke-mun chief of the Lac du Flambeau—Sub-chiefs, and war-chiefs—Death of the war-chiefs Yellow Head, and Wolf's Father in battle with the Dakotas—Shawano prophet, brother of Tecumseh—He raises an excitement among the Ojibways—His creed—One hundred and fifty canoes of Ojibways start from Shaug-a-waum-ik-ong to visit him at Detroit —They are turned back at the Pictured Rocks by Michel Cadotte—Anecdote respecting the deceptions of the prophet—Ojibways pillage Michel Cadotte's trading post at Lac Coutereille—Causes and consequence of this act—Cadotte curtails his trade—In 1823 he sells out his trading interest, and retires to private life—Brief review of his pioneer life.

AMONG the different bands of the Ojibways, occupying the country drained by the currents of the Wisconsin and Chippeway Rivers, something like a regular system of governmental polity existed at this time. The dangers of their position (being continually subject to the attacks of the powerful Dakotas) linked them together, in a bond of brotherhood, which remained unbroken in its natural simplicity, till the fur traders entered their country in opposition to one another, and to forward their own views and interests, sowed dissensions among them, and eventually almost broke the beautiful system which had held them bound to one another like brothers. This remark is applicable to the whole tribe, but at this stage of our history, we refrain from entering into a discussion of this important question.

At the great convocation of tribes, held by the French nation at Sault Ste. Marie, in 1671, the traditions of the Crane family assert that Ke-che-ne-zuh-yauh, the head of their family, was recognized as principal chief over the

Ojibway tribe; and a golden[1] medal was placed on his breast, as a badge of his rank. He resided at La Pointe, and at his death left two sons, A-ke-gui-ow (Neck of Earth), and She-da-wish (Bad Pelican), the eldest of whom succeeded him in his rank, and continued to reside at La Pointe, while the youngest became the first pioneer towards the headwaters of the Wisconsin River.

A-ke-gui-ow, after his death, was succeeded by his son, Waub-uj-e-jauk (White Crane), who could rightfully claim the first chieftainship in his tribe; but who, being of an unambitious and retiring disposition, neglecting his civil duties, and attending only to those of the chase, he became at last superseded by a noted character of his time, named Au-daig-we-os (Crow's Flesh), the head or chief of the Loon family, who is justly celebrated in the traditions of his people, for wisdom, honesty, and an unvarying friendship to the whites. During his lifetime, his influence extended over the whole tribe, and his descendants to this day have upheld in some respects the position which their illustrious ancestor attained. The Cranes did not fully regain their former rank in the tribe, till the convocation of the northwestern tribes, held at Prairie du Chien by the United States government in 1825, at which Hon. Lewis Cass acted as commissioner. This treaty was held for the purpose of promoting peace between the different belligerent tribes, and that a just partition might be made between them, of the country which they occupied. The Ojibway tribe was fully represented; chiefs and warriors being present from the Upper Mississippi, Lake Superior, St. Croix, Chippeway and Wisconsin Rivers. Shin-ga-ba-ossin (Spirit Stone), was acknowledged to be the representative of the Crane family, and his name was signed to the treaty,

---

[1] There is no official record of a golden medal having been given at that time.—E. D. N.

as head chief of the tribe. He came from Sault Ste. Marie, over which band, or village, he was resident chief.

Prior to this event, the dignity and influence of the Cranes had been upheld by Keesh-ke-mun (Sharpened Stone), the son of Sha-da-nish, the first Ojibway pioneer towards the Wisconsin. He is first mentioned by the old men and traders of the tribe, as having attained a prominent position as chief, between forty and fifty years ago. He made it his home, or permanent village, at Lac du Flambeau, and from this point he ruled over that division of his tribe, who occupied the midland country, between Lake Superior, southwest to the Mississippi. Under him was a chief of the warriors, whose business it was to carry out, by force, if necessary, the wishes of his chief. Next in rank to the war-chief was the pipe bearer, or Osh-ka-ba-wis, who officiated in all public councils, making known the wishes of his chief, and distributing amongst his fellows, the presents which the traders occasionally gave to the chief to propitiate his good-will.

Keesh-ke-mun was not only chief by hereditary descent, but he made himself truly such, through the wisdom and firmness of his conduct, both to his people and the whites. During his lifetime, he possessed an unbounded influence over the division of his tribe with whom he resided, and generally over the Lake Superior bands and villages.

On the Chippeway River, the traders had recognized as a chief Mis-ko-mun-e-dous (Little Red Spirit), a man noted for courage in war, and especially for great success in the chase. He belonged to the Marten family. At Lac Coutereille, Mon-so-ne (Moose Tail), of the Catfish family, presided as resident chief; and in fact over each separate community, one, either noted for courage in war, success in hunting, wisdom, or age, was recognized, as head man, or chief. All these acted under and listened to the wishes of Keesh-ke-mun. And to this day (even after their former simple and natural civil polity had been so entirely broken up, that it is a doubt in the minds of many whether the Indians ever possessed any form of government), the descendants of this chief still retain the shadow of their former ascendancy and real chieftainship.

Waub-ish-gang-aug-e (White Crow), the son and successor of Keesh-ke-mun, fully sustained the influence of his deceased father over the inland bands, till his death in 1847. His son Ah-mous (the Little Bee), though lacking the firmness, energy, and noble appearance of his fathers, and though their formerly large concentred bands are now split up by the policy of traders and United States agents into numerous small factions headed by new-made upstart chiefs, yet virtually, in the estimation of his tribe, he holds the first rank over the Lac du Flambeau and Chippeway River division, and his right to a first rank in the councils of his people is unquestioned.

The war-chiefs, though second in rank to the civil chiefs, have often attained a paramount influence over the villages or sections of the tribe with whom they resided; but this influence (before they learned to follow some of the evil ways of the whites) they always used towards sustaining and strengthening the hereditary civil chiefs. The war chieftainship was usually obtained by courage and exploits in war, and success in leading a war party, through spiritual vision, against the enemy. It sometimes descended from father to son, in fact always, where the son approved himself in a manner to secure the confidence of the warriors.

Half a century ago, in the Chippeway River district, Yellow Head, of Lac Coutereille, was a noted war-chief, and so also, Ke-dug-e-be-shew (Speckled Lynx), who first founded the village on Lac Shatac. The father of Maheen-gun (Wolf), at present a chief of Chippeway River, was also a noted chief. These men guided the war and peace movements of their respective villages, and they were prominent actors in all the most important rencontres which occurred between their section of the Ojibways, and the Dakotas.

It was a day of deep mourning amongst their people, when the brave war-chiefs, Yellow Head and Wolf's Father, fell fighting side by side, against immense odds of Dakotas. With a small party of their fellows they had been hunting deer by torchlight, during the hot nights of summer, on the Red Cedar River. During the course of their hunt, being both men " not knowing fear," they had approached too near the haunts of the Dakotas, and being discovered, one morning, while engaged in curing meat at the mouth of Hay River, a large party of the enemy stealthily surrounded and suddenly attacked them. The two war-chiefs escaped the first volley of bullets; and bade the young men, who were with them, to save themselves by flight, while they withstood the attack. Fighting against immense odds, they were at last forced into the river, where, in crossing to an island which lay close to the scene of action, Wolf's Father received a bullet through his brains, while Yellow Head, having reached the shelter of the island, sustained the unequal fight till his ammunition failed him, and the Dakotas, after a severe struggle, gloried in the possession of his long much-coveted scalp. The saying of the people, is, that " on their journey to the land of spirits, these two warriors went well attended by Dakotas, whom they slew at the time of their departure (or death)."

After this occurrence, and the usual levying of war parties, and consequent bloody revenge which followed it, no event of any immediate importance occurred on the Chippeway and Wisconsin Rivers till the year 1808, when, under the influence of the excitement which the Shaw-nee prophet, brother of Tecumseh, succeeded in raising, even to the remotest village of the Ojibways, the men of the Lac Coutereille village, pillaged the trading house of Michel

Cadotte at Lac Coutereille, while under charge of a clerk
named John Baptiste Corbin. From the lips of Mons.
Corbin, who is still living[1] at Lac Coutereille, at the advanced age of seventy-six years, and who has now been
fifty-six years in the Ojibway country, I have obtained a
reliable account of this transaction:—

Michel Cadotte, after having fairly opened the resources
of the fur trade of the Chippeway River district, and having approved himself as a careful and successful trader,
entered into an arrangement with the Northwest Fur Company, who at this time nearly monopolized the fur trade
of the Ojibways. Mons. Cadotte located a permanent post
or depot on the island of La Pointe,[2] on the spot known at
the present time as the " Old Fort." He also built a trading house at Lac Coutereille, which in the year 1800, was
first placed in charge of J. B. Corbin. To supply these
posts, he procured his outfit from the Northwest Company
at Grand Portage. It is said that his outfit of goods each
year amounted to the sum of forty thousand dollars, which
he distributed in different posts on the south shores of Lake
Superior, Wisconsin, Chippeway, and St. Croix Rivers.
He resided himself at La Pointe, having taken to wife the
daughter of White Crane, the hereditary chief of this village. Cadotte, though he continued to winter in different
parts of the Ojibway country from this time, always considered La Pointe Island as his home, and here he died in
1836, at the advanced age of seventy-two years.

In the year 1808, during the summer while John B.
Corbin had charge of the Lac Coutereille post, messengers,
whose faces were painted black, and whose actions appeared
strange, arrived at the different principal villages of the

---

[1] A. D. 1852.

[2] Isle De Tour or St. Michel is the name given to La Pointe Island by Franquelin in 1688, which it retained until after the year 1800. Madeline Island
is a comparatively modern designation.—E. D. N.

Ojibways. In solemn councils they performed certain ceremonies, and told that the Great Spirit had at last condescended to hold communion with the red race, through the medium of a Shawano prophet, and that they had been sent to impart the glad tidings. The Shawano sent them word that the Great Spirit was about to take pity on his red children, whom he had long forsaken for their wickedness. He bade them to return to the primitive usages and customs of their ancestors, to leave off the use of everything which the evil white race had introduced among them. Even the fire-steel must be discarded, and fire made as in ages past, by the friction of two sticks. And this fire, once lighted in their principal villages, must always be kept sacred and burning. He bade them to discard the use of fire-water—to give up lying and stealing and warring with one another. He even struck at some of the roots of the Me-da-we religion, which he asserted had become permeated with many evil medicines, and had lost almost altogether its original uses and purity. He bade the medicine men to throw away their evil and poisonous medicines, and to forget the songs and ceremonies attached thereto, and he introduced new medicines and songs in their place. He prophesied that the day was nigh, when, if the red race listened to and obeyed his words, the Great Spirit would deliver them from their dependence on the whites, and prevent their being finally down-trodden and exterminated by them. The prophet invited the Ojibways to come and meet him at Detroit, where in person, he would explain to them the revelations of the "Great Master of Life." He even claimed the power of causing the dead to arise, and come again to life.

It is astonishing how quickly this new belief obtained possession in the minds of the Ojibways. It spread like wild-fire throughout their entire country, and even reached the remotest northern hunters who had allied themselves with the Crees and Assiniboines. The strongest possible proof which can be adduced of their entire belief, is in their obeying the mandate to throw away their medicine bags, which the Indian holds most sacred and inviolate. It is said that the shores of Sha-ga-waum-ik-ong were strewed with the remains of medicine bags, which had been committed to the deep. At this place, the Ojibways collected in great numbers. Night and day, the ceremonies of the new religion were performed, till it was at last determined to go in a body to Detroit, to visit the prophet. One hundred and fifty canoes are said to have actually started from Pt. Shag-a-waum-ik-ong for this purpose, and so strong was their belief, that a dead child was brought from Lac Coutereille to be taken to the prophet for resuscitation. This large party arrived on their foolish journey, as far as the Pictured Rocks, on Lake Superior, when, meeting with Michel Cadotte, who had been to Sault Ste. Marie for his annual outfit of goods, his influence, together with information of the real motives of the prophet in sending for them, succeeded in turning them back. The few Ojibways who had gone to visit the prophet from the more eastern villages of the tribe, had returned home disappointed, and brought back exaggerated accounts of the suffering through hunger, which the proselytes of the prophet who had gathered at his call, were enduring, and also giving the lie to many of the attributes which he had assumed. It is said that at Detroit he would sometimes leave the camp of the Indians, and be gone, no one knew whither, for three and four days at a time. On his return he would assert that he had been to the spirit land and communed with the master of life. It was, however, soon discovered that he only went and hid himself in a hollow oak which stood behind the hill on which the most beautiful portion of Detroit City is now built. These stories became current among the Ojibways, and each succeeding year developing more fully the fraud and warlike purpose of the Shawano, the excitement gradually died away among the Ojibways, and the medicine men and chiefs who had become such ardent believers, hung their heads in shame whenever the Shawano was mentioned. At this day it is almost impossible to procure any information on this subject from the old men who are still living, who were once believers and preached their religion, so anxious are they to conceal the fact of their once having been so egregiously duped. The venerable chiefs Buffalo, of La Pointe, and Esh-ke-bug-e-coshe, of Leech Lake, who have been men of strong minds and unusual intelligence, were not only firm believers of the prophet, but undertook to preach his doctrines.

One essential good resulted to the Ojibways through the Shawano excitement—they threw away their poisonous roots and medicines; and poisoning, which was formerly practised by their worst class of medicine men, has since become almost entirely unknown. So much has been written respecting the prophet and the new beliefs which he endeavored to inculcate amongst his red brethren, that we will no longer dwell on the merits or demerits of his pretended mission. It is now evident that he and his brother Tecumseh had in view, and worked to effect, a general alliance of the red race, against the whites, and their final extermination from the "Great Island which the great spirit had given as an inheritance to his red children."

In giving an account of the Shawano excitement among the Ojibways, we have digressed somewhat from the course of our narrative. The messengers of the prophet reached the Ojibway village at Lac Coutereille, early in the summer of 1808, and the excitement which they succeeded in raising, tended greatly to embitter the Indians' mind against the white race. There was a considerable quantity of goods stored in Michel Cadotte's storehouse, which was located on the shores of the lake, and some of the most foolish of the Indians, headed by Nig-gig (The Otter)—who is still[1] living—proposed to destroy the trader's goods, in accordance with the prophet's teachings to discard the use of everything which the white man had learned them to want. The influence of the chief Mons-o-ne at first checked the young men, but the least additional spark to their excitement caused his voice to be unheard, and his influence to be without effect. John Baptiste Corbin, a young Canadian of good education, was in charge of the post, and through his indiscretion the flame was lighted which led to the pillage of the post, and caused him to flee for his life, one hundred miles through a pathless wilderness, to the shores of Lake Superior. As was the general custom of the early French traders, he had taken to wife a young woman of the Lac Coutereille village, related to an influential family. During the Shawano excitement, he found occasion to give his wife a severe beating, and to send her away almost naked, from under his roof, to her parents' wigwam. This act exasperated the Indians; and as the tale spread from lodge to lodge, the young men leaped into their canoes and paddling over to the trading house, which stood about one mile opposite their village, they broke open the doors and helped themselves to all which the storehouses contained. Mons. Corbin, during the excitement of the pillage, fled in affright. An Ojibway whom he had befriended, followed his tracks, and catching up with him, gave him his blanket, moccasins, and fire-works, with directions to enable him to reach La Pointe, Shag-a waum-ik-ong, on Lake Superior, which he did, after several days of hardship and solitary wandering.

This act, on the part of the Lac Coutereille band, was very much regretted by the rest of the tribe. Keesh-ke-

---

[1] A. D. 1852.

mun, the chief at Lac du Flambeau, was highly enraged against this village, and in open council, he addressed the ringleaders with the most bitter and cutting epithets. It came near being the cause of a bloody family feud, and good-will became eventually restored only through the exertions of the kind-hearted Michel Cadotte, who, by this stroke, became crippled in his means as an Indian trader, and who from this time gradually curtailed his business, till in the year 1823 he sold out all his interests in the Ojibway trade to his two sons-in-law, Lyman M. and Truman A. Warren, and retired to a quiet retreat at La Pointe, after having passed forty years in the arduous, active and dangerous career of a pioneer fur trader. In 1784 we find him wintering with a small outfit of goods on the Num-a-ka-gun River, and year after year moving his post further westward, leading the Ojibways into richer, but more dangerous hunting grounds. In 1792 we find him wintering on Leaf River of the Upper Mississippi, and in company with his elder brother, opening a vast area of Indian country, to the enterprise of fur traders.

The marks of his wintering posts are pointed out at Thief River, emptying into Crow Wing, at Leech, Winnipeg, and Cass Lakes, at Pokaguma Falls, and at Oak Point, on the Upper Mississippi, where he is said again to have narrowly escaped the bullets of the wild Indians. At Yellow Lake, Snake River, Po-ka-guma (in the St. Croix region) and at different points on the Chippeway and Wisconsin Rivers, the marks of this old pioneer are still visible. Like all other traders who have passed their lifetime in the Indian country, possessing a charitable heart and an open hand, ever ready to relieve the poor and suffering Indian, he died poor, but not unlamented. He was known among the Ojibways by the name of Ke-che-me-shane (Great Michel).

CHAPTER XXVIII.

AFFAIRS OF THE OJIBWAYS ON THE ST. CROIX.

State of affairs between the Ojibways and Dakotas on the St. Croix River—
Two Ojibways, carrying a peace message, are killed by the Dakotas—Revenge of the Ojibways—Battle on " Sunrise Prairie"—Dakotas attack a
camp of Ojibway hunters during a term of peace—Ojibways raise a war
party—They make a midnight attack on a Dakota village at the mouth of
Willow River—A slight sketch of Waub-ash-aw, a noted Ojibway warrior—
Bi-aj-ig, "the lone warrior"—Anecdote of his hardihood and bravery—
Slight sketch of Shosh-e-man—Be-she-ke—Names of living chiefs of hereditary descent.

DURING the middle and latter part of the eighteenth century, the hunting camps of the Dakotas and Ojibways
often met on either banks of the St. Croix River, as far
down as the Falls. Spots are pointed out, on Sunrise,
Rush, and Snake Rivers, where bloody fights, massacres,
and surprises have taken place, and where lives of helpless
women and children, as well as stalwart warriors, have
been sacrificed to their implacable warfare. It happened,
sometimes, that the camps of either tribe would meet in
peace, in order that the hunters might pursue the chase
during the winter in security. But no sooner did spring
again make its appearance, than the peace was treacherously broken, by either party, and war raged again during
the summer, full as deadly as ever.

They did not always succeed in their attempts, each fall,
to smoke the pipe of peace together. On one occasion the
Ojibway chief, Mons-o-man-ay, sent two of his young men
with a peace pipe to a large camp of Dakotas who were, as
usual in the fall, approaching to make their winter hunts
on the St. Croix River. These young men were received
in the enemies' lodges and treacherously killed. They were
relatives of the Ojibway chieftain, and he made prepara-

tions during the winter to revenge their death. He collected a large party of warriors, and when the snow melted from the ground, he followed the trail of the Dakotas as they returned towards their villages on the Mississippi. He caught up with their camp, at a prairie on Sunrise River. They numbered many lodges, and around their camp they had thrown up an embankment of earth about four feet high. In order to more readily accomplish his vengeance, the chief approached the encampment in open day, after the Dakota hunters had dispersed for the day's chase. He approached with the semblance of a peace party, carrying the white man's flag at the head of his long line of warriors. The enemy for a time appeared uncertain how to receive him, but as they saw the Ojibways continue slowly to advance to the very foot of their defences, two warriors, unarmed, rushed forth to meet them, thinking that they came in peace. Without waiting for the orders of their chief, some of the young Ojibway warriors immediately fired on them. One succeeded in making his escape, while the bleeding scalp of the other dangled on the belt of a warrior.

The Ojibways ran up to the Dakota defences, from behind which they fired repeated volleys into the defenceless lodges within, thus turning to their own advantage the embankment of earth which the enemy had formed with such great labor. The Dakota hunters, hearing the noise of the battle, flew back to their camp, and the fight every moment, as their ranks increased, became more hotly contested. Towards evening the Ojibways were dislodged from their position, and forced to retreat, with the loss of several killed and many wounded. The loss to the Dakotas which was much greater, judging from long rows of graves they left on the spot, and which my informants assert, are still plainly discernible within the inclosure of the earthen embankment.

Several years after this occurrence, the Dakotas, after having made a formal peace with the Ojibways, and agreed to hunt in peace and friendship, suddenly attacked a small camp of hunters and killed several women and children. During the summer following, the Ojibways collected to the number of sixty warriors, and proceeded down the St. Croix River, to revenge this act of perfidy. They discovered their enemies encamped in a large village near the mouth of Willow River. They approached the camp during the middle of a pitchy dark night, and the chiefs placed two or three men to stand by each lodge, into which, at a given signal, they were to fire a volley, aiming at the spots where they supposed the enemy were lying asleep. Immediately loading their guns, when the inmates of the lodges would jump up in affright, they were to fire another volley and immediately retreat, as even the lodges of the Dakotas many times outnumbered the warriors of the Ojibways, and the enemy were too strong to risk with them a protracted fight. They judged also that the Dakotas were preparing to go on a war party, from the warsongs, drumming, and dancing which they had kept up throughout the village during the evening.

The orders of the Ojibway leader were strictly adhered to, and but two volleys were poured into the enemies' lodges, when the party suddenly retreated. The Dakotas, however, recovering from the first surprise of the sudden and unexpected attack, grasped their arms and rushing forth, a hundred warriors were soon on the rear of the midnight invaders. The Ojibways, anxious for a fight, made a stand, and a fierce fight ensued in the darkness, the combatants aiming at the flashes of their enemies' musketry. The bravest warriors gradually approached to within a few feet of one another, in the midst of the darkness, when a Dakota chief was heard to give orders to his people in a loud voice, to divide into two parties, and making circuits to the right and left, surround the enemy and cut off their retreat. An Ojibway warrior, who had been a captive among the Dakotas, understanding these orders, quietly informed his fellows, and when the enemy's fire slackened in front, they made a silent but quick retreat.

They had arrived but a short distance from the scene of action, when they suddenly heard the firing and yelling of a fierce fight, at the spot which they had just left. The noise lasted for some minutes, and the Ojibways learnt afterwards, that their enemy, dividing into two parties, with intent to surround them, had met in the darkness and mistaking one another for Ojibways, they had fired several volleys into each other's ranks, and continued to fight till, by their manner .of yelling the war-whoop, they had discovered their mistake. The Dakotas, on this occasion, suffered a severe loss, infinitely aggravated from the fact of their having inflicted a portion of it on themselves. They consequently abandoned the war party, for which they had been making preparation. The slightest rebuff of this nature, always leads to the disorganization of a war party when on the point of starting. The slightest accidents, or evil omens, will send them back even when once fairly started on their expedition.

Several warriors have arisen from the ranks of the St. Croix Ojibways who have distinguished themselves by deeds of great bravery, and whose names consequently live in the traditions and lodge stories of their people. Waub-ash-aw was the name of one, of part Dakota extraction, who flourished as a brave and successful war-leader, during the middle of the past century. He fought in many engagements, and was eventually killed at the battle of St. Croix Falls. He was one of the spiritual, or clairvoyant, leaders of the war party who fought on this occasion, and is said to have predicted his own death.

BI-A-JIG, THE LONE WARRIOR.

When the Ojibways first took possession of the St. Croix River region, four generations ago, while still carrying on an active war with the Odugamies (Foxes), a warrior named Bi-a-jig became noted for the bravery and success with which he repelled the oft-repeated attacks of the Foxes and Dakotas.

He was accustomed to leave his family at Sha-ga-waum-ik-ong, or some other place of safety, and, entirely alone, he would proceed to the hunting grounds of his enemies, and in their very midst pursue his hunts. Numberless were the attacks made on his isolated little lodge by the Foxes, but he as often miraculously escaped their bullets and arrows, and generally caused many of their warriors to "bite the dust." Each spring he would return to his people's villages with nearly as many human scalps dangling to his belt as there were beaver skins in his pack.

So often did the Foxes attack him without success, by night and day, that they at last considered him in the light of a spirit, invulnerable to arrows and bullets, and they allowed him to pursue the chase wherever he listed, unmolested. Such a fear did they have of his prowess, that whenever they attacked a camp of Ojibways, if the defence appeared unusually desperate, they would call out to inquire if Bi-a-jig was present, and on that warrior showing himself, the assailants would immediately desist from the attack and retreat.

The following characteristic anecdote is related, illustrating the hardihood and bravery of Bi-a-jig: After the Foxes had been driven by the Ojibways from the midland country between the Mississippi and Lake Superior, they retired towards Lake Michigan, and on Green Bay they located themselves in a large village. They sued for peace with the Ojibways, which, being granted, it became customary for parties from either tribe, to pay one another visits of peace. On one occasion, Bi-a-jig joined a small party of his people, who proceeded to pay a visit to the village of the Foxes on Green Bay. They were well received, and entertained with divers feastings and amusements.

One day the Foxes proposed a grand war-dance, where the warriors of each tribe should have license to relate their exploits in war. The dance was held in a long lodge erected purposely for the occasion. The men of the Ojibways were seated on one side of this lodge, while the more numerous Foxes occupied the other. A red stake was planted in the centre, near which was also planted a war-club, with which each warrior, wishing to relate his exploits, was to strike the red stake, as a signal for the music and dancing to cease. The dancing commenced, and as the warriors circled the stake, occasionally yelling their fierce war-whoop, they soon became excited, and warrior after warrior plucked the club and told of bloody deeds.

Among the Ojibways was an old man, bent with age and sorrow. In the course of the late war with the Foxes he had lost ten sons, one after another, till not a child was left to cheer his fireside in his old age. Often had he gone on the war trail to revenge his losses, but he always returned without having seen the enemy. On the occasion of this dance, he sat and listened to the vaunts of his children's murderers, and he could not ease the pain at his heart, by being able to jump up and tell of having in turn killed or scalped a single Fox.

Among the Foxes was a warrior noted far and wide for his bravery and numberless deeds of blood. He was the first war-chief of his tribe, and his head was covered with eagle plumes, each denoting an enemy he had slain, a scalp he had taken, or a captive whom he had tortured to death. This man again and again plucked the war-club to relate his exploits. He related, in the most aggravating manner, of having captured an Ojibway youth and burnt him at the stake, vividly describing his torments. From the time and place where this capture was made, the old Ojibway knew that it was one of his sons, and under a feeling of deep aggravation, he jumped up, and grasping the war-club, he struck the red stake, but all he could say, was : "I once packed my little mat (war-sack), and proceeded towards the country of my enemies," then take his seat in silence.

The Fox warrior judged from this that he was the father of the youth whom he had tortured ; and again grasping the club, he told of another whom he had captured and burnt with fire ; then dancing in front of the old man, he yelled his war-whoop in aggravation. In quick succession he told of another and another he had taken, and treated in like manner, addressing himself to the bereaved father, of whose children he knew he was telling, vividly describing their tortures, and enjoying the deep anguish which his words caused in the breast of the poor old man, whose sorrowing and aged head hung lower and lower between his knees. Aggravated beyond measure, once more he jumped up, but all he could say was as before: "I once packed my little mat, and proceeded to the country of my enemies," and as he took his seat, he was jeered with laughter by the Foxes, who revelled in his distress. Once more, amidst the encouraging yells of his fellows, the Fox war-chief grasped the war-club, and dancing before the old man, he told of another of his sons whom he had treated with aggravated tortures.

Bi-a-jig had sat calmly by, smoking his pipe. Not joining in the dance, he had taken silent notice of the whole scene. His heart yearned for his old comrade, whose sorrows were being so wantonly opened afresh, by the cruel and ungenerous Foxes. His party was but a handful in the midst of their numerous enemies, but this did not deter him from following the impulse of his good nature. He had borne the aggravating yells of the Foxes as long as his patience could last, and the moment the Fox war-chief returned the club to its place, amidst the cheers of his fellows, Bi-a-jig sprang up, and grasping the club, he struck the vaunting warrior in the mouth, and brought him to the ground, exclaiming, "My name is Bi-a-jig; I too am a man!" As the Fox warrior. arose to his feet, Bi-a-jig again struck him on the mouth, and exclaimed. "You call yourself a man. I too am a man! we will fight, to see who will live to tell of killing a warrior!"

During this scene the Foxes had grasped their arms, and the Ojibways, though far outnumbered even within the lodge, jumped up and yelled their war whoop, all of course supposing that the Fox war-chief, who had made himself so conspicuous, would resent the blow of Bi-a-jig, which act would have led to a general battle. The disgraced warrior, however, disappointed their expectation. He quietly arose and left the lodge, with the blood gushing from his battered mouth. The old man, whose feelings he had been so unwarrantably harrowing, pointed at him with his fore-finger, and yelled a jeering whoop. His revenge was sweet.

The name of Bi-a-jig had become a common household word with the Foxes, with which mothers quieted their children into silence, and scared them into obedience. Their knowledge of his prowess, and belief in his being invulnerable, saved his Ojibway peace party from total destruction on this occasion.

Shosh-e-man (Snow Glider) became noted as a war-chief during the latter part of the eighteenth century. He belonged to the Awause Totem Clan. He was much loved by the traders, for his unvarying friendship to the whites. In company with John Baptiste Cadotte, he often encount-

ered great danger in attempts to make peace with the Dakotas. He was also noted for great oratorical powers, and
he is mentioned by some of the old traders who knew him
as being the most eloquent man the Ojibways have ever
produced. No-din, his son, succeeded him in his rank as
chief of a portion of the St. Croix district. He is also dead,
and none are now living to perpetuate the chieftainship of
this family.

Buffalo, of the Bear Clan, also became noted as a chief
of the St. Croix Ojibways, in fact superseding in importance and influence the hereditary chiefs of this division.
Having committed a murder, he originally fled from the
Sault Ste. Marie and took refuge on the St. Croix. The
traders, for his success in hunting, soon made him a chief
of some importance. His son, Ka-gua-dash, has succeeded
him as chief of a small band.

The descendants of the hereditary chief of the Wolf Totem, are, Na-guon-abe (Feather End), and Mun-o-min-ik-a-
sheen (Rice Maker), chiefs of Mille Lac ; I-aub-aus (Little
Buck), chief of Rice Lake, and Shon-e-yah, (Money), chief
of Pokaguma.

As has been remarked in a former chapter, the Ojibway
pioneers on the St. Croix first located their village at
Rice Lake, and next at Yellow Lake. The villages at
Pokaguma and at Knife Lake are of comparative recent
origin, within the memory of present living Indians.

About thirty years ago [1820] the Ojibways were, many
of them, destroyed by the measles, or the " great red skin,"
as they term it, on the St. Croix ; whole communities and
families were entirely cut off, and the old traders affirm
that at least one-third of the " Rice Makers," or St. Croix
Indians, disappeared under the virulence of this pestilence.
Other portions of the tribe did not suffer so much, though
some villages, especially that of Sandy Lake, became nearly
depopulated.

CHAPTER XXIX.

THE PILLAGERS.

Present number of the Pillager warriors—Their reputation for bravery—Severe
fight with the Dakotas at Battle Lake, and great sacrifice of their warriors
—Exploit of We-non-ga—Night attack on a camp of Dakotas at Chief's
Mountain.

NOTWITHSTANDING the continual drain made in their
ranks by their inveterate and exterminating war with the
Dakotas, the large band of the Ojibways who lived on
Leech Lake, and had become known by the name of Pillagers, continued gradually to increase in numbers, through
accessions from the more eastern villages of their tribe.
Their men capable of bearing arms (most of whom have
actually seen service) number, at the present time,[1] about
three hundred.   They have ever borne the reputation of
being the bravest and most warlike division of the Ojibways, from the fact of their ever having formed the vanguard of the tribe, and occupied the most dangerous ground
in their westward advance and conquests.   As a sample of
their bravery and hardihood, we shall devote this chapter
in giving an account of one of their numerous and bloody
rencontres with the Dakotas, wherein they lost many of
their bravest warriors.

About fifty-seven years ago, John Baptiste Cadotte (who
has already been mentioned in previous chapters) arrived
at Red Cedar, or Cass Lake, late in the fall, with a supply
of goods, ammunition, and other necessaries, intending to
pass the winter in trading with the Pillagers and northern
Ojibways.   The Pillagers, at their village on Leech Lake,
were preparing to go on a grand war party against the Da-

------

[1] A. D. 1852.

kotas, but being destitute of ammunition, the men repaired in a body to Cass Lake, to procure a supply from the trader who had so opportunely arrived. It being contrary to his interests as a trader, that the Indians should go to war at this season of the year, Mons. Cadotte endeavored to dissuade them from their purpose. He invited them to council, and after stating to them his wishes, he presented some tobacco, and a small keg of liquor to each head, or representative chief, of the several grand clans, or totems, and promised them, that if they would give up their present warlike intentions, and hunt well during the winter, in the spring he would give them all the ammunition he might have on hand, to use against their enemies.

These rare presents, and promise, in connection with Cadotte's great influence among them as their relative, induced the Pillagers to promise to give up their general war party. With their present of fire-water, they returned to their village at Leech Lake, to hold a grand frolic, which, in those early days, were seldom and far between. When their revel had been ended, and all had once more become sober, one morning at sunrise Uk-ke-waus, an elderly man who had that fall returned to his people after a long residence among the Crees of Red River, walked slowly through the village from lodge to lodge, proclaiming in a loud voice that he was determined on going to war, and calling on all those who considered themselves *men* to join him, and pay no attention to the words of the trader.

The next day this obstinate old warrior, with his four sons, left the village, and proceeded on the war-path against the Dakotas. He was followed by forty-five warriors, many of whom, it is said, went with great reluctance. To sustain this assertion, an anecdote is told of one, who, that morning, had determined to raise camp, to proceed on his fall hunt for beaver. He requested his wife to pull down their lodge, and gum the canoe, preparatory to leaving, but the wife appeared not to notice his words. He spoke to her a second time, and she still remaining unmindful, the husband got up, and taking down his gun he left the lodge, remarking, " Well, then, if you refuse to do as I wish you, I will join the warriors." He never returned to his disobedient wife, and his bones are bleaching on the sandy shores of Battle Lake.

After four days' travel to the westward, the war party arrived in the vicinity of Leaf Lake, within the country of their enemy, and discovered fresh signs of their hunters. In the evening they heard the report of Dakota guns booming in the distance. Early in the morning of the fifth day, they came across a beaten path, following which led them towards a large lake, which, from the ensuing fight, has borne the name of Lac du Battaile, or Battle Lake. As they neared this lake, they again heard the report of the enemy's guns, gradually receding in the distance, as if they were moving away from them. Uk-ke-waus, the leader of the party, insisted that the Dakotas must have discovered them, and were running away, and he importuned the party to quicken their steps in pursuit. The leading, and more experienced warriors, however, halted, and filling their pipes, gravely consulted amongst themselves the best course to be pursued. From the repeated firing of guns, in almost every direction, it was argued that the enemy must be occupying the country in great force, and probably some of their hunters, having discovered their trail, were preparing to cut off their retreat. A return home was seriously talked of under these circumstances, but Uk-ke-waus, being a passionate and withal a determined man, violently opposed this measure, and upbraided his fellows for their faint-heartedness in unmeasured terms. On this, the determination of their warriors was instantly formed, for none could brook the reproval of cowardice.

The party continued their onward course, and followed up the enemy's trail with quickened steps. Arriving on the lake shore, they beheld the late deserted encampment of their enemies, who had just moved off, and whose lodge fires were still brightly burning. As the Pillagers made their appearance on a rise of ground overlooking the deserted camp, three young men of the Dakotas suddenly jumped up from around a fire, where they had been sitting, and casting their eyes on the group of warriors who were fast approaching, and recognizing them for Ojibways, they fled towards the lake shore. Urged on by the old warrior, the Pillagers increased their speed to a full run. On arriving at the lake shore, they perceived in the distance the moving camp of their enemies, winding along the sandy beach, which stretched for two miles to their right. Some were on horseback, others on foot, and all packing along their leathern lodges, traps, and various camping equipage. It was not long before the moving Dakotas perceiving warrior after warrior collecting in their rear, apparently in full pursuit of them, and seeing the three young men who had been left as a rear guard, running and occasionally throwing up their blankets in warning, became panic-stricken, and dropping their loads, a general flight commenced.

Urged on by the apparent confusion and fear caused by their presence, amongst the ranks of their enemies, the Pillagers rushed on as if to a feast, and "first come was to be best served." About half their number, thinking to head the fleeing enemy, left the sandy beach of the lake, and ran around a swamp which lay between the narrow beach and the main land. This intended short cut, however, only led them astray, as they could not get around the swamp without going a great distance out of the way which the enemy were pursuing. In the mean time the Dakotas disappeared one after another in a deep wood which stood at the extreme end of the sand beach. Three

Pillager braves, who, being excellent runners, kept some distance ahead of their fellows, fearlessly followed after them. They ran through the woods and emerged upon an open prairie, where they were struck with surprise, at suddenly perceiving long rows of Dakota lodges. The fleeing camp had joined another, and together they numbered three hundred lodges. Guns were firing to call in the straggling hunters, drums were beating to collect the warriors, many of whom, already prepared for battle, their heads decked with plumes and their bodies painted in red and black, made a terrific appearance as they ran to and fro, marshalling the younger warriors and hurrying their preparations.

One look was sufficient for the three panting Pillagers, and amid a shower of bullets which laid one of them in death, the survivors turned and ran back, and as they met their fellows, they urged on them the necessity of immediate flight, for it was impossible to resist the numbers which their enemies were about to turn against them. Heated, tired, and panting for breath, the Pillagers could not think of flight. Their utmost exertions had been spent in a foolish and fruitless chase, and they could now do no more than die like men. Deliberately they chose their ground, at a place where a small rivulet connected the lake, through the narrow neck of sand beach, with a wide swamp. Here they could not be surrounded, and when half of their number had collected, they hid in the tall grass which grew on either side of the little creek, and here, entirely commanding the narrow pass, they awaited in ambush the coming of the Dakota warriors, who soon appeared from the woods, and marshalled in long lines on the lake shore, dressed and painted for battle. Their advance was imposing. They were led on by a prominent figure who wore a blue military coat, and who carried conspicuous on his breast a large silver medal, denoting his rank as chief. In one hand he brandished only a long spear, while in the other he carried aloft the war ensign of plumes, and as he came on, running from side to side, in front of his warriors, to keep them in line and check, he exhorted them to act like men with a loud voice.

Breathlessly the tired Pillagers crouched in the grass, awaiting the onset. The imposing array of their enemies had already reached within range of their bullets, but still they kept quiet, unseen in their ambush. The remainder of their fellows who had attempted to run around the swamp, finding out their mistake, had returned, and were now running up the sandy beach to the support of their fellows. On these the Dakotas turned their attention, and, unsuspecting, they marched right on their hidden enemies. The first gun fired by the Pillagers brought down the noble form of their leader. A yell of rage issued from the ranks of the Dakotas, and instead of dodging here and there, hiding behind trees, or throwing themselves in the tall grass, as they generally do in battle, they rushed forward in a body, determined to annihilate at one blow their feeble and tired enemy. Their front ranks, however, fell before the united volleys of the Pillagers, and the battle now commenced in earnest.

Retiring behind the shelter of trees, the Pillagers for a time kept up the hopeless contest, being every moment joined by their fellows who had been left behind. Last of the stragglers, when over one half of his comrades had been shot down, came Uk-ke-waus, the old warrior who had urged them on to the foolish chase. He had four sons engaged in the fight, the youngest of whom had been killed before the Dakota lodges. As he came up and took his stand beside his surviving warriors, the death of his favorite son was proclaimed to him, and bitter reproaches were addressed to him, for causing the untimely death of so many brave men. Determined to save some of his fel-lows, if possible, the old warrior called out in a voice distinctly heard above the din of battle, " Let those who wish to live, escape by retreating, while singly I shall stand in the path of our enemies!" The surviving Pillagers, all but his three brave sons, took him at his word, and leaving them to withstand the pursuit of the Dakotas, they turned and fled. For a long time the yells of those devoted warriors could be heard, as, at each crack of their guns, an enemy bit the dust. Volley after volley were fired on them in vain. They appeared to have a charmed life, but their strength and ammunition failing, the few remaining friends to whom by their self-sacrifice they had given life, heard from a great distance the exultant yells of the Dakotas as they silenced them forever, and tore the reeking scalps from their heads.

Not one-third of that Pillager war party ever returned to their people. Their bones are bleaching, and returning to dust, on the spot where they so bravely fought and fell. We-non-ga (the Vulture), one of the leaders of this ill-fated war party, though sorely wounded, returned home in safety. He was still living a few years since, honored and respected by all his people. It was his boast as he struck the war-pole, to relate his exploits, that on this bloody occasion, he shot down, one after another, seven Dakotas. The slaughter in their ranks must have been very considerable.

The beautiful sheet of water where the above related event took place, has since then been named by the Ojibways, Ish-quon-e-de-win-ing (where but few survived). The French, from the same circumstance, named it Lac du Battaile, interpreted in " Nicollet's map of the Mississippi Valley," into Battle Lake.

Esh-ke-bug-e-coshe, the venerable chief[1] of the Pillagers, from whose lips I have obtained the above account, was a young man when the fight at Battle Lake took place. He

---

[1] A. D. 1852.

was returning to Leech Lake, after a long residence among his Cree relations in the north, and was stopping to hunt with some friends at Red Lake, when, about midwinter, the news of the above battle reached them. There being many relatives of the old man Uk-ke-waus and his sons residing at Red Lake, at the news of their death, a war party was immediately raised, consisting of one hundred and thirty warriors, who marched on snow shoes towards the hunting grounds of the Dakotas. The young Pillager chief joined this party, and proceeded with them to the southern base of O-ge-mah-mi-jew, or Chief's Mountain, where they made a night attack on a large camp of the enemy, consisting of over fifty lodges. Several volleys were fired into the defenceless lodges, and many of the inmates killed and wounded, when, the warriors of the Dakotas briskly firing back, the Ojibways retreated.

The young chief, with two others, remained for some hours in the vicinity of the camp, after their fellows had gone, and he vividly describes the plaintive wailing of those who had lost relatives in the late attack. There was deep mourning in the camp of the Dakotas that bloody night! Stealthily approaching the lodges in the darkness, the young chief, with his two companions, once more discharged their guns at their weeping enemies, then turning homewards, they ran all night to rejoin their fellows.

Esh-ke-bug-e-coshe relates as a curious fact, that this war party left Red Lake on snow shoes, the ground being covered with deep snow. They marched directly westward, and having reached the great western plains, they found bare ground, left their snow shoes, and walked whole days through immense herds of buffalo.

CHAPTER XXX.

OJIBWAYS OF THE UPPER MISSISSIPPI.

The Sandy Lake band are nearly destroyed by the Dakotas—Battle of Cross
Lake, and destruction of an Ojibway camp—Captives taken—Escape of a
young woman by climbing into a pine tree—The Mississippi Ojibways are
reinforced through accessions from Lake Superior—Account of the chieftain
" Curly Head"—He takes possession of the Crow Wing hunting grounds—
Vain efforts of the Dakotas to destroy his camp—Chiefs of the Mississippi—
Lieut. Pike's journey to the sources of the Mississippi—He visits Leech Lake,
and takes possession of the country for the United States.

WE will once more return to the division of the Ojibways, who had made their homes on the waters forming
the sources of the Mississippi River. It has already been
related how, in the year 1782, the village of Sandy Lake
became nearly depopulated by the dreadful ravages of the
smallpox. This band, however, gradually recovered their
former strength and numbers, through accessions from the
villages of their people located on Lake Superior, who
were drawn to the Mississippi country by the richness of
the hunting grounds, and facilities of obtaining a plentiful
and easy livelihood.

In the year 1800 (as near as can be judged from the Indian mode of counting time), the ill-fated village of Sandy
Lake again received a severe blow, which cut off its inhabitants nearly to a man. On this occasion, however, they
suffered from the implacable hatred of the Dakotas. As
it had become customary, in the fall of the year, the hunters with their families, had gone down the Mississippi,
and joining with the Pillager camp at Crow Wing, they
had proceeded to the rich hunting grounds in the vicinity
of Long Prairie, to pursue the chase during the winter.
This year the Dakotas did not approach them for the pur-

pose of making a temporary peace, as they had been accustomed to do for some years previous. On the contrary,
they kept a wary watch over the movements of the Ojibway camp, for the purpose of obtaining an opportunity of
inflicting on them a sudden blow, which might have the
effect of deterring them from again encroaching on their
favorite hunting grounds.

As spring approached, the Ojibways again turned their
faces homewards, and made slow marches towards their
villages. The Dakotas collected their warriors, and to the
number of four hundred men, they stealthily followed the
return trail of their enemies. At Crow Wing the Pillager
and Sandy Lake camps, as usual, parted company, and
moved in different directions. The Dakotas followed the
smaller camp, which led towards Mille Lac and Sandy
Lake, and at Cross Lake, thirty miles northeast of Crow
Wing, they fell on the Ojibways, and destroyed nearly the
whole camp. The Ojibways, perfectly unaware that the
enemy was on their tracks in such force, as it was not the
season of the year when they usually carried on their warfare, had leisurely moved their camp from place to place,
without taking any precautions to guard against sudden
attack or surprise. In camping about in a dangerous
neighborhood, they were accustomed to cut down trees and
pile logs about their wigwams for defence against midnight attacks; but on this occasion, the fated Ojibways
failed to follow the usual precautions which might have
saved them from almost total destruction.

They encamped one evening at Sa-sub-a-gum-aw, or Cross
Lake, on a long narrow point covered with pine trees,
which ran across the lake nearly dividing it in two. They
numbered eight long, or double wigwams, besides several
smaller ones, altogether containing over two hundred men,
women, and children. Luckily, several families residing
at Mille Lac, had that day parted from the main camp,

and had gone in the direction of their village, consequently escaping the fate which awaited their fellows. Early the next morning, also, a number of women left the camp, to carry heavy loads of meat some distance ahead towards their next camping ground, intending to return after other loads. On their return, hearing the noise of the battle, which commenced soon after their departure, they succeeded in making their escape.

Soon after the sun had arisen on this fated morning, several of the Ojibway hunters sallied out of their wigwams for the usual day's hunt, intending to rejoin their families at the next encampment. On reaching the ice on the lake, they perceived several wolves sitting a short distance off, apparently watching the encampment. The hunters ran towards them, but as they did so, the seeming wolves got up and retreated into the woods which skirted the lake. The hunters instantly recognized them for human beings, who, covered with wolf skins, had quietly been reconnoitring their camp, and counting their lodges. They ran back and gave the alarm, but the Ojibway warriors were given but a few moments to make preparations for the coming onslaught.

On being discovered, the Dakotas immediately marshalled their forces on the ice, and in long lines, dressed and painted for battle, they slowly approached the Ojibway encampment. So unusual was this mode of attack, that for a moment the Ojibways were deceived into the belief that they came for the purpose of making peace, and under this impression two of their bravest warriors, Be-dud and She-shebe, ran out upon the ice to meet them. They were welcomed with a shower of bullets and arrows. They, however, bravely stood their ground, and returned the fire of the enemy, and their fellow warriors joining them, a fierce fight ensued on the ice, which soon became crimsoned with blood.

Many times outnumbered by their enemies, the few surviving warriors of the Ojibways were finally forced to take shelter near their wigwams, but the Dakotas entirely surrounded them. After a brave, but hopeless, defence, their guns were silenced forever, and their scalps graced the belts of their victorious enemies. After annihilating the men, the Dakotas rushed into the perforated wigwams, and massacred the women and children who had escaped their bullets. Some few children were spared, who were afterwards adopted into the families of their captors. Some have since returned to their people and are still living,[1] who speak the Dakota tongue with great fluency. A grandson of the chief Bi-aus-wah was captured on this occasion, and he is said to be still living[1] amongst his captors, at an advanced age, and much respected by them.

The narrative of this bloody event was related to the writer by an aged woman, who is now[1] the mother and grandmother of a large and respectable family of half-breed children. She was a young maiden at the time of the massacre, and being present, she witnessed all its terrible incidents. She escaped the fate of her fellows by climbing into a pine tree, the thick foliage of which effectually screened her from the eyes of the bloody Dakotas. After they had finished the work of scalping and mutilating the dead, and setting the wigwams on fire, they left their bloody work, and returned homeward, singing songs of triumph. The young woman descended from her perch in the pine tree, and vividly she describes the scene which presented itself to her eyes as she walked about the encampment, weeping bitter tears for her murdered relatives. The defence had been so long and desperate, that not a lodge pole, or shrub about the late encampment, but what had the marks of bullets or arrows.

[1] A. D. 1852.

This was a terrible blow on the Ojibways who had taken possession of the Upper Mississippi country, and they felt it severely. But it did not have the effect of causing them to evacuate the hunting grounds, which cost them so much blood. On the contrary, they held their vantage ground against the Dakotas with greater determination and tenacity, and their warriors who had been slain at Cross Lake being soon replaced by others from Lake Superior, they were enabled, in a few years, to inflict a terrible retribution on the Dakotas.

It is at this time that the celebrated chief, Ba-be-sig-aun-dib-ay, or "Curly Head," first made his appearance on the Upper Mississippi. He belonged to the Crane family, and removed to this region with a small camp of his relatives from the shores of the Great Lake. He did not stop at Sandy Lake, but proceeded down the Mississippi, and located his camp in the vicinity of Crow Wing, on a plentiful hunting ground, but in dangerous proximity to the Dakotas. The bravest warriors and hunters of the Mississippi Ojibways joined his camp and they soon formed a formidable body of hardy and fearless pioneers, who, ever wary against the advances of their enemies, were never attacked by them with impunity. Twice the Dakotas endeavored to destroy this daring band by sudden night attacks, but each time they were repulsed with severe loss.

Curly Head was much respected and loved by his people. In the words of one of their principal warriors, " He was a father to his people ; they looked on him as children do to a parent ; and his lightest wish was immediately performed. His lodge was ever full of meat, to which the hungry and destitute were ever welcome. The traders vied with one another who should treat him best, and the presents which he received at their hands, he always distributed to his people without reserve. When he had plenty, his people wanted not."

His band increased in numbers, and they eventually held the Crow Wing country without incurring the yearly and continued attacks of the Dakotas, who were thus finally forced to give up this portion of their hunting grounds and retire further down the Mississippi. The present Mississippi and Gull Lake band proper, now[1] numbering about six hundred souls, are the descendants of this hardy band of pioneers.

Curly Head became the third principal chief on the Upper Mississippi. He ruled the "men of the great river," while Ka-dow-aub-e-da (Broken Tooth), son of Bi-aus-wah, ruled the Sandy Lake village, and Esh-ke-bug-e-coshe, better known as Flat Mouth, presided over the Pillagers.

These three noted chiefs are mentioned by Lieut. Zebulon M. Pike, in his narrative of a journey to the sources of the Mississippi in 1805. The visit of this officer is an event of considerable importance to the Ojibways of the Upper Mississippi, as they date from it their first intercourse with the "Long Knives," or citizens of the United States. Previous to this time, they had been altogether under British influences, and all their chiefs wore the badges and medals of Great Britain, and her flag. They held intercourse only with British traders of the Northwest and Hudson's Bay companies, as the Americans had not as yet commenced to compete with these powerful companies in the fur trade. The object of the United States government in sending this expedition to the sources of the Mississippi, was to explore the country and take formal possession.

Lieut. Pike proceeded up the Mississippi with a party of soldiers in batteaux. Cold weather and ice prevented his further progress at the foot of Pike's Rapids, about thirty miles below the confluence of the Crow Wing with

---

[1] A. D. 1852.

the Mississippi, and here he was obliged to pass the winter, erecting comfortable quarters for his people, and collecting an ample supply of provisions from the abundance of game, buffalo and elk, which at that time covered this portion of the Upper Mississippi country. During the winter he proceeded with a party of his people to Leech Lake, where the Northwest Fur Company held a stockaded trading post, and here he formally proclaimed our right to the country, by planting a flag staff on which waved, for the first time, the stars and stripes. On this occasion, the young Pillager chief and warrior, Esh-ke-bug-e-coshe, who already held unbounded influence over his fellows, exchanged his British flag and medal for the flag and medal of the United States; and as the now aged chief expresses himself, " he ceased to be an Englishman, and became a Long Knife."

During this journey, Lieut. Pike had intercourse also with the chiefs, Curly Head and Broken Tooth, and recognized their rank and authority by bestowing on each a medal and flag.

CHAPTER XXXI.

OJIBWAYS OF THE UPPER MISSISSIPPI.

Waub-o-jeeg, 2d, killed by the Dakotas at Mille Lac—Curly Head and Flat
Mouth collect a war party to avenge his death—Attack on a Dakota camp at
Long Prairie—"Strong Ground" first distinguishes himself for bravery—
Dakotas evacuate the Long Prairie River country—Battle at Pembina between Ojibways and Dakotas—Son of the chief "Little Clam" killed—Revenge of the father—Death of Ta-bush-aw—Ojibway hunters congregate on
the Red River—Extent of the border on which the warfare of the Ojibways
and Dakotas is carried on—Origin of the name for Thief River.

HALF a century since, there flourished as one of the principal leaders of the Ojibway warriors on the Upper Mississippi, a man whose name was Waub-o-jeeg, or White
Fisher (namesake to the celebrated chief who, eighty years
ago,[1] led his people against the allied Foxes and Dakotas at
the battle of St. Croix Falls). Waub-o-jeeg was a warrior of
some distinction. He possessed much influence with, and
was loved and respected by his people. His lodge was
ever filled with the fruits of the successful chase, to which
the hungry were always welcome. His social pipe was
ever full, and the stem often passed around among his fellows. He was always foremost in defence of his people,
when, as it too often happened, the startling war-whoop of
their enemies fearfully broke on the morning stillness of
their sleeping encampment! A successful and adventurous
hunter, a brave and daring warrior, Waub-o-jeeg, who was
ever foremost on the dangerous hunting grounds of the
Dakotas, at last, in the prime of life, fell a victim to his
courage.

A few years after the battle and massacre at Cross Lake,
one summer, while encamped near Mille Lac, in company

---

[1] A. D. 1852.

with another warrior named She-shebe (who had distinguished himself on this bloody occasion), a Dakota war
party suddenly fell on them early one morning, and being
unprepared to resist the attack, they, with their wives and
children, were killed and scalped. Waub-o-jeeg suffered
death at the first fire; but She-shebe had time to grasp his
gun, and as his foes were eagerly rushing forward to finish
their work and secure his scalp, he fired in their midst,
killing one Dakota and wounding another, according to
their after acknowledgment. The death of these two noted
warriors, with their families, created a general excitement
throughout the villages of the whole tribe, and the relatives
of Waub-o-jeeg lost no time in making preparations to revenge the blow on their enemies. Ba-he-sig-au-dib-ay, or
Curly Head, chief of the Lower Mississippi, or Gull Lake
Ojibways, took the matter especially in hand, and late in
the fall he collected the Sandy Lake warriors at Gull Lake.
During the summer, Esh-ke-bug-e-coshe, or Flat Mouth,
the Pillager chief, had lost a nephew at the hands of the
Dakotas, and to revenge his death, he also collected his
warriors, and these two noted chiefs met by appointment,
and joined their respective forces at Crow Wing, from
which place they jointly led one hundred and sixty warriors into the Dakota country.

In those days, the lands which the Ojibways lately sold
to the United States government, lying between Long
Prairie and Watab Rivers, on the west side of the Mississippi, and now[1] forming the home of the Winnebagoes,
were favorite hunting grounds of the Sisseton and Warpeton Dakotas. They were accustomed to rove through it
each autumn, congregated in large camps, for greater security against the Ojibways. On this occasion, the war
party of Curly Head and Flat Mouth first discovered the
Dakota trail, at the western extremity of Long Prairie,

[1] A. D. 1852.

near the present site of the Winnebago agency. Following the trail, they discovered a Dakota encampment consisting of about forty lodges, located on the banks of Long Prairie River, which they determined to attack.

The encampment was surrounded during the night, and at a given signal, early in the morning, the Ojibways fell on the sleeping Dakotas. They fired volley after volley into the defenceless lodges, before a single warrior appeared to resist the attack. The sharp yell of defiance was at last heard issuing from the lips of a Dakota warrior, as he rushed bleeding from his lodge, and took a stand to return the fire of the assailants. Yell after yell succeeded his, and following his brave example, form after form were seen issuing from the perforated lodges, till nearly sixty Dakotas stood forth to confront their foes, and defend their families. The fight is said to have been close and most fiercely contested. It lasted till nightfall, when all the Dakota warriors but seven had been shot down, and silenced forever. Of these seven men, the most daring acts of valor are related. Retreating into the lodges, they actually kept off the united force of the Ojibways, and finally compelled them to retreat, leaving behind the rich harvest of scalps which they had hoped to reap.

On this bloody occasion the Dakotas sustained a heavy loss of life—fully as great as their enemies had suffered at Cross Lake. Song-uk-um-ig, or Strong Ground, the elder brother of the late celebrated war-chief Hole-in-the-day, first distinguished himself for bravery in this fight. Though but a mere lad, he was one of the few who daringly ran into the very ranks of the Dakotas to secure the scalp of a fallen warrior. This brave man, who died a few years since, could boast in his time, thirty-six eagle plumes on his head-dress, each denoting an enemy whom he had slain, or a scalp which he had secured in battle, the first of which he earned at Long Prairie fight.

As it afterward appeared by following the movements of the remnants of the Dakota camp, their forty lodges had been reduced, by the attack of the Ojibways, to but five. The loss of the Ojibways was seven killed, besides many severely wounded. Fighting from behind the shelter of trees and embankments of earth hastily thrown up, they had suffered a small loss, considering the length and sanguinary nature of the fight. They captured thirty-six horses, which, however, not being used to manage, they eventually destroyed. The bleaching bones of horse and man are still[1] to be seen on the spot where this bloody occurrence took place. From this event may be dated the final evacuation of the Long Prairie River country by the Dakotas. Enticed by the richness of the hunting grounds, they would sometimes return, in force, but after suffering repeated blows at the hands of the Mississippi war-chiefs, Strong Ground and Hole-in-the-day, they eventually gave up possession and all claim on the country which now[1] forms the home of the Winnebagoes.

It happened that on the same day in which the battle at Long Prairie took place, a large Dakota war party levied from another camp, and attacked a party of Ojibway hunters near Pembina, on the Red River of the north. The Ojibways, under the guidance of their chief Ais-sance, or Little Clam, made a fierce resistance, and succeeded in beating them away from their encampment. The favorite son of the Ojibway chieftain was, however, killed, and he was rifled of a large British medal which he wore conspicuous on his breast. Ais-sance, in the excitement of battle, had not noticed the fall of his beloved son, and he became so exasperated when the Dakotas displayed in the midst of battle the scalp and medal of his son, that he rushed furiously in the midst of their ranks, shot down the boasting Dakota, and cutting off his head, retreated holding it up

[1] A. D. 1852.

in triumph, and yelling his war-whoop till he reached a
secure shelter behind a tree. So struck were the enemy
by this sudden and daring act of valor, that they fired not
a shot at the brave warrior till he had reached a place of
safety.

The Ojibways were so exasperated at the loss of their
young chief, that they fought with unusual fierceness and
hardihood, and pursued the Dakotas some distance as they
retreated, notwithstanding they were many times outnumbered by them. An Ojibway hunter named Ta-bush-aw,
whose wigwam stood some distance from the main camp of
Ais-sance, arrived too late on the field to join the fight, but
determined to have his share of the sport, and withal a
scolding wife causing life to be a burden to him, he followed up the retreating war party on horseback, at night,
accompanied by another hunter, named Be-na. They
headed the Dakotas, and lying in ambush on their route,
they fired into their ranks. Be-na, pursuant to the request
of his fellow hunter, immediately retreated, while Ta-bush-
aw kept up the fight with the whole Dakota war party,
till he fell a victim to his bravery.

Instances are not rare, where warriors have sacrificed
their lives in this manner, either for the sake of being
mentioned in the lodge tales of their people as brave men,
to wipe off the slur of cowardice, which for some cause,
some one of their fellow warriors might have cast on them,
or more often, through being tired of the incessant scold-
ings of a virago wife, and other burdens of life equally
unendurable, as was the case with Ta-bush-aw.

At this time, the Ojibways occupying the sources of the
Mississippi and Red River, had forced the Dakotas to retreat west of these two streams. Hunters from Lake Superior, and even from the Ottoways of Mackinaw, had
found their way to the Red River of the North, to trap
beaver, and chase the buffalo, which abounded in these

regions in great abundance. Thus, a formidable body of
the tribe had gradually congregated on this remote northwest frontier, who flourished under the alliance of the Kenisteno and Assineboin tribes, to whom, properly, the country belonged. They joined their wars against the Yanc-
ton Dakotas; and thus, on an uninterrupted line from
Selkirk's settlement to the mouth of the Wisconsin River,
over a thousand miles in length, the Ojibways and Dakotas
carried on against one another their implacable warfare, and
whitened this vast frontier with each other's bones.

For a number of years, on the headwaters of Thief River
(which empties into Red River below Otter Tail Lake), a
camp of ten Dakota lodges, succeeded in holding the country by evading or escaping the search of the Ojibway war
parties. Here, loth to leave their rich hunting grounds,
they lived from year to year in continual dread of an attack
from their conquering foes. They built a high embankment of earth, for defence, around their lodges, and took
every means in their power to escape the notice of the
Ojibways—even discarding the use of the gun on account
of its loud report, and using the primitive bow and arrows,
in killing such game as they needed. They were, however, at last discovered by their enemies. The Crees and
Assineboines, during a short peace which they made with
the Dakotas, learned of their existence and locality, and
informing the Ojibways, a war party was raised, who went
in search of them. They were discovered encamped within
their earthen inclosure, and, after a brave but unavailing
defence with their bows and arrows, the ten lodges, with
their inmates, were entirely destroyed. The embankment
of earth is said, by Wa-won-je-quon, the chief of Red Lake
(who is my informant on this subject), to be still[1] plainly
visible. From this circumstance, the Ojibways named the
stream (the headwaters of which the Dakotas had so long

[1] A. D. 1852.

secretly occupied), Ke-moj-ake-se-be, literally meaning, "Secret Earth River," which the French, pronouncing Ke-mod-ake, meaning Stealing Earth, has been interpreted into Thief River, by which name it is laid down on Nicollet's Map.

CHAPTER XXXII.

OJIBWAYS OF THE UPPER MISSISSIPPI.

The Dakotas make unusual advances to effect a peace with the Ojibways—
Shappa, the Yankton Dakota chief—He effects a peace with the Red River
Ojibways—Dakotas and Ojibways meet on Platte River—Disturbance of the
peace—Bloodshed is prevented by Wa-nah-ta, son of Shappa—Flat Mouth,
the Pillager chief, refuses to accept the peace—He mistrusts the intentions
of the Dakotas—His narrow escape, and discovery of a war trail on Otter
Tail Lake—Murder of his two cousins—Their brave defence against the
Dakotas—Flat Mouth prepares for war—Shappa sends him his peace pipe,
and appoints when and where to meet him—Flat Mouth keeps the appointment—He refuses to shed blood on a white man's door-step—Death of
Shappa, with two of his warriors—He is succeeded by his son, Wa-nah-ta,
who becomes a noted warrior—Threats of Col. Dickson against Pillagers—
Fierce battle between Dakotas and Ojibways at Goose River—Black Duck
distinguishes himself for bravery—Characteristic manner of a peace effected
between an Ojibway camp, and Dakota war party on Platte River—The
chief of Sandy Lake makes a peace visit to the Dakotas—His party narrowly
escapes destruction—They are saved by the trader Renville—Dakotas kill an
Ojibway on Gull Lake, and leave the war-club on his body—Quick revenge
of Curly Head—Five women killed—War-club returned.

THE year after the battle at Long Prairie, the Dakotas,
along the whole line of their eastern frontiers, made an
unusual attempt to enter into a general peace with the
Ojibways. Shappa (the Beaver), head-chief of the Yankton Dakotas, the most numerous section of this extensive
tribe, and occupying the most northern position, first made
advances of peace to the Ojibways on Red River. Some
years previous he had taken captive a young Ojibway
woman, who soon became his favorite wife. This woman
he now placed on a fleet horse, and giving her his peace
pipe, he bade her to go to her people at Pembina, and tell
them that in so many days, Shappa would come and
smoke with them in peace and good-will.

On the day appointed, the Dakota chief, with a large number of his people, made his appearance, and the Red River Ojibways accepted his offers of peace. At the same time the Sisseton, Warpeton, and M'dewakanton Dakotas, in a large camp, approached the Ojibways of the Mississippi and Sandy Lake, and Mille Lac. The two parties met on the banks of Platte River, near its junction with the Mississippi, and the peace pipe was formally smoked between them, and games of various kinds was played between the young men of the two camps. The feeling of hatred, however, which rankled in the breasts of the Dakotas against the Ojibways, could not altogether be restrained. At a grand game of ball, or Baug-ah-ud-o-way, played between the young men of either tribe for a large stake, a disturbance nearly leading to a scene of bloodshed occurred.

One of the seven Dakota warriors who had survived the battle at Long Prairie, picked a quarrel with an Ojibway, by striking him for some trivial cause, with his ball-stick The blow was returned, and the fight would soon have become general, had not the young Wa-nah-ta, son of Shappa, rushed in, and forcibly separated the combatants, inflicting a summary punishment and scolding on his fellow Dakota who had commenced the fight. This is the first occasion in which Wa-nah-ta is mentioned by the Ojibways. He afterwards became celebrated as a warrior, and a chief of vast influence over the wild Yankton Dakotas.

While peace parties thus met above and below him, Flat Mouth, the Pillager chief, quietly hunted beaver on Long Prairie River. The peace pipe had been sent to him, but he had not as yet determined to accept it, for he mistrusted the intentions of the Dakotas in thus unusually making the first advance to bury the war-club. The wary chieftain could not think them sincere in their proffers of good-will and fellowship, so soon after suffering such a severe blow as the Ojibways had inflicted on them at Long Prairie. He suspected from his knowledge of their character, that some deep design of treachery was concealed beneath this guise of peace, and he hesitated to place the stem of the sacred peace pipe to his lips.

Flat Mouth, pursuing his hunts, proceeded to Otter Tail Lake, and was one evening encamped at the outlet of Otter Tail Creek, dressing a bear skin, when a feeling of fear suddenly came on him, and in the darkness of night he ordered his family to raise camp, for he " felt that the Dakotas were in the vicinity." They embarked in their canoe, and passing the night on the lake, the next morning he landed to reconnoitre. On the prairie which skirted the lake shore, he discovered a wide, fresh, Dakota war trail! Having left some hunters in his rear towards Leaf Lake, and fearing that they might be attacked (as from the late reports of peace they hunted in apparent security), he followed the trail to satisfy himself as to the direction the war party would take. They had passed close to his last evening's encampment, where, had he remained, they would doubtless have discovered and attacked him. He saw their encampment of the past night, and from the marks left, he judged the party to be fully four hundred strong, marching under the direction of four different leaders, who left their respective marks on the trees. One of these was a beaver, which satisfied Flat Mouth that the false Yankton chief, Shappa, was now working out his treachery, after having lulled the habitual caution of the Ojibways by his false songs of peace.

When satisfied that the enemy had gone in the direction of Battle Lake, where he knew there were no Ojibways, he returned to his family, and again embarking, he proceeded down towards Leaf Lake, to warn his people of the threatened danger. He was, however, wind-bound one day on Otter Tail Lake, and the next morning as he entered the creek, he perceived a huge smoke arising in a direction where he supposed his two cousins, Nug-an-ash, and Blue Eagle, were hunting beaver in an isolated little lake. A smoke in a dangerous vicinity is never without meaning, and satisfied that something serious had befallen his cousins, Flat Mouth returned to a party of his people who were gathering wild rice in an adjacent lake, and immediately sent out a party to go and view the spot from whence the ominous smoke had arisen. They soon returned and reported that they had discovered the mutilated remains of his two cousins; with them had been left three Dakotas in a sitting position, facing the west, whom they had killed.

The Dakotas afterwards related to Flat Mouth that while their war party was stealthily approaching to attack the lodge of his two cousins, which stood on the borders of a little lake, the two hunters first perceived them, from a high wooded promontory of the lake where they happened to be busy in cutting poles for stretching beaver skins. They first fired on the Dakotas, killing one of their number, on which they were furiously attacked, but they defended themselves on the narrow point, and kept off their assailants, till one became wounded, when they quickly embarked in their canoe, and paddled to a small rock islet, standing in the lake, but which could be reached by bullets, or even arrows, from the point which they had just left. They, however, made partial defences by piling stones around them, from which they kept up the fight. The Dakotas surrounded them on all sides, and approached their defences by rolling large logs into the water, and swimming behind them, gradually pushed them towards the island. The two hunters kept them off till their ammunition failed, when they fell an easy prey to their numerous enemies. Three Dakotas were left on the ground whom they killed, and many more were wounded, some of whom afterwards died.

The Pillager chief was very much exasperated at the death of his two cousins, and he lost no time in collecting a war party to avenge them. His war-pipe and war-club were carried by fleet messengers from village to village of his people, to inform them of his intention, and inviting the warriors to join him. In the mean time a messenger came to him from a trading post on Red River, belonging to Col. Dickson, with a message from the Yankton chief Shappa, denying all participation in the late war party of his people, and appointing a day when he should meet him at the trading post for the purpose of smoking the peace pipe and strengthening good-will between their respective people. Flat Mouth chose thirty of his best warriors, and on the appointed day he arrived at the trading post on Red River, where he found four Frenchmen who had charge of the establishment. On the next day, the Yankton chief arrived, accompanied by only two men.

The warriors of Flat Mouth made demonstrations to kill them at once, but Flat Mouth ordered them to desist, as he did not wish " to sully the door-steps of a white man with blood." He refused to smoke from the proffered pipe-stem of the Dakota chief, and Shappa knew from this that his treachery was fully known, and his enemies had met to punish him. All night it rained and thundered heavily, and mingled with the roaring of the storm without, there arose the voice of the doomed chieftain, as he prayed and sang to the spirits of his belief for protection against the threatened danger. Early in the morning, Sha-wa-ke-shig, the principal warrior of Flat Mouth, asked his chief for permission to kill the three Dakotas. The Pillager chief answered: " You know that since the death of my cousins, my heart has been sore; the road which I have followed in coming here, is red with blood. The

Great Spirit has placed these men in our hands that we might do with them as we please. Do, therefore, as you wish, only do not shed blood on the steps of these white men, nor in their presence. Though it is my doing, yet I shall not be with you."

The Ojibways waited till the Dakotas left the shelter of the trading post, and escorting them out on the prairie, towards their country, they shot them down, and cutting off their heads, they caught up with their chief, who had gone on his road homewards, unwilling to witness the scene which he knew his warriors were determined to perpetrate. Sha-wa-ke-shig is noted as having killed the chief Shappa, and secured his scalp. The chief's medal which he wore on his breast, was secured by Wash-kin-e-ka (Crooked Arm), a warrior of Red Lake.

Col. Dickson. who had married a sister of the Yankton chief, was very much exasperated at his death, and he sent a message to Flat Mouth, that henceforth the smoke of a trading house would never more arise from among the Pillagers; and within four years the village would be swept away." The Pillager chieftain laughed at his threats, and he now[1] remarks, that "the traders came to him as usual, and his village continued to grow larger, notwithstanding the big words of the red-headed Englishman." It is doubtless a fact, that Col. Dickson's future treatment of this powerful northern chieftain conduced greatly to alienate him from the British interest, and to strengthen his predilections to the American government. He peremptorily refused to join the British in the late war against the people of the United States.

Shappa, the Yankton chief, was succeeded by his son Wa-nah-ta, who became one of the most influential and celebrated warriors that the Dakotas can boast of. During his lifetime he amply revenged the death of his father,

[1] A. D. 1852.

by inflicting repeated blows on the Ojibways of Red River. On the death of Shappa, the war again raged on the whole frontier between the two belligerent tribes. Wa-nah-ta led a large party of his warriors into the Ojibway country, towards Red Lake. He was accidentally met by a war party of his enemies, headed by the chief, Wash-ta-do-ga-wub, and at the entry of Goose River into the Red River, a severe fight ensued, which lasted nearly a whole day, and which resulted in the retreat of both parties with severe loss. Two scouts of the Ojibways, who always kept ahead of the main body while on the march, were suddenly fired on by the Dakotas, and one killed. In the sanguinary battle which ensued, the Ojibways were so hard pressed by the superior numbers of their enemies, that they were forced to dig holes in the ground for shelter and defence against their missiles. An Ojibway warrior named " Black Duck" distinguished himself for bravery in this fight. He fought in the foremost ranks, recklessly exposing his person, and with his own hand killed and scalped seven Dakotas.

The summer following this eventful year in the annals of the Ojibways, the farce of a temporary peace was again enacted on Platte River, a short distance below Crow Wing. The scouts of a large camp of Ojibways discovered a Dakota war party approaching their encampment, evidently for the purpose of attack. On account of their women and children, who would be the main sufferers in case of a battle, the Ojibways determined on a bold manœuvre, which, if it failed, they were determined to fight to the last. A piece of white cloth was attached to a pole, and a brave warrior, who offered himself for the purpose, sallied out singly to meet the enemy. He saw them stealthily approaching the encampment, and when perceived by them, he dropped his gun, and with nothing but his flag he fearlessly rushed into their ranks. He was

caught in the arms of the foremost warriors, many blows
of war-clubs were aimed at him, and he expected every
moment to suffer death; but a tall Dakota defended him,
warding off the blows of his angry comrades. After the
excitement had somewhat cooled down, and the tall warrior had addressed a few words to his fellows, a Dakota
whose face was painted black, denoting mourning, for
whose benefit, probably, the war party were now bent on
their errand of blood, stepped forth and throwing down
his arms, he took hold of the Ojibway and offered to
wrestle with him. The Dakota was thrown to the ground,
on which he got up, and laughing, he tried his more powerful adversary another hold. He was again thrown, on
which he shook the Ojibway by the hand and exchanged
with him his pipe, gun, and clothing. The brave man
who had thus conquered a peace, led the party to the wigwams of his people, where they saluted one another with
the firing of guns. The peace pipe was smoked, and for
several days they literally " eat out of the same dish," and
" slept under the same lodge covering."

Shortly after this Dakota war party had returned to
their homes, emboldened by the cordial and unexpected
manner in which they had met their advances for peace, a
small war party of Ojibways, under Broken Tooth, the
chief of Sandy Lake, proceeded in their birch canoes down
the Mississippi to the mouth of the Minnesota, to pay the
Dakotas a visit of peace at their own villages. On the low
point over which now towers the American fortress known
as Fort Snelling, the Ojibways first discovered their old
enemies congregated in a large camp. Broken Tooth, to
denote his rank, approached with the American flag hanging over the stern of his canoe. On their being perceived,
the wildest excitement ensued in the camp. The men ran
out of their lodges with guns in their hands. The Dakotas
were preparing to go on a war party against the very people

who now made their appearance, and the warriors made demonstrations to fire on them. Their chiefs interfered, but with little effect, and bullets were already flying about the ears of the Ojibways, when Renville, an influential Dakota trader and half-breed, made his timely appearance, and with a loud voice quelled the disturbance, and took the peace party under his protection. The excited warriors, however, insisted on firing a salute, and their bullets, for some minutes, spattered the water in every direction around the canoes of the Ojibways, and even perforated the flag which hung over the head of their chief. The old men, still living,[1] who were present on this occasion, describe it as the most dangerous scene in their lives. They would much rather have met their enemies in open fight than bear the long suspense between life and death which they perceived hanging over them, the wild excitement among the Dakotas, and the bullets whizzing past their heads. They all acknowledge that they owed their deliverance to the timely interference of the trader Renville.

Broken Tooth and his party made but a short stay in the midst of a people who were so anxious to spill their blood, and handle their scalps. Under an escort provided by the kind trader, who guarded them some distance towards their country, they succeeded in reaching their homes in safety, and felt thankful for escaping from such a fearful predicament. They had been at home but a few days, when a Dakota war party who had followed on their tracks, waylaid an Ojibway hunter on the shores of Gull Lake. They left a war-club, with a sharp iron spearhead, sticking in the mutilated body of their victim. Curly Head, the Mississippi chief, immediately collected such warriors as were camping with him on Gull Lake, and in their canoes, they floated down the swift current of "the great river." They crossed the portage around the Falls of St. Anthony during the night, and arrived at the mouth

---

[1] A. D. 1852.

of the Minnesota River, the morning after the return of
the Dakota war party. On the point just below Fort
Snelling, which was then covered with trees and brush,
they pulled up, and hiding their canoes, they laid in ambush, commanding the confluence of the Minnesota with
the Mississippi.

They could distinctly hear the drums beating in an adjacent village of their enemies, as they held rejoicings over
the scalp which their warriors had brought home. Towards
evening a canoe load of young women came floating .lei-
surely down the sluggish current of the Minnesota, chat-
ting and laughing, in anticipation of the magnificent scalp
dance which they were going to join, after having adorned
their persons with profuse ornaments, and painted their
cheeks with vermilion. Little did they dream of the fate
that awaited them—that their own long scalp-locks would
so soon dangle in the belt of the fierce Ojibway warriors,
and that the women of their foe would so soon be rejoicing
over them.

When the canoe had reached opposite the Ojibway ambuscade, at a whistle from the leader, a volley of bullets
was fired into it, and the men, rushing into the water, a
struggle ensued, who should secure the scalps. Five Dakota women suffered on this occasion, and their bodies
being dragged on shore, the war-club which their people
had left sticking in the body of their victim at Gull Lake,
was left, with peculiar marks, on the body of one, to warn
the Dakotas that the revenge of the Ojibway was quick
and sure.

The party returned in safety to their village, and their
exploit, though comparatively of trivial importance, is
mentioned by their people to this day with great satisfaction. The quick revenge was sweet, and withal it acted as
a check in some measure to the continually repeated forays
and war parties of the bloodthirsty Dakotas.

CHAPTER XXXIII.

ENDEAVORS OF THE BRITISH TO ENTICE THE OJIBWAYS OF LAKE SUPERIOR AND MISSISSIPPI TO JOIN THEIR ARMS IN THE WAR OF 1812.

Mistaken impression respecting the position of the Ojibways during the last war—Efforts of British agents to induce them to break their neutrality—Col. Dickson sends a messenger to the Pillagers to induce them to join the British—Laconic reply of Flat Mouth—Great Cloud, an Ojibway warrior, helps the arms of Great Britain—Anecdote of his first acquaintance with Col. Dickson, who makes him a chief—Michel and John Baptiste Cadotte, Jr., act as British interpreters—Ojibways collect in large numbers at Mackinaw—British attempts to induce them to fight the Americans—Opposition of the chieftain Keesh-ke-mun—He is called to council, and reprimanded by the British commandant—The chieftain's answer—We-esh-coob, the Pillager war-chief—He refuses to join the British—His bitter reply to their taunt of cowardice.

It has been a general impression throughout the United States, that the Ojibways, as a tribe, fought under the flag of Great Britain, during the war of 1812. It is not so; and it can be stated as a fact, that of the nine thousand which this tribe number on Lake Superior, and the Mississippi, not more than one or two warriors are mentioned as having joined the British. There are several villages of Indians in Upper Canada, who are sometimes denominated as Ojibways, but who are more properly the remnants of the original Algonquins who have always been in the interest of the British, and aided them in their wars. The connection existing between these and the Lake Superior and Mississippi Ojibways, is not very close, though they speak the same language, and call one another relatives.

If any of the Ojibways living within the boundaries of the United States fought for the British during the last war, it was more through coercion than otherwise, and

they belonged to small bands who lived among the Ottaways at Mackinaw, and who were scattered in Michigan
among the Pottawatumies and other tribes. The main
body of the tribe occupying Lake Superior, and the waters
of the Mississippi firmly withstood every effort made by
the British to induce them to enter into the war, and it is
thus they have succeeded in holding their own in numbers,
and in fact, gradually increasing, while other tribes, who
have foolishly mingled in the wars of the whites, have become nearly extinct.

Agents were sent by the British government to the
principal villages of the Ojibways, to invite them to join
their arms against the Americans. Col. Dickson,[1] who
had long been a trader amongst the Dakotas, and northern
Ojibways, is mentioned as one of the most prominent and
active of the British agents in levying the savage tribes,
in an exterminating warfare against the men, *women, and
children* of the United States.

He sent the British interpreter, St. Germain, in a light
canoe, fully manned with Canadian voyageurs, from Fort
William to Leech Lake, to obtain the co-operation of the
Pillagers. He gave presents to Esh-ke-bug-e-coshe (Flat
Mouth), the chief of the warlike band, and in public council he presented the wampum belts of the British agent,
and delivered his message. The Pillager chieftain sent
back the belts with the laconic answer: " When I go war
against my enemies, I do not call on the whites to join my
warriors. The white people have quarrelled among themselves, and I do not wish to meddle in their quarrels, nor
do I intend ever, even to be guilty of breaking the window-
glass of a white man's dwelling."

St. Germain next urged him to visit Col. Dickson at Ft.
William, but the chief refused to go, and of all his war-

[1] For notices of Dickson, see Neill's *History of Minnesota*, 5th edition, 1883,
Minnesota Historical Collections, Vol. I. p. 390.

riors, but one obeyed the summons of the British agent. This one was a noted warrior named Ke-che-aun-o-guet, or Great Cloud, whose attachment had been secured by Col. Dickson, in the following characteristic manner:—

Great Cloud was one time, early in the spring, hunting in company with a Frenchman near Leaf Lake, while the Dakotas still claimed the country about it as their own. Early one morning, hearing the report of a gun towards Leaf Lake, Great Cloud told his comrade that he knew it must be the Dakotas, and he must go and see what they were about. Bidding the Frenchman good-bye, saying that he would try and return during the night, but not to wait for him longer than noon the next day, the Indian started on his dangerous expedition. Arriving at the outlet of Leaf River from the lake, he noticed some maple trees freshly tapped, and he soon fell on a beaten path, following which he soon discovered a log house, surrounded by a fence of felled trees. He hid by the roadside between the forks of a fallen tree, and there patiently awaited the appearance of some Dakota, whose scalp would add another eagle plume to his head-dress.

A woman came from the house to examine the maple trees, and gather the sap. She was dressed like a white man's squaw, and not wishing to kill a woman, Great Cloud did not molest her, but still continued in his ambush. Soon after, two other women, apparently mother and daughter, issued from the hut, came close to his hiding place, to gather sap. They were both apparently the women of some white man, as they were much cleaner and dressed far better than squaws usually are, and again the warrior refrained from attacking them. Towards evening he saw a man going towards the house, carrying some swans and ducks on his back, and Great Cloud prepared for an onset, but the hunter passed close to the lake shore, and out of bullet range. Tired of waiting, he at last crawled up to the house and posted himself directly in front of the gateway, amongst a clump of stumps. He saw a lodge standing within the inclosure on the other side of the house, and this he determined to watch till a Dakota should issue from it. It was now dusk, and he had remained in his new position but a moment, in fact had but just lighted his pipe, when the two women he had seen in the afternoon again came out of the house, and were examining a canoe which lay close to him, when they discovered the ambushed warrior. They immediately ran screaming into the house, from whence a white man with a large head of red hair soon issued, carrying a tremendous sword under his arm, and a gun in his hand. This was Col. Dickson. He walked up to Great Cloud, who was quietly smoking his pipe, and presenting his gun to his breast, demanded in broken Ojibway, " who he was, and what he wanted?"

The Indian answered, that " he was Great Cloud, an Ojibway warrior, and he had come to look for Dakota scalps." The trader then told him that the Dakotas were all gone, and that there was no one with him but a Menominee Indian. He inquired if there were any more of his people with him, and on answering in the negative, Dickson laughed, took Great Cloud by the hand, called him a brave man, and invited him into his house, where he was well treated. The Menominee Indian soon came in, and together they took a social smoke. Great Cloud related his adventures, and so pleased was his host at his having spared his women, that he gave him a flag and placed a medal on his breast, besides loading him with a present of goods.

On his return, Great Cloud found his French comrade had fled to Leech Lake, where he himself soon arrived, dressed as a chief, and instead of fur, loaded with merchandise, to the great surprise and wonder of his people. From this time he always showed a deep attachment to Col. Dickson, and though his people refused to recognize him as a chief, yet he always assumed the dignity and was treated as such by the British. Great Cloud proceeded to Fort William with St. Germain, and he was in nearly all the principal battles which took place between the British and Americans, during the last war, in Canada. He remained in the east some time after the closing of the war, and we find his name attached to most of the treaties which from this time the United States government made with the allied Ottaways, Pottawatumies, and eastern Ojibways, at Detroit, Vincennes, and Sault Ste. Marie.

Of the Ojibway half-breeds, John Baptiste and Michel, sons of Michel Cadotte, Sr., of La Pointe, were captured or enticed by the British of Isle Drummond, and there given the option, either to go into confinement during the war, or act as interpreters, and use their influence to collect the Ojibways. They accepted the latter alternative, and were actors in all the principal Canadian battles, and were present on the occasion of Tecumseh's death. John Baptiste was severely wounded, and is now[1] a pensioner on the British government. Michel is also living,[1] minus one arm, at La Pointe, on Lake Superior.

After the taking of Fort Howard, on the island of Mackinaw, the Ojibways of Lake Superior and the inland country towards the Mississippi, being deprived of their usual resident traders and supplies, congregated in unusual numbers on the island. The British took this occasion again to renew their attempts to induce them to join their arms. They, however, signally failed to make an impression on their minds, as the Ojibways were influenced by one of their principal chiefs, who was noted both for wisdom and great firmness of character. His name was Keesh-ke-mun, already mentioned in a previous chapter. On discovery that the councils of this chief was the cause of the failure

---

[1] A. D. 1852.

of their attempts to induce the Ojibways to war against the Americans, the British officers sent for him to come to their council room. The chief obeyed the summons, accompanied by a numerous guard of his warriors. Michel Cadotte, Jr., acted as interpreter, and from his lips have these items and speeches been obtained by the writer.

The British officers. in full uniform, were all collected in the council room, when the Ojibway chieftain and his train entered and silently took the seats allotted to them. Mr. Askin, a British agent, opened the council by stating to the chief that his British father had sent for him, understanding that his councils with his red brethren had shut their ears against his words, and cooled their hearts towards him. " Your British father wishes to know who you are, that you should do these things—that you should dare to measure yourself against him." After an interval of silence, during which the chieftain quietly smoked his pipe, he at last arose, and shaking hands with the British commandant, he answered as follows :—

" Englishman ! you ask me who I am. If you wish to know, you must seek me in the clouds. I am a bird who rises from the earth, and flies far up, into the skies, out of human sight; but though not visible to the eye, my voice is heard from afar, and resounds over the earth!

"Englishman ! you wish to know who I am. You have never sought me, or you should have found and known me. Others have sought and found me. The old French sought and found me. He placed his heart within my breast. He told me that every morning I should look to the east and I would behold his fire, like the sun reflecting its rays towards me, to warm me and my children. He told me that if troubles assailed me, to arise in the skies and cry to him, and he would hear my voice. He told me that his fire would last forever, to warm me and my children.

" Englishman ! you, Englishman, you have put out the

fire of my French father. I became cold and needy, and you sought me not. Others have sought me. Yes, the *Long Knife* has found me. He has placed his heart on my breast. It has entered there, and there it will remain!"

The chieftain here pulled out from his decorated tobacco pouch, an American George Washington medal, which had been given him by a former commandant of Fort Howard, and placing it around his neck, it lay on his breast, as he quietly returned to his seat.

Somewhat excited at the vehement address of the chief, and at the act of seeming bravado which closed his harangue, the British officer replied to him:—

"You say true. I have put out the fire of the French men; and in like manner am I now putting out the fire of the Long Knife. With that medal on your breast, you are my enemy. You must give it up to me, that I may throw it away, and in its stead I shall give you the heart of your great British father, and you must stand and fight by his side."

Keesh-ke-mun, without arising from his seat, answered:

"Englishman! the heart of the Long Knife, which he placed on my breast, has entered my bosom. You cannot take it from me without taking my life."

The officer, exasperated at the unflinching firmness of the chieftain, now exclaimed, in anger, addressing the interpreter: "Tell him, sir, that he must give up his medal, or I shall detain him a prisoner within the walls of this fort." This threat, being duly interpreted to him, the chief grasped his medal in his hand, and once more arising from his seat, he addressed the excited officer, himself not showing the least marks of emotion:—

"Englishman! I shall not give up this medal of my own will. If you wish to take it from me, you are stronger than I am. But I tell you, it is but a mere bauble. It is only an emblem of the heart which beats in my bosom;

to cut out which you must first kill me! Englishman! you say, that you will keep me a prisoner in this your strong house. You are stronger than I am. You can do as you say. But remember that the voice of the Crane echoes afar off, and when he summons his children together, they number like the pebbles on the Great Lake shore!"

After a short consultation between the officers and Mr. Askin, the commandant again addressed the chief:—

"Your words are big, but I fear them not. If you refuse to give up the medal of the Long Knives, you are my enemy, and you know I do not allow my enemies to live."

The chief answered: "Englishman! you are stronger than I am. If you consider me an enemy because I cherish the heart which has been placed on my bosom, you may do so. If you wish to take my life, you can take it. I came into your strong house because you sent for me. You sent for me wishing to set me on to my father the Long Knife, as a hunter sets his dogs on a deer. I cannot do as you wish. I cannot strike my own father. He, the Long Knife, has not yet told us to fight for him. Had he done so, you Englishmen would not now be in this strong house. The Long Knife counsels us to remain quiet. In this do we know that he is our own father, and that he has confidence in the strength of his single arm."

After some further consultation among the officers, who could not help admiring his great firmness, the chief was dismissed. The next morning, Michel Cadotte (his grandson), was again sent to him to call him to council. Keesh-ke-mun, with a score of his warriors again presented themselves. A large pile of goods and tobacco was placed before him. Mr. Askin addressed him as follows:—

"Your English father has not sent for you to take your life. You have refused to accept the badge of his heart. You have refused to join him in putting out the fire of the Long Knives who are stealing away your country.

Yet he will not detain you. He will not hurt a hair of your head. He tells you to return to your village in peace. He gives you wherewith to warm your children for the coming winter. But he says to you, remain quiet—remember if you join the Long Knives, we shall sweep your villages from the earth, as fire eats up the dry grass on the prairie."

Keesh-ke-mun, without answering a word, accepted the presents and returned to his village. To his influence may be chiefly attributed the fact that the Ojibways of Lake Superior and Mississippi remained neutral during the progress of the last war.

Another anecdote is told by my informant, who acted as the British interpreter for the Ojibways during the last war; which further illustrates the attachment which this tribe had conceived for the American people.

About the same time that Keesh-ke-mun so firmly withstood the inducements and threats of the British officers at Fort Howard, We-esh-coob, the war-chief of the Pillagers, with a party of his people from Leech Lake, happened to be present at the island of Michilimacinac. He was vainly urged by the British agents to join their arms with his band of warriors, who were noted as being the bravest of the Ojibway tribe. At a council held within the fort, this chief was asked, for the last time, by the British commandant, to array himself under their flag. We-esh-coob, in more decided terms than ever, refused, and his words so exasperated the commandant, that he rose from his seat, and forgot himself so far as to say to the Pillagers:—

"I thought you were men, but I see that you are but women, not fit even to wear the breech-cloth. Go back to your homes. I do not wish the assistance of women. Go, put on the clothing which more befits you, and remain quiet in your villages."

As he delivered this violent speech, he was proceeding to leave the council room, when We-esh-coob, having quietly listened to the interpretation thereof, rose to his feet, and approaching the angry Englishman, he put his hand on his epaulette and gently held him back. " Wait," said he, " you have spoken ; now let me speak. You say that we should not wear the breech-cloth, but the dress of women." Then pointing to the opposite shore of the lake, towards the site of the old English fort which the Ojibways had taken in 1763, We-esh-coob exclaimed :—

" Englishman ! have you already forgotten that we once made you cry like children ? yonder ! who was the woman then ?

" Englishman ! you have said that we are women. If you doubt our manhood, you have young men here in your strong house. I have also young men. You must come out on some open place, and we will fight. You will better know, whether we are fit, or not, to wear the breech-cloth.

" Englishman ! you have said words which the ears of We-esh-coob have never before heard," and throwing down his blanket in great excitement, he pointed to different scars on his naked body, and exclaimed : " I thought I carried about me the marks which proved my manhood."

The English officer whose irritation had somewhat abated during the delivery of this answer, grasped the unusually excited Indian by the hand, and requested the interpreter to beg him to forget his hasty words. Peace and good-will were thus restored, but this bitter taunt tended greatly to strengthen the minds of the Ojibways against the agents who were continually engaged amongst them, to draw them into the war.

CHAPTER XXXIV.

A BRIEF SKETCH OF THE FUR TRADE AND FUR TRADERS AMONG
THE OJIBWAYS FROM THE FORMATION OF THE NORTHWEST
COMPANY IN 1787 TO 1834.

Origin of the Northwest Fur Company—Departments of their trade in the
Ojibway country—Depot at Grand Portage—Yearly meetings of the partners
—Names of the original partners—Sir Alex. McKenzie—He forms the X. Y.
Company, and opposes the Northwest—The two companies join issues—
Opposition of the Hudson's Bay Co.—Bloody struggle between the two rival
companies—Northwest becomes merged in the Hudson's Bay Co.—Names of
their Ojibway traders—Astor's American Fur Co.—Amount of their outfits in
1818—Policy of their trade—Names of their principal traders—W. A. Aitkin
—Lyman W. Warren—Names, motives, and conduct of the American traders.

AMONG the first traders who pushed their enterprise to
the villages of the Ojibways on Lake Superior, after France
had ceded the Canadas to Great Britain, the names of
Alexander Henry and the Cadottes appear most conspicuous. The Northwest Fur Company was not formed till
the year 1787. It originated in the following manner:—

Three or four rival traders, or small companies, had proceeded from Montreal and Quebec, and located trading
posts on the north coast of Lake Superior, about the mouth
of Pigeon River, up which stream they sent outfits to the
" Bois Fort" and Muskego Ojibways, and then to the Kenisteno and Assineboines of Red River. The rivalry between these different traders became extremely bitter, and
at last resulted in the murder of Waddon, who was shot
in cold blood, within his trading house, at Grand Portage.
This outrage brought the most sensible portion of the
traders to their senses, and they immediately made efforts
to compromise their difficulties, and to join their interests
into one. These efforts resulted in the formation of the

Northwest Company, which soon became so rich and powerful that for a long time they were enabled to monopolize the northern fur trade, and cope with the most powerful and favored combinations which the capitalists of Great Britain could bring against them.

In the year 1792, immediately after the noted expedition of John Baptiste Cadotte to the Upper Mississippi, the Northwest Company extended their operations over the whole Ojibway country within the limits of the United States, on Lake Superior and the Mississippi. Their trade in these regions was divided into four departments:—

The Fond du Lac department consisted of the country at the head of Lake Superior, and the sources of the St. Louis and Mississippi Rivers. The Folle Avoine department consisted of the country drained by the waters of the St. Croix. The Lac Coutereille department covered the waters of the Chippeway; and the Lac du Flambeau department, the waters of the Wisconsin.

The depot for this portion of their trade was located at Fond du Lac, but their great depot was at Grand Portage on the north coast of Lake Superior and within the limits of what is now known as Minnesota Territory. From this point they sent their outfits up Pigeon River, towards the northwest, and occupied the country of the Kenisteno and Assineboines. Here, each summer, the partners and clerks of the company, who had passed the winter amongst the inland posts, collected their returns of fur, and were met by the partners from Montreal with new supplies of merchandise. These yearly meetings were enlivened with feastings, dancing, and revelry, held in the great hall of the company. In the style of the feudal barons of old, did these prosperous traders each year hold their grand festival surrounded by their faithful and happy " coureurs du bois" and servitors. The eyes of an " old northwester," while relating these happy scenes of by-gone times, will sparkle with excitement—his form will become momentarily erect as he imagines himself moving off in the merry dance, and his lips will water, as he enumerates the varied luxuries under which groaned long tables in the days of these periodic feastings.

Amongst the different partners of this company on its first formation, the names of Frobisher, McTavish, Pond, Gregory, and Pangman are mentioned as most conspicuous. In their future operations, the names of Sir Alex. McKenzie and McGilvray soon became prominent as the most active partners. They were early opposed at some of their northern posts by the Forsyths and Ogilvys, but were not much troubled by the rivalry of these men till, through some unfortunate misunderstanding with members of the company, Sir Alex. McKenzie was forced to draw out his means and leave the firm. He thereupon joined with the Forsyths, and under the denomination of the X. Y. Company, through his great tact and experience in the trade, he caused the Northwest for several years to suffer severe losses. After his death, the two rival companies came to an amicable understanding, and joined as partners.

It is about this time that the Northwest first began to be materially harassed by the Hudson's Bay Company, who not only met them in their most lucrative northern posts, from the direction of Hudson's Bay, but followed them up, through their usual route from Canada. This company, formed principally of influential lords and gentlemen in England, supported by the favor of government and possessing a charter, eventually proved too powerful for the old Northwest. They, however, did not crush this old firm till after a protracted and severe struggle. The Northwest Company, by the honorable and humane course which they are noted as having pursued towards the Indians, and also towards their numerous Canadian and half-breed servitors and dependants, were, in return, loved by them, and in the efforts of these people to retain them in their country, blood was unfortunately made to flow.

On the 17th of June, 1816, Governor Semple, of the Hudson's Bay Company, with some British troops, in trying to prevent the march of a body of mounted half-breeds, was suddenly cut down, and his troops killed, by a sweeping charge of these hardy buffalo hunters. A bloody partisan warfare was only prevented by the strong interference of the British government. In 1819 the Northwest became merged into the Hudson's Bay Company, and ceased to exist. With it may be said to have ended the Augustan age of the fur trade. With deep regret do the old voyageurs and Indians speak of the dissolution of this once powerful company, for they always received honorable and charitable treatment at their hands. The principal traders who operated among the Ojibways during the era of the Northwest Company, and who may be mentioned as contemporary with John Baptiste and Michel Cadotte, are Nolin, Gaulthier, McGillis, St. Germain, Bazille Beauleau, Chabolier, Wm. Morrison, Cotte, Roussain, Bonga, J. B. Corbin, and others. These early pioneer traders all intermarried in the tribe, and have left sons and daughters to perpetuate their names. Wm. Morrison of Montreal, and J. B. Corbin, of Lac Coutereille, are now[1] the only survivors of all these old traders.

For the above brief account of the early fur trade, I am indebted to Hon. Allan Morrison of Crow Wing, who has been for upwards of thirty years a trader among the Ojibways, and who is a grandson of Waddon, whose murder led to the formation of the Northwest Company.

To Mr. Bruce, of St. Croix Lake, now in his seventyninth year, mostly passed in the northwest, I am also indebted for information. At the dissolution of the Northwest Company, citizens of the United States began seriously

[1] A. D. 1852.

to turn their attention to the Ojibway fur trade, and from this time a new class of individuals, as traders, began to penetrate to the remotest villages of this tribe. In the year 1818, the Astor Fur Company first commenced their operations on Lake Superior. They confined themselves, however, during the years 1816 and 1817, to trading posts at Sault Ste. Marie, Grand Island, and Ance-ke-we-naw. John Johnston, with a capital each year, of $40,000, managed this portion of their trade.

In 1818, the company sent outfits to cover the whole Ojibway country, within the limits of the United States. William Morrison, Roussain, Cotte, and others, as traders on salary, with an outfit amounting to $23,606, were sent to the Fond du Lac department, which included the Upper Mississippi country. These traders continued during the years 1819–20–21–22, with small increase of capital. The department of Lac du Flambeau was placed in charge of Bazil Beauleau and Charatte as traders, on salary, in 1818, with a capital of $5100; Hawley and Durant, with a capital of $5299.

For the Lac Coutereille department, the company outfitted John Baptiste Corbin, as a trader on salary, with goods to the amount of $5328. For the St. Croix district, Duchene acted as trader, on salary, for the company in 1818. Capital $3876.

In 1822, the capital of the Lac Coutereille and St. Croix departments amounted to $19,353, in charge of Duchene as trader. In 1818, the Ance department was placed in charge of John Holliday as trader on salary; his capital, or amount of outfit, averaged till 1822, $6000 per annum.

In 1822, the Astor Fur Company made a slight change in the system of their trade in the Ojibway country. The Fond du Lac department was given to Wm. Morrison on halves, and this arrangement continued to 1826, when Messrs William A. Aitkin and Roussain took charge with a share of one-sixth each. In 1820, Mr. Aitkin bought out Roussain, and for one year he had charge, with a share of one-third. In 1831, Mr. Aitkin took charge of this important department on halves with the Astor Company, and continued thus till 1834.

In 1824, Lyman M. Warren, after having traded in opposition to the American Fur Company for six years, in the Lac du Flambeau, Lac Coutereille and St. Croix departments, entered into an arrangement with them, and took charge as a partner, and under a salary of these three departments, making his depot at La Pointe. He continued with the same arrangement till the year 1834.

These items respecting the fur trade are here introduced to give the reader an idea of the importance of the trade amongst the Ojibways, and to introduce the names of the principal traders who, at this time, were remaining in the country. The Astor Fur Company followed the example of the Northwest Company in hiring as traders, men whom they found already in the country, holding influential positions among the Ojibways, and in some cases connected with them by marriage. Some of these men had traded in connection with the old Northwest Company, as William Morrison, Cotte, Roussain, Corbin, and others,while others of more recent date had traded as opposition traders, and distinguished themselves by their success. Among these may be mentioned Wm. A. Aitkin, Esq., who first came into the Chippeway country about 1815, a mere boy, and as a servant for a trader named John Drew. Intermarrying into an influential Indian family, he was soon enabled to trade on his own account, and he gradually increased his business till, in 1831, he takes charge of the important department of Fond du Lac, on halves, with John Jacob Astor. Mr. Aitkin's name is linked with the history of the Upper Mississippi Ojibways for the last half century. He was one of the old pioneers of the northwest. He died in the fall of the year 1851, and lies buried at Aitkinsville (Swan River), on the banks of the Upper Mississippi.

Among others may be mentioned the names of Lyman M. and his brother Truman A. Warren. They first came into the Ojibway country from Vermont, in 1818. They hired the first year in charge of small outfits, to Charles Ermitinger, at the rate of $500 per annum. They soon took outfits on their own account, and traded with great success in the Lac Coutereille and Lac du Flambeau departments. In 1821, they married each a daughter of the old trader Michel Cadotte, and their trade increased to such a degree that in 1824, Lyman Warren made an apparently advantageous arrangement with the Astor Fur Company, becoming a partner thereof, besides receiving a handsome salary. Truman died in 1825, on board a vessel bound from Mackinaw to Detroit, from a severe cold caused by the extreme exposure incident to an Indian trader's life. He died much lamented by the Ojibways, who had already learned to love him for his many gentle and good traits of character.

Lyman M. Warren, the elder brother, located his permanent residence on La Pointe Island, and continued with slight interruptions and varied success, to trade with the Ojibways till his death in 1847. He lies buried at La Pointe, and his name may now well be mentioned among the early American pioneers of the northwest. Half a century hence, when the scenes of their wild adventures and hardships shall be covered with teeming towns and villages, these slight records of individuals who still live in the memory of the present generation, will be read with far greater interest than at the present day.

Samuel Ashmun, Daniel Dingley, Charles H. Oakes, and Patrick Conner, may be mentioned as prominent traders among the Ojibways during the early part of the nineteenth century. Some of these gentlemen commenced their career in opposition to the Astor Fur Company, but in accordance to the policy of this rich firm, they were soon bought out and engaged in its service.

When John Jacob Astor entered into arrangements with the British Fur Companies for the monopoly of the Ojibway trade within the United States territory, a new era may be said to have occurred in the fur trade. The old French Canadian traders so congenial to the Indians, who had remained in the country after the closing of the French supremacy, had all nearly died away, and disappeared from the stage of active life, and a new class of men, of far different temperaments, whose chief object was to amass fortunes, now made their appearance among the Ojibways. They were of the Anglo-Saxon race, and hailed from the land of the progressive and money-making " Yankee." To some degree the Indian ceased to find that true kindness, sympathy, charity, and respect for his sacred beliefs and rites, which he had always experienced from his French traders.

The Ojibways were more deserving of respect in those days, while living in their natural state, and under the full force of their primitive moral beliefs, than they are at the present day, after being degenerated by a close contact with an unprincipled frontier white population. The American fur traders, many of whom were descended from respectable New England families, did not consider their dignity lessened by forming marital alliances with the tribe, and the Ojibway women were of so much service to their husbands, they so easily assimilated themselves to their modes of life, and their affections were so strong, and their conduct so beyond reproach, that these alliances, generally first formed by the traders for present convenience, became cemented by the strongest ties of mutual affection. They kindly cherished their Indian wives, and for their sakes, as well as for the sake of children whom they begat, these traders were eventually induced to pass their lifetime in the Ojibway country. They soon forgot the money-making mania which first brought them into the country, and gradually imbibing the generous and hospitable qualities of the Indians, lived only to enjoy the present. They laid up no treasure for the future, and as a general fact, which redounds to the honor of this class of fur traders, they died poor. The money which has been made by the fur trade has been made with the sweat of their brows, but it has flowed into the coffers of such men as John Jacob Astor.

It is a fact worthy of notice, that the Anglo-Saxon race have mingled their blood with the Ojibways to a much greater extent than with any other tribe of the red race.

It reflects honor on this tribe, as it tends greatly to prove the common saying, that they are far ahead of other tribes in their social qualities, and general intelligence and morality. Of French and American extraction, the Ojibways number about five thousand persons of mixed blood, who are scattered throughout Canada, Michigan, Wisconsin, Minnesota, and the British possessions. Many of the Ojibway mixed bloods are men of good education and high standing within their respective communities.

The American Board of Foreign Missions early established a mission school on the island of Mackinaw, to which most of the Ojibway traders sent their half-breed children. The school was sustained on the manual labor system, and great good was disseminated from it, which spread over the whole northwest country. Many of our most prominent half-breeds, now engaged as missionaries, or in mercantile pursuits, and women who figure in the best of civilized society, received their education at the Mackinaw mission. After its dissolution, such of the traders as were pecuniarily able, usually sent their children to receive an education in some of the Eastern States.

CHAPTER XXXV.

EVENTS FROM 1818 TO 1826.

In 1818, Black Dog, a Pillager war-leader, marches into the Dakota country, with a party of sixteen warriors—Desperate fight, from which but one Pillager escapes death—In 1824, four white men are murdered on the shores of Lake Pepin by an Ojibway war party—Unsuccessful pursuit of the murderers—The traders demand them at the hands of their chiefs—Chief of Lac du Flambeau delivers three of the ring-leaders into the hands of Truman A. Warren—The principal murderer is secured by Wm. Holliday—They are taken to Mackinaw and confined in jail, from which they make their escape—Convention at Fond du Lac in 1826, between commissioners on the part of the United States, and the Ojibways—Objects thereof.

FOR several years after the closing of the last war between Great Britain and the United States, no event of sufficient importance to deserve record, occurred to the Ojibways. Their warfare continued with the Dakotas, but no important battle was fought, nor striking acts of valor and manhood performed, such as find a durable place in the lodge tales and traditions of the tribe, till the year 1818, when the hardy Pillagers again lost a select band of their bravest warriors.

A noted war-leader, Black Dog, having lately lost some relatives, at the hands of the Dakotas, raised a small but select band of warriors to go with him in pursuit of vengeance. They numbered but sixteen men, but being all of determined character, they marched westward, and proceeded further into the country of their enemies, than any Ojibway war party had ever done before them. After having travelled all one night in crossing a wide prairie, early in the morning they discovered a large encampment of Dakotas, whose lodges were located on a prairie, close by the banks of a small river. The Ojibways were unfortunately discovered by a party of buffalo hunters who were scouring the prairie on horseback, and their presence was immediately reported to the grand encampment, whose warriors prepared to turn out in irresistible numbers against them. It was useless for them to think of flight, for their enemy, being on horseback, would soon overtake and surround them. They could but sell their lives as dearly as possible.

The leader lost not his presence of mind, though perfectly satisfied that the fate of his party was fully sealed. Addressing a few words of encouragement to his warriors, he led them to a small clump of poplar trees which grew on a knoll on the prairie, in plain view of the Dakota encampment. Here, they each dug a hole in the ground, from which they determined to keep up the fight with their numerous enemies, as long as their ammunition might last. They had hardly finished their preparations, when the Dakota warriors made their appearance in a formidable array on the open prairie. They were fully painted and dressed for battle, and a large number were on horseback, who quickly rode forward and completely surrounded the knoll of trees in which the Ojibways had taken shelter. The battle commenced, and lasted without intermission till midday, the Dakotas suffering a severe loss from the unerring aim of their desperate enemies, who threw not a single shot away. So well were they posted, that it was impossible to approach or dislodge them. At last their scanty supply of ammunition gave out, and the Dakotas discovering it by the slackening of their fire, and by one of their number being wounded with a stone which an Ojibway had substituted in his gun for a bullet, a simultaneous rush was made on them, and after a short hand to hand struggle, the sixteen Pillager warriors, with but one exception, were killed. This one, named Bug-aun-auk, re-

turned safely to his people, but he never would give but
the most supernatural account of his manner of escape—
tales that were not believed by his own people.   It was at
first the general impression that he had deserted his party
before the fight came on, but the Dakotas, at a future peace-
meeting with the Ojibways, stated that there were sixteen
warriors who went into the poplar grove, as counted by
their scouts, and there were found sixteen holes from
which the warriors fought, in one of which remained only
the bundle of the man who had so miraculously escaped.
The Dakotas acknowledged that they lost thirty-three of
their warriors in this desperate engagement, besides many
maimed for life.

Since the execution of the Indian at Fond du Lac in
1797, by the northwestern traders for killing a Canadian
" coureur du bois," the life of a white man had been held
sacred by the Ojibways, and one could traverse any portion
of their country, in perfect safety, and without the least
molestation.   In the year 1824, however, four white men
were killed by the Ojibways, under circumstances so peculiar, as to deserve a brief account in this chapter.

An Ojibway named Nub-o-beence, or Little Broth, residing on the shores of Lake Superior near the mouth of Ontonagun River, lost a favorite child through sickness.   He
was deeply stricken with grief, and nothing would satisfy
him but to go and shed the blood of the hereditary enemies of his tribes, the Dakotas.   He raised a small war
party, mostly from the Lac du Flambeau district, and they
floated down the Chippeway River to its entry, where, for
several days they watched without success on the banks of
the Mississippi, for the appearance of an enemy.   The
leader had endured hardships, and came the great distance
of five hundred miles to shed blood to the manes of his
dead child, and long after his fellows had become weary of
waiting and watching, and anxious to return home, did he

urge them still to continue in their search. He had determined not to return without shedding human blood.

Early one morning, as the warriors lay watching on the
shores of Lake Pepin, they saw a boat manned by four
white men land near them, and proceed to cook their morning meal. Several of the party approached the strangers,
and were well received. The white men consisted of a Mr.
Finley, with three Canadian boat men, who were under
the employ of Mons. Jean Brunet, of Prairie du Chien, an
Indian trader. They were proceeding up the Mississippi
to Ft. Snelling on some urgent business of their employer,
and Mr. Finley had with him a number of account books
and valuable papers.

The assault and massacre of these men was entirely un-
premeditated by the Ojibway war party, and contrary to
the wishes of the majority. They had paid them their
visit and begged some provisions, receiving which, they
retired and sat down in a group on a bank immediately
above them. The leader here commenced to harangue his
fellows, expressing a desire to shed the blood of the white
man. He was immediately opposed, on which he commenced to talk of the hardships he had endured, the loss
of his child, till, becoming excited, he wept with a loud
voice, and suddenly, taking aim at the group of white men,
who were eating their breakfast, he fired and killed one.
Eight of his fellows immediately followed his example, and
rushing down to the water-side, they quickly dispatched
the whole party, and tore off their scalps. Taking the
effects of their victims, they returned towards their homes.
At Lac Coutereille they attempted to dance the scalp dance
before the door of J. B. Corbin, the trader, who immediately ran out of his house, and forcibly deprived them of
the white men's scalps which they were displaying, order-
ing them at the same time to depart from his door. The
trader was supported by the Indians of his village, and the

murderers now for the first time beginning to see the consequences of their foolish act, skulked silently away, very much crestfallen.

The remains of the murdered white men were soon discovered, and the news going both up and down the river, a boat load of fifty soldiers was sent from Prairie du Chien to pursue the murderers. At Lake Pepin they were met by three boats laden with troops from Ft. Snelling, and the party, including volunteers, numbered nearly two hundred men. Mons. Jean Brunet was along, and had been most active in raising this force. They followed the Ojibway war-trail for some distance, till, coming to a place where the warriors had hung up their usual thanksgiving sacrifices for a safe return to their homes, a retreat was determined on, as the party had not come prepared to make a long journey, and it was folly to think of catching the murderers, scattered throughout the vast wilderness which lay between Lake Superior and the Mississippi.

The matter was subsequently left in the hands of the traders among the Ojibways. Truman A. Warren, the principal trader of the Lac du Flambeau department, demanded the murderers, at the hands of the chiefs of this section of the tribe. The celebrated Keesh-ke-mun had died a short time previous, and had left his eldest son Mons-o-bo-douh to succeed. This man was not a whit behind his deceased father in intelligence and firmness of character. He called a council of his band, and insisted on the chief murderers being given up by their friends. He was opposed in council by a man noted for his ill-tempered and savage disposition, who even threatened to take his life if he attempted to carry his wishes into effect. A brother of this man had been one of the ring-leaders in the murder, and now stood by his side as he delivered his threats against the young chief. As they again resumed their seats, Mons-o-bo-douh arose, and drawing his knife, he

went and laid hold of the murderer by the arm and intimated to him that he was his prisoner.   He then ordered
his young men to tie his arms.   The order was immediately obeyed, and accomplished without the least resistance
from the prisoner or his brother, who was thunderstruck
at the cool and determined manner of the chief.

Shortly after, two more of the murderers were taken,
and Mons-o-bo-douh delivered them into the hands of the
trader.   The leader of the party, who lived on the shores
of Lake Superior, was secured by Mr. William Holliday,
trader at Ance Bay.   The four captives were sent to Mackinac, and confined in jail.   While orders were pending
from Washington respecting the manner of their trial,
they succeeded in making their escape by cutting an aperture through the logs which formed their place of confinement.

The ensuing year (1826), the Hon. Lewis Cass was com-
missioned by the United States, to proceed to Lake Superior, and convene the Ojibways in council, to treat with
them for the copper and other mineral, which was now
found to abound in their country.   This important convention was held at Fond du Lac, which was then considered as about the centre of the Ojibway country.   Boat
loads of provisions were taken from Mackinaw and collected at this point, to feed the assembly of Indians, who
were notified through messengers to collect.   The Ojibways had not collected in such large numbers for a long
time.   Delegations arrived from their most remote villages
towards the north.   Shin-ga-ba-ossin, chief of the Crane
family, from Sault Ste. Marie, was also present, and took
a most prominent part in the proceedings, in behalf of his
tribe.   He is said to have made a speech to his fellows,
wherein he urged them to discover to the whites their
knowledge of the minerals which abounded in their country.
This, however, was meant more to tickle the ears of the

commissioners and to obtain their favor, than as an earnest appeal to his people, for the old chieftain was too much imbued with the superstition prevalent amongst the Indians, which prevents them from discovering their knowledge of mineral and copper boulders to the whites. The objects of the commissioners were easily attained, but the Ojibways, who felt a deep love for the offspring of their women who had intermarried with the whites, and cherished them as their own children, insisted on giving them grants of land on the Sault Ste. Marie River, which they wished our government to recognize and make good. These stipulations were annexed by the commissioners to the treaty, but were never ratified by the Senate of the United States. It is merely mentioned here to show the great affection with which the Ojibways regarded their half-breeds, and which they have evinced on every occasion when they have had an opportunity of bettering their condition.

A stipulation was also annexed to the treaty, wherein some of the relatives of the murderers of Finley and his party, agreed to deliver them within a given time. This, however, was never carried into effect, and as the traders took no further interest in the matter, the murderers were allowed to run at large. The leader is still[1] living at Ontonagun, and another named "the Little Eddy," is living[1] at La Pointe. Both are noted for their quiet and peaceable disposition.

At the treaty of Fond du Lac, the United States commissioners recognized the chiefs of the Ojibways, by distributing medals amongst them, the size of which were in accordance with their degree of rank. Sufficient care was not taken in this rather delicate operation, to carry out the pure civil polity of the tribe. Too much attention was paid to the recommendation of interested traders who

[1] A. D. 1852.

wished their best hunters to be rewarded by being made chiefs. One young man named White Fisher, was endowed with a medal, solely for the strikingly mild and pleasant expression of his face. He is now a petty sub-chief on the Upper Mississippi.

From this time may be dated the commencement of innovations which have entirely broken up the civil polity of the Ojibways.

INDEX

In constructing this index, the compilers have used accepted 20th century spellings for names of persons, places, and tribes followed by Warren's spelling in parentheses. Each entry is indexed according to Warren's version and cross-referenced to the modern spelling. The names of individual Indians appear in English translation, if known, and are cross-referenced from the Indian version.

Petun 116

axes belong to women 73   Naud-o-wa-se = DAKOTAS 280

after death 73   Copper 392

Chippewas separate from Odawa 81, Origin 82

Chequamehity 87-9   St. Lawrence Algonquins 124

Traders first 122   great Island 138

La Crosse ball = word 202   no war in winter 251, 252

women made sugar while men hunted 264 —

Cause of war - Condolence 264 women pick berries 265

Ojibways intermarry with whites more than any other tribe 386